Arabella Boxer's
Book of English Food

# ARABELLA BOXER'S BOOK OF ENGLISH FOOD

*A Rediscovery of British Food from Before the War*

FIG TREE
*an imprint of*
PENGUIN BOOKS

FIG TREE

Published by the Penguin Group
Penguin Books Ltd, 80 Strand, London WC2R ORL, England
Penguin Group (USA) Inc., 375 Hudson Street, New York, New York 10014, USA
Penguin Group (Canada), 90 Eglinton Avenue East, Suite 700, Toronto, Ontario, Canada M4P 2Y3
(a division of Pearson Penguin Canada Inc.)
Penguin Ireland, 25 St Stephen's Green, Dublin 2, Ireland (a division of Penguin Books Ltd)
Penguin Group (Australia), 250 Camberwell Road, Camberwell, Victoria 3124, Australia
(a division of Pearson Australia Group Pty Ltd)
Penguin Books India Pvt Ltd, 11 Community Centre, Panchsheel Park, New Delhi – 110 017, India
Penguin Group (NZ), 67 Apollo Drive, Rosedale, Auckland 0632, New Zealand
(a division of Pearson New Zealand Ltd)
Penguin Books (South Africa) (Pty) Ltd, Block D, Rosebank Office Park, 181 Jan Smuts Avenue,
Parktown North, Gauteng 2193, South Africa

Penguin Books Ltd, Registered Offices: 80 Strand, London WC2R ORL, England

www.penguin.com

First published by Hodder and Stoughton 1991
Revised and updated edition published by Fig Tree 2012
001

Text copyright © Arabella Boxer, 1991, 2012
Illustrations copyright © Cressida Bell, 2012

The moral right of the author and of the illustrator has been asserted

Set in 11.5/14.75 pt Bembo Book MT Std
Typeset by Palimpsest Book Production Limited, Falkirk, Stirlingshire
Printed in Great Britain by Clays Ltd, St Ives plc

A CIP catalogue record for this book is available from the British Library

ISBN: 978–1–905–49099–8

www.greenpenguin.co.uk

ALWAYS LEARNING                    PEARSON

In memory of my father, who died in 1943.

# CONTENTS

# ACKNOWLEDGEMENTS

I should like to thank all the authors and publishers who have given me permission to quote from their books, and all the friends and acquaintances who have looked out recipes, lent me books, and generally given support and encouragement. In particular, I am deeply grateful to the following:

Mark Amory; Hilary Arnold; Mrs Jonathan Blackburn; Kate Boxer; Hugh Cecil; Chatto & Windus, for recipes from *Party Food and Drink* by Rosemary Hume; Mrs Dorothy Child; Glynn Christian; Condé Nast Publications Ltd, for recipes from *Vogue*, and *Vogue's Cookery Book*; Constable Publishers, for recipes from *Eat at Pleasure: Drink by Measure* by Olof Wijk; *Country Life*, for recipes from *Lightning Cookery* by Countess Morphy; Lillie Davies; J. M. Dent and Sons Ltd, for recipes from *Come into the Garden, Cook*, by Constance Spry, and *The Constance Spry Cookery Book* by Constance Spry and Rosemary Hume, and *Good Cookery* by W. G. R. Francillon; André Deutsch Ltd, for a recipe from *Personal Choice* by Ambrose Heath; Polly Devlin; the Duchess of Devonshire; Duckworth Ltd, for recipes from *When the Cook Is Away* by Catherine Ives, and *Be Your Own Chef* by Lucie Marion; Catherine Forshall; James Fox; Hamish Hamilton Ltd, for recipes from *The Complete Hostess* by Quaglino; the late Lady Harrod; the late Lady Dorothy Heber-Percy; Harrods Ltd, for recipes from *A Year's Dinners* by May Little; William Heinemann Ltd, for recipes from *What Shall We Have Today?* and *What Shall We Have To Drink?* by X. Marcel Boulestin, reprinted by permission of the Peters Fraser and Dunlop Group Ltd; Adrian Higham, for recipes from *Vegetable Cultivation and Cookery* by Eleanour Sinclair Rohde; the late Lady Anne Hill; Lord Hindlip, for the recipe from *Minnie Lady Hindlip's*

*Cookery Book*; Houghton Mifflin Company, for recipes from *June Platt's Plain and Fancy Cookbook*; the late Lord Kelvedon, for material from the diaries of his father, Sir Henry 'Chips' Channon; the late Mrs Nancy Lancaster; Mrs Elizabeth Lewthwaite; the late Loelia, Lady Lindsay of Dowhill; Jane Longman; Macdonald Group, for recipes from *Food in England* by Dorothy Hartley; the late David McKenna CBE; the late Lady John Manners; Paul Manousso; Methuen & Co., for recipes from *The Perfect Hostess* by Rose Henniker Heaton; Michael Joseph Ltd, for recipes from *The Alice B. Toklas Cook Book*, and *Wheeler's Fish Cookery Book* by Macdonald Hastings and Carole Walsh; Joyce Molyneux; the late Nigel Nicolson OBE; the Nonesuch Press, for recipes from *Lovely Food* by Ruth Lowinsky; the late Tom Parr; the late Frances Partridge; the late Jennifer Paterson; Max Reinhardt; Mrs Maud Shimwell; Mrs Michael Stanley, for recipes from *English Country House Cooking*; Mrs Oliver Steele; Sir Tatton Sykes; the *Vogue* Library; Lucy Ward; Francis Wyndham.

INTRODUCTION

# INTRODUCTION

I

Twenty years have passed since I first wrote this book on rediscovering the English food of the 1920s and 30s, and it must be harder than ever for readers now to understand how things were, in that brief interval between the two world wars.

In the years between the wars English food underwent a brief flowering that seems to have gone almost unremarked at the time, and later passed into oblivion. The pomposity of the Edwardian meals that dominated the early years of the century was a thing of the past; meals became shorter and more informal, and the dishes themselves more light-hearted. Meals were rarely more than three courses, except for a formal dinner, and a more relaxed attitude became the norm.

It is regrettable that this trend was cut short by the outbreak of the Second World War in 1939. Such things take time to reach all levels of society, and this one had hardly had time to spread beyond the sophisticated world in London and the south before war was declared, and the country was plunged into austerity. Food rationing dragged on for fifteen years, and when Elizabeth David's first book, *A Book of Mediterranean Food*, was published in 1950, it found a public starved of foreign travel and of interesting food – for monotony, not hunger, was the curse of our wartime diet. The reading public embraced this vision of a Mediterranean world wholeheartedly, and with an enthusiasm that has never abated. Restaurants with names like Le Matelot sprang up, with strings of garlic and fishing nets incorporated in their decor. These were soon followed by a rash of Italian trattorias, and our own English food was forgotten.

The misplaced passion for foreign food still continues; today it is north Italian food that dominates the scene, with its robust dishes of sausage and polenta, Parmesan and olive oil, while the more exotic cuisines of the Far East may tempt the more adventurous cook. All this is intrinsically good, and enjoyable in the extreme when eaten in Tuscany, or in a good restaurant, but it does seem slightly ridiculous that pesto should have become a national dish.

The English are a strange mixture of complacency and insecurity, for they genuinely don't seem to value their own culinary inheritance. Foreigners know better, and I learnt many years ago that the way to please visiting French, Italians, Americans or Swiss is to present them with a meal composed entirely of classic British delicacies. Some oysters or smoked eel to start with, then some lightly roasted game with all the traditional accompaniments, or a sirloin of Scotch beef, or a saddle of Welsh mountain lamb. A salad of mixed green leaves to follow, and don't be misled into thinking that mâche, rugola and pourpier have always been foreign imports, for all three were commonly grown in England in medieval times under their English names: lamb's lettuce (or corn salad), rocket and purslane. With the salad, two or three unusual English cheeses: a Single Gloucester, a Cornish Yarg, and a Spenwood made with ewes' milk; with them, some Miller's Damsel wheaten wafers made on the Isle of Wight, unsalted English farm butter, and hearts of celery. Then, in summer, a fruit fool made with raspberries or blackcurrants, served partly frozen, with a thinly iced lemon cake. In winter, a marmalade tart, served warm, with Devonshire cream.

Few people today seem aware that a discreet revolution in food took place in the 1920s and 30s. As Constance Spry wrote in 1942, looking back: 'the decade before the war seems to have had uncomplicated elegance as its keynote.

The criterion of good food was subtlety of flavour and contrast, combined with that perfection of simplicity which is the hardest thing to achieve. That intelligent aim in food towards fewer courses and more discernment in their choice was in no sense dictated by austerity. On the contrary, it indicated a high level of epicurean taste.'

By the 1950s, this clearness of vision had been lost by all but very few. As Ruth Lowinsky, herself the author of three excellent pre-war cookery books, wrote, 'a palate is dwindling into a thing of the past'. And this is why, presumably, having lost touch with their own traditions as the English are wont to do, they went overboard for Mediterranean food.

English food of the 1920s and 30s is curiously hard to define, partly because it is understated. It lies at the other end of the spectrum from robust peasant dishes, for it is basically bland in flavour, although the accompanying sauces and garnishes are often sharp, sour or spicy. Since a contrast in flavour was often the aim, the individual foods were almost always cooked and served separately, so that they met for the first time on the plate. This is in direct opposition to the French traditions, whereby different foods are encouraged to merge in the cooking process, and where sauces are an intrinsic part of the dish. The English food of the period demanded skill in execution, and elegance in presentation. It was above all careful cooking, requiring first-rate ingredients, precise timing, and stylish presentation. When practised without due care, it could be the worst food in the world, as many will remember to their cost.

Even when it was well done, the food of the time had its weaknesses, judged by today's standards. For their criteria were different from ours; there was not the same wish for variety, for a start. Every middle-class family had a cook, albeit a modest one, whereas people living at a comparable level today do the cooking themselves. Most families had the same dish for lunch every Sunday, either a roast chicken, or a joint of beef or mutton, and the same series of dishes to follow. Even the very best cooks had a more limited range than good cooks do today. The professional cook who went out to cater for dinner parties, arriving with her sauces already made lest a prying kitchen maid should learn her secrets, did not offer a very wide range, whereas most cooks in private practice prided themselves on their specialities, which favoured guests of the household seemed happy to eat time after time. This was in direct contrast to the post-war habit, whereby hostesses were urged to keep a notebook of menus, and when they were served, to avoid serving guests the same dish more than once.

Mrs Woodman, the redoubtable cook to the Mildmays for fifty years, had an asparagus ice for which she was famous. When the Queen Mother, then the Queen, was staying at Flete she asked for the recipe, but Mrs Woodman stoutly refused to part with it. 'Yer husband asked me for that,' she said, 'but I wouldn't give it to him.'

There were two significant outside influences on our food during this period: both affected only a small section of society, basically the moneyed upper classes and the intel-ligentsia, yet they had lasting effects and would have spread further had it not been for the outbreak of war. The first came from the United States, for a number of American women had married Englishmen and come to live over here. Some, like Nancy Astor and Emerald Cunard, had married before the First World War; others, like Lady Astor's niece Nancy Lancaster, married during the inter-war years. Many of these young women were talented exponents of the minor arts: interior decoration, entertaining and clothes. Almost without exception, they seemed to have a social ease and a lack of shyness that many Englishmen found irresistible. Their high spirits, wit and sense of fun put many of their English contemporaries in the shade. A prime example was Wallis Simpson, a clever and manipulative woman who knew just how to amuse the Prince of Wales and his friends by providing the sort of relaxed and frivolous ambiance he craved, in striking contrast to the stuffy family circle at Sandringham and Windsor. Wallis Simpson was a perfectionist who prided herself on always being immaculately turned out, and having exquisite food.

Although the dishes Mrs Simpson served at her table were hardly typical, being a highly sophisticated version, American food was not widely divergent from our own, in that both shared common roots. Many of the early settlers who went out to America in the 1620s and subsequent years must have taken their receipts with them, and in some ways their food had stayed closer to its past than our own. Dishes like pumpkin pie and cheesecake are clear descendants from Stuart times, while some American recipes for mincemeat still include minced steak, as ours once did. Words like broil, skillet, grind and scallion have stayed the same, while the US pint still holds 16 fluid ounces, as ours did until 1878.

Once the first war was over, young American women came over in hordes, hoping to find a titled husband. In some cases, this took the form of a bargain: he provided the title while she brought the fortune. To digress for a moment and tell you about my mother's case, she was in a different situation, for she had no fortune to bring, nor had she set her sights on an English peer. It was 1924, and she was rather fed up, staying alone in a hotel in Paris, buying clothes. She was twenty years old, and had just returned to Europe from a fabulous journey in the Far East with a school friend, and her friend's mother and brother.

During the trip she and the brother had become secretly engaged, but before the voyage was over he changed his mind, saying she was not serious enough for him to marry. While not exactly heartbroken, she was understandably put out, and was dreading the return to New York for a third debutante season.

Then my father turned up, on his way to shoot game in Kenya. They had met the previous winter in New York, where he had spent a brief visit. He must have fallen in love with her then, and when they met again in Paris he proposed. In her impulsive way, she accepted, and they were married within a few weeks. Her aged parents came over from New York, rather flummoxed by the turn of events; my father's mother came from Scotland, travelling to the Continent for the first time in her life.

What was a twenty-year-old American girl thinking of, to commit herself to a life in a country (Scotland) she did not know, surrounded by a family she had never met?

After a honeymoon in Venice, my parents arrived at what was to be their first home, Donibristle, a charming house, not very big, on the edge of the sea on the south coast of Fife, steeped in history and romance; here the 2nd Earl of Moray had been murdered by his rival, Huntly, in 1592, as recounted in the ballad 'The Bonny Earl of Moray'.

I doubt if any of the young American women who came to marry in England were more accomplished than my mother was; but many of them were bright, and socially ambitious. She, on the other hand, was bored by the subject of food and completely ignorant on the subject. She told me how, in her first weeks at Donibristle, she had gone shopping in Edinburgh and come back with a leg of Canterbury lamb. Misled by the name, which conjured up images of salt marshes in Kent, she was unaware that it was frozen, imported from New Zealand; one can imagine the sniggers in the servants' hall as Lady Doune makes a fool of herself again.

A young woman marrying into a big house was in a perilous situation. Coming into a large establishment with no experience (I doubt that my mother had hardly ever set foot in the kitchen at her parents' house), she found herself faced with a phalanx of servants ranged against her, quick to intimidate her and laugh at her mistakes. It was not considered necessary to give her any sort of training, just as she was not given any help or advice in dealing with married life. All was left to chance.

## II

The second influence on English cooking of the 1920s and 30s came from France, in the endearing personality of Marcel Boulestin. Boulestin arrived in London as a penniless young man in 1906, having escaped from the clutches of Willy, Colette's first husband, for whom he had worked as a general dogsbody. In London he worked first as a journalist, then as a decorator. When war broke out in 1914, he enlisted in the French army, where he made friends with the painter and illustrator Jean-Emile Laboureur.

Once the war was over Boulestin returned to London, where he tried to re-establish himself as a decorator, but without success. Several of his former clients, like Syrie Maugham, had become professional decorators themselves; others were beginning to feel the effects of the coming recession.

In 1923 Boulestin published his first cookery book, with illustrations by Laboureur. This small book, *Simple French*

*Cooking for English Homes*, was an instant success, and was to be the first of many. The same year, Boulestin wrote cookery articles for the *Manchester Guardian*, the *Daily Express*, the *Morning Post*, the *Spectator* and *Vogue*. (He wrote regularly for *Vogue* until the end of 1928.) In 1925 he opened his first restaurant on the corner of Panton Street and Leicester Square; a few years later it moved to Southampton Street, where it stayed until it closed for good in 1994. Also in 1925, he started a cookery school where society ladies went, taking their cooks with them; in 1937 he became the first ever person to demonstrate cookery on television.

In 1932 André Simon and A. J. A. Symons founded the Wine and Food Society. André Simon, its president, was a French wine historian living in England, an anglophile who delighted in helping to spread knowledge of good food and wine. The Society published regular newsletters, and its influence was considerable.

At a certain level, there had always been a French influence on food and drink in this country. Some of the best cooks, like the Duke of Devonshire's, had trained under French chefs. (Mrs Tanner, cook at Chatsworth in the 1920s and 30s, had been sent by her former employer, Lord Savile, to learn under Escoffier while he was chef at the Hotel Cecil in London and in the south of France. She in turn trained her daughter Maud, who succeeded her mother as cook to the Devonshires.)

It was the practice to have menu cards on the table in the evening, for weekend parties in the big country houses, and for dinner parties in London, and these were always written in French. French wine, especially claret, was the most highly prized, while French brandy, Cognac, Armagnac and other digestifs, also sweet liqueurs like crème de menthe, were extremely popular.

Yet Marcel Boulestin was the first person to introduce the English to the cuisine bourgeoise. He was the ideal exponent of French family cooking, being at the same time sophisticated and down to earth. The dishes he taught his pupils and wrote about were far removed from those of the haute cuisine as served in his restaurant. They were simple, homely dishes, well within the capabilities of a modest cook. Thanks to him, unpretentious dishes like canards aux navets and veau braisé aux carottes began to find their way into the homes of the English middle class.

In 1934, Boulestin's place as food writer for *Vogue* was taken by June Platt, a cosmopolitan American who had lived for some years in France. Her recipes were an appealing blend of French and American which fitted in well with the mood of the time. This new style of food caught on with the fashionable set, a narrow circle of people who could afford to travel, and who were as much at home in New York or Paris as in London. They lived for the most part in London, in houses or flats, or in medium-sized country houses, or divided their time between the two. These were not the aristocracy, whose lifestyle seemed to remain in a semi-permanent status quo, about twenty-five years behind the times, where only the smallest changes were allowed to ruffle the surface. (At Flete, the Mildmays' house near Plymouth, years after electricity had been installed, the footmen still continued to carry the lamps in each evening, and remove them next morning, just as they had done with oil lamps which needed to be cleaned and refilled.)

Many of the great landowners, rich as they were, had been forced to retrench after the end of the First World War, as a result of increased taxation and the growing agricultural depression which preceded the recession. Almost without exception, they chose to do this by selling off their London properties, rather than diminish the size, or the style, of their country estates, or impoverish their collections of furniture and paintings. Most of the great private houses in London were sold to property developers and demolished between the wars, while others were destroyed by bombs during the second war. Devonshire House was sold for one million pounds in 1919, and demolished in 1924. This great house was built by William Kent in the eighteenth century; it stood in Piccadilly, opposite the Ritz, taking up a whole block, with a vast garden stretching away behind it. Hotels like Grosvenor House and the Dorchester, and blocks of flats like Brook House – in its turn destroyed by bombs – were erected on the sites of the great family houses, often bearing the same name. By the end of the Second World War only a few remained, like Apsley House, Spencer House and Londonderry House.

In the vast country houses like Blenheim, Chatsworth and Eaton Hall, there had been little change since Edwardian times. Like cumbersome ocean liners which continue to move days after their engines have been switched off, these huge establishments ploughed on majestically. As Lord Lambton remarked, recalling his youth at Lambton Castle and Fenton: 'The meals consisted of five courses, where they used to be six or seven.'

Few people thought of modernizing their kitchens until after the Second World War. It took the butler at Chatsworth six minutes to walk from the kitchen to the dining-room. Most of the cooking was still done on Aga-style solid-fuel ranges; a thermostatically controlled gas oven was introduced in 1923, but there was no gas supply in the country. Electric thermostatically controlled ovens appeared on the market in 1933; Mrs Tanner, the cook at Chatsworth, persuaded the Duke of Devonshire to install one near the dining-room, so that she could serve soufflés. But her plan failed, for it took the butler too long to walk around the huge table, and the soufflé collapsed before it could be served. It was not here, in the houses of the mega-rich, that the move towards a new simplicity began, but in the more modest homes of a younger, more fashionable set.

The food in our own home was a good example of Scottish country house food. We lived in a fairly remote part of north-east Scotland, with little social life apart from shooting parties. My father was a purist about food, and liked only the very plainest things. He had a horror of rich sauces, butter and cream, which literally made him ill. As I have said, my mother had little interest in food, unlike so many of her American contemporaries who came to live in Britain in the 1920s. But she learnt to cook after the Second World War, and thoroughly enjoyed it. We lived for the most part on prime ingredients, very simply cooked. We had our own farms, and a large kitchen garden, salmon river and grouse moor, so that we were almost self-supporting.

Each Sunday we had roast beef: a sirloin with the fillet attached. My father was an expert carver, and gave each person a thickish slice of the fillet, with one or two thinnish slices of the sirloin. For the next two or three days we ate cold roast beef, rather rare, which we adored. I don't remember ever having it hashed up or reheated in any form. Salmon was always poached; when hot, it came with a sauce made from its cooking liquor, reduced. When cold, with mayonnaise. We ate a lot of salads, for my father loved cold food. He insisted on making the salad dressing himself; bottles of olive oil and vinegar, salt, pepper, sugar and Worcestershire sauce were laid out on a side table. My father was terribly fussy about his food; the only comments I remember hearing were criticisms.

Each winter, before the war, my parents would spend two months travelling to warm places like Mexico or South

America, or sailing with friends. My father had had tuber-culosis as a young man, and had been advised to winter abroad. Then my sisters and I would have food that seemed even duller than when our parents were at home. For good as our food was, in its way, it was not the sort to appeal to a child. It never occurred to me then that food could be fun, or in any way enjoyable.

In the 1930s my parents had a small house in St James's Place, and each summer my mother would travel south to enjoy herself. My father would join her for a little while, then he would go back to Scotland with a sigh of relief. For although he loved travelling, he disliked London and social life equally. In the early 30s, before I was born, my sisters would also go to London, but they had to stay with Nanny in the Stafford Hotel next door, for the house was too small to hold them all. In London the two little girls found them-selves thrown into another world without warning, with terrifying ordeals like Lady Astor's fancy-dress parties, and dancing classes with the little Princesses. Our Scottish nanny took it all in her stride, and remained unimpressed. When one of the smart nannies at the dancing class enquired whether we were going away for the summer, Nanny replied dourly: 'We're away the noo.' My elder sister was less phlegmatic. When faced with a crowded London street for the first time, she burst into tears, wailing: 'All these people, and nobody knows us.'

This privileged way of life changed abruptly – and for good, in our case – with the outbreak of war in 1939. Our house in Scotland was turned into a hospital for wounded soldiers and the family moved into one end of it. Our cook, Mrs Jones, found herself cooking for about a hundred people, including patients and nurses. It was to her credit, and to the nature of our somewhat austere diet, that our food changed hardly at all. (Mrs Jones was later awarded the OBE.)

After only eighteen years the country found itself again in the grip of food rationing. But this time the Government was prepared, and ration books were already printed, awaiting distribution. Much had been learnt during the First World War, when rationing had only been introduced halfway through, in 1916. By 1920 it was already coming to an end, unlike the aftermath of the Second World War, when rationing dragged on for almost ten years. The study of our national diet brought about by the First World War was to prove of immense value, not only in combating the war to come, but also in the Depression of the early 30s. By 1931 the nation's health was causing grave concern, especially in poor mining districts like Yorkshire and Lancashire. The Ministry of Health set up an Advisory Committee on Nutrition, which issued a series of pronouncements, urging the British to eat more fruit and raw vegetables, cheese, milk and oily fish. As usual, their advice was largely ignored, for, as George Orwell pointed out in *The Road to Wigan Pier*, it is only the rich who want to eat healthy food and breakfast on orange juice and Ryvita. The poor, living on the breadline in a permanent state of lassitude and depression, needed the quick lift they got from food like sliced white bread and jam, sweet tea, and fish and chips.

For the well-off, and especially for the young, the end of the First World War was followed by a period of euphoria. Everyone wanted to enjoy themselves and to live, at least for a time, purely hedonistic lives. As Loelia Lindsay recalled in her memoirs: 'Wounded soldiers in their blue suits and red ties disappeared from the square gardens and hospital wards became ballrooms again. London was dancing mad – it seemed we couldn't have enough of it.'

The same mood, influenced by the United States, brought in its wake such things as gramophones, dinner jackets, cocktails, sports cars, nightclubs and jazz. Cocktail parties became fashionable, and buffet dinners replaced the formal dinners of the past. Meals were held later than ever before. Staying at Fort Belvedere, country home of the Prince of Wales, in 1930, Diana Cooper wrote to Conrad Russell: 'Everything is a few hours later than in other places. (Perhaps it's American time.) A splendid tea arrived at 6.30. Dinner was at 10. Emerald (Cunard) arrived at 8.30 for cocktails.'

Fort Belvedere was an exaggerated case, but even in traditional country houses the meals were served later than in other places, and this still goes on today. Breakfast at nine, or nine thirty on Sundays, lunch at one thirty, tea at five, and dinner at eight thirty was, and still is, considered normal.

There was a general resolve among the younger generation never to return to the stuffy formality of pre-war days, or seven-course meals, and batteries of servants. This coincided with a growing reluctance on the part of the working classes to spend their lives in domestic service, as many had been happy to do before the First World War. Most of the men who had served in the armed forces showed little inclination to go back into service; having tasted independence, they preferred to find jobs in factories. It became progressively harder to find male living-in staff for the big houses, and the balance of indoor servants became predominantly female. For young women, domestic service for a good employer still offered a fairly enjoyable life, with chances of improvement, and the possibility of finding a husband among the male employees. Lady Anne Hill remembered the servants in her parents' house in Suffolk in the 1920s: 'They were tremendously overworked and underpaid, but they had great fun. I knew the maids frightfully well – I used to play whist with them. I remember roars of laughter.'

The number of living-in servants seems unbelievable today. In a sense, it became a vicious circle, for the more numerous they were, the more junior servants were needed to wait on them. At Chatsworth in 1930 there were thirty-nine living-in servants, with about twenty more coming in each day. At times like Christmas, when all the family came to stay, they must have been kept busy, for this meant six rival nurseries installed, with six resident nannies and nursery-maids, for the old Duke had twenty grandchildren at that time. While the nursery-maids were responsible for making breakfast and tea, both the main meals had to be carried up to the various nurseries by the footmen.

Chatsworth was exceptional, even among country houses, but in more modest establishments the number of staff was still considerable. In 1928, Sir Roderick Jones and his wife, the writer Enid Bagnold, were living in London and Rottingdean. The Joneses were not especially rich, although Sir Roderick must have been earning a good salary as head of Reuters, yet they employed thirteen indoor servants and five outdoor ones, including a chauffeur, two grooms and two gardeners. All were ruled by Cutmore, the butler/valet, who supervised the weekly move from London to Sussex. The cook and most of the servants were sent ahead by train, with a taxi to meet them, while the Joneses and their children, Cutmore and the silver canteen were conveyed in two cars. Milk and papers were stopped in one house and started in the other. For longer periods, caretakers were installed in the empty house.

All things considered, life below stairs must have been more fun in the really big houses. Flete had about fifty bedrooms, and a living-in staff of eighteen. A Devon lady who had been second kitchen maid there from 1936 to 1938 spoke to me nostalgically of their life, which involved travelling round the three great Mildmay houses at different times of year, leaving a skeleton staff behind in each one. The maids had alternate evenings off, unless there were people staying, and alternate Sundays, with two weeks' holiday a year. This gave them lots of time to visit their families, and a bus was sometimes laid on to take them to the local hops. She told me she left regretfully after two years, to 'better herself'. She had to do this, she explained, as there was no future for advancement if you stayed in the same house all the time, especially one like Flete, where the housekeeper, cook, butler and valet all stayed for fifty years.

In less old-fashioned houses, the decreasing number of servants was offset by the advances in domestic technology. Central heating began to replace the endless series of coal fires, while refrigerators simplified the preparation and storage of food. Gas and electric cookers gradually ousted the old black ranges, which had to be cleaned every day. By 1939 there were 9 million gas cookers throughout the UK, and 1½ million electric cookers. Both, by this time, boasted thermostatically controlled ovens.

The standard of cooking varied from house to house, just as it always has. In many, the food must have been tedious in the extreme, with menus that rarely changed except in detail, based on a series of culinary clichés. In others, it was exceptional, as described by one writer in 1929: 'Clean, tasty English cooking – the fruits of a thousand years of civilization.'

Few of my contemporaries seem to be aware of the good food that existed, at least in certain circles, before the war. When asked the subject of this book, I was met with general incredulity. 'Good food before the war – was there any?' was a typical response. 'Rather a non-starter, surely?' was another. 'Bangers and mash? Toad-in-the-hole?' enquired a third, while another, getting his timespan confused, ventured: 'Woolton pie?'

Yet every now and then a random hint surfaces, suggesting that here and there, in unexpected corners, this sort of cooking still goes on, hidden from public scrutiny, just as it always has been. While writing this book in the 1990s, I read in *Tatler* an account of staying with the Duke of Beaufort at Badminton. 'Three large cooks toil permanently in the kitchen, with a brief to produce top quality English dishes. You do not find elaborate cuisine at Badminton, which the Beauforts regard as "restaurant food" which you would have "during the week, in London". In the country they eat fish pie with white sauce, hard-boiled eggs in cheese sauce, rather a lot of lamb and pheasant, and chops in aspic with minted peas arranged concentrically around the plate.'

Does this sort of cooking still go on today, I wonder, in the kitchens of the grand houses that we never see? I doubt it, fearing that the dread hand of *Masterchef* may have taken over.

## Hostesses and Food Writers

Entertaining in the country houses did not change much, except the visits became shorter. Apart from Christmas and the summer holidays, guests came for weekends which were called 'Saturday to Monday', and for shooting parties. These usually lasted for three days in the middle of the week, which meant that no serious 'shot' could hold down a job and still be free to accept invitations to shoot.

One of the hardest things for us to envisage nowadays is the sheer scale of life in the big houses. At their first dinner party after their marriage in 1930, the Duke and Duchess of Westminster entertained seventy-two guests to dinner. They were all seated at one table, covered with a single damask cloth. This was at Eaton Hall, in Cheshire, where they could put up forty weekend guests. In London, at her house in Charles Street, Mrs Ronnie Greville had fifty-six guests to dinner in 1928. They had an eight-course meal, and Ambrose's band played throughout. In the same year, in the process of changing and redecorating their house at Rottingdean, Sir Roderick and Lady Jones commissioned Alan Walton, the fashionable decorator of the day, to marble two dining tables for them, to seat twenty-eight guests. Lady Astor was another hostess who liked to entertain on a massive scale, although not always successfully, according to Harold Nicolson's diaries. In 1930 he wrote: 'Down to Cliveden. A dark autumnal day. Thirty-two people in the house. Cold and draughty. Little groups of people wishing they were alone: a lack of organisation: a desultory drivel. The party is in itself good enough. (Duff and Diana Cooper, Tom and Cimmie Moseley, Harold and Dorothy Macmillan, Bob Boothby etc.) But it does not hang together. After dinner, in order to enliven the party, Lady Astor dons a Victorian hat and a pair of false teeth. It does not enliven the party.'

Behaviour was different in those days, when to be entertaining was considered a social duty. As Cynthia Asquith remarked, in her memoirs: 'We were brought up to believe that silence is never golden.' In his book of Anne Fleming's letters, Mark Amory described social life at Stanway in the 1920s. 'The atmosphere to be created was gaiety this side of boisterousness, of wit but not self-conscious exhibitionism. Serious topics were treated lightly, light matters given serious consideration, solemnity banned. Politicians might be present but they would not discourse on politics. Conversation should be general but sparkling.' At the table, guests would start to eat as soon as they had been served; only the governess waited until everyone had helped themselves. Women rarely drank spirits, or even much wine; barley water was always much in evidence. In many houses, as at Flete and Eaton Hall, drinks were never served before dinner, while at Cliveden, alcohol at any time was banned outright.

Although there had been notable hostesses in earlier times, they had mostly operated within specific fields, like Trollope's Lady Glencora and her political soirées in the Palliser novels. In the 20s a new sort of entertaining became fashionable; one might call it entertaining for entertaining's sake. No longer did its proponents seek power, either for themselves or for their protégés. Entertaining had become an end in itself.

Few of the hostesses were beauties, or even especially good-looking. Beauties had other things to do. The talents that made a good hostess were the very ones that a clever woman could cultivate, as a compensation for lack of beauty. What was needed was wit, originality, a light touch, boundless energy and a lot of money. A streak of frivolity and driving ambition also helped. Armed with most of these, a worldly and intelligent woman could create an amusing life for herself and her friends, while the beauties sat back and led a passive existence, receiving compliments, invitations and proposals of marriage from all sides.

In London, Paris and New York, standards of entertaining grew higher and higher. People in society were restless, spoilt, easily bored. The leading hostesses of the day were smart in the American sense, adept at creating an elegant and stylish ambiance, with interesting men and amusing, pretty women, sparkling conversation and delicious food.

The two most successful hostesses between the wars were indubitably Lady Cunard and Lady Colefax. Neither wrote a cookery book, but both were reputed to have excellent food. Yet food was only one of the important assets a host-ess needed to have up her sleeve: the talent to amuse, or to entertain, certainly ranked higher, and this both ladies possessed in abundance. Both were intelligent and cultivated women, although both were sometimes portrayed as silly geese by their acquaintances, for each had their own camp, with their champions as well as their detractors. Lady Cunard's field of activities was primarily musical, for the love of her life was the conductor Sir Thomas Beecham. Lady Colefax had a passion for royalty and high society, but she also loved and prized intellectuals, and numbered Virginia Woolf among her friends. (Which did not stop Virginia Woolf being extremely malicious about her on occasion.)

Lady Cunard was American, born Maud Burke. In 1895 she married Sir Bache Cunard, of the shipping fortune, and came to live in England. Sir Bache was twenty years older than Lady Cunard, and by 1911 she had fallen in love with Thomas Beecham, and left Sir Bache. She installed herself and her daughter Nancy, later to become a symbol of the 1920s, in a large house in Grosvenor Square, and concentrated her energies on entertaining, for which she had a genius. Like most of the great hostesses, Lady Cunard had little time for domestic – or family – life. In later years, when Nancy was looking for a house, her mother remarked: 'Only the banal need a home.' Relations between mother and daughter grew steadily worse. Nancy felt she had been neglected by her mother as a child, and never forgave her. Once, as an adult, Nancy startled other guests during after-dinner games in a country house when she met the query, 'Who would you most like to see come into the room?' with the chilling reply: 'Lady Cunard, dead.'

Yet Emerald Cunard (she changed her name from Maud in 1926, at the age of fifty-four) was dearly loved by friends of all ages. Loelia Lindsay, in her memoirs *Grace and Favour*, writes: 'Beloved Emerald Cunard. From my gawky schoolgirl days onwards she was always kind and fun-providing, and of all the people I have known well, I am most grateful for having had Emerald as a friend.'

Osbert Sitwell paid tribute to her qualities as a hostess. 'Her airy and rather impersonal alertness, her wit, made her drawing room unlike any other. Lady Cunard loves to be amused, but she tires so quickly of dullness that she has her own method of dealing with it. She can goad the conversation like a bull, and she a matador, and compel it to show a fiery temper.' Sitwell also praises her dedication: 'It was largely her support and the way she marshalled her forces, that enabled the wonderful seasons of opera and ballet to materialise. Her will power was sufficient, her passion for music fervent enough to make opera almost compulsory for those who wished to be fashionable.'

As we have already noted, the great hostesses were rarely, if ever, beauties, and Lady Cunard was no exception. Loelia Lindsay describes her appearance: 'She has yellow, fluffy hair, a sharp little beaked nose, eyes swimming in mascara, and she has been unkindly described as "a canary of prey".' Siegfried Sassoon, never the most charitable of men, refers to 'that bobbed and bedizoned blonde with startled and unspeculative eyes in a clown-painted face'.

During the latter part of her life, Lady Cunard showed great courage in facing adversity from two directions. Persecuted by her daughter Nancy's vindictive campaign in print, and deserted by Sir Thomas Beecham for a younger woman, she sailed back from New York in the middle of the war to find her house in Grosvenor Square had been destroyed by bombs. She sold off her possessions, moved into the Dorchester, and proceeded to entertain with all her old verve until her death in 1948.

Lady Colefax was inevitably in competition with Lady Cunard. They each had their own circles, which overlapped here and there, and their own admirers, but were rarely to be found in each other's houses. One of Lady Colefax's camp was Harold Nicolson, who commented in his diary: 'I think Sybil Colefax is a clever old bean who ought to concentrate on intellectuals and not social guests.' Like Lady Cunard, Lady Colefax was married to a much older man, the barrister Sir Arthur Colefax. They lived in Argyll House in the King's Road (opposite the fire station today), which is a hostess's dream, with its romantic façade, wrought-iron gates, stone-flagged courtyard and lovely garden. But Lady Colefax was another redoubtable character who showed courage in adversity, for in 1930 they lost all their capital in the New York stock market crash. The same year Sir Arthur became deaf, and was forced to retire. Undaunted by this dramatic change in their fortunes, Sybil Colefax set herself up as an interior decorator, doing much of the work herself. She made £2,000 in her first year, which was no mean sum for those days, while continuing to entertain in Argyll House. By 1934 she started her own firm, Sybil Colefax, with premises in Bruton Street, and in 1938 she took on John Fowler, a Chelsea neighbour, as her partner. (In 1950 she was bought out by Nancy Lancaster, and the firm continues today as Colefax and Fowler.)

Sybil Colefax continued to live, and to entertain, at Argyll House until her husband's death in 1936, when she gave a series of 'last dinners' before quitting the house. Desmond MacCarthy describes one of these in his diaries: 'Sybil had excelled even her own standards of lion hunting by assembling for dinner Harold Nicolson, Winston and Clementine Churchill, Duff and Diana Cooper, Somerset Maugham, Artur Rubinstein and many others.'

In the immediate circle of the Prince of Wales and Mrs Simpson, Lady Cunard and Lady Colefax found themselves in direct rivalry, both deeply disapproved of by the rest of the royal family, who considered them a bad influence.

Both were guests at a dinner party given by Mrs Simpson for the King in 1936. Luckily for us, that inveterate diner-out Harold Nicolson was there to record the scene: 'It is evident that Lady Cunard is incensed by the presence of Lady Colefax, and that Lady Colefax is furious that Lady Cunard should have been asked. Lady Oxford appears astonished to find either of them at what was to have been a quite intimate party.'

Another successful hostess-turned-decorator was Syrie Maugham, who lived next door to her rival Sybil Colefax in the King's Road, and immediately opposite the other fashionable decorator, John Fowler. The daughter of Dr Barnardo, Syrie had been married briefly – and unhappily – to Somerset Maugham. After the breakdown of her marriage, she started working as a professional decorator. Of all the decorators of her day, she was one of the most brilliant, and the most innovative. As Ursula Wyndham recalls in her memoirs, *Astride the Wall*, 'Syrie Maugham was the first society decorator who started the fashion for the all-white drawing room, celadon green having been the previous "safe" colour, not likely to be mocked by sardonic friends.'

Syrie Maugham was a gifted hostess, as was the American-born decorator Elsie de Wolfe. Unlike the others, Elsie de Wolfe was a decorator first, before going on to become a social figure. Like Ladies Colefax and Cunard, she married a rich English husband much older than herself: Sir Charles Mendl, the Paris representative in the News Department of the Foreign Office. The Mendls had two homes in France: an apartment in the Rue de Rivoli, and the exquisite Villa Trianon at Versailles. They entertained ceaselessly, both in

France and in London during the season. Lady Mendl published a small cookery book under her maiden name, *Elsie de Wolfe's Recipes for Successful Dining*, filled with good recipes and outrageous comments: 'At Christmas time 1931, I had a table of gold (lamé), hoping that it might in some way draw us all back to the old gold standard . . .' Yet the recipes themselves are excellent, and grounded in common sense.

Lady Astor was primarily a political hostess, as was Margot Asquith, later to become Lady Oxford. Born Margot Tennant, she was the second wife of Herbert Asquith, the Liberal Prime Minister who was later made Lord Oxford. Each weekend, according to *Edith Olivier's Journals*, Margot Asquith 'collected together fourteen people who had little in common, and who she hardly knew herself'.

Then there was the racing world: rich philistines for the most part, who were prepared to spend vast sums of money on their parties. Desmond MacCarthy describes one such event at the house of Mrs Rupert Beckett, in 1931: 'I enjoyed the glitter and splendour. It was a new "set" for me, rich, smart, racing people and I was amused. The enormously rich Lady Granard was there in ropes of pearls and her mild, exquisitely clean husband with a pearl the size of an electric button in his shirt.'

Some of the hostesses operating on a more modest scale were authors of contemporary cookery books. One of the most accomplished was Lady Jekyll, whose *Kitchen Essays* first appeared in *The Times* on Saturdays in 1921 and 1922. Agnes Jekyll was a remarkable woman; the youngest daughter of William Graham, a friend and patron of the pre-Raphaelites, she had been brought up in an intellectual and artistic environment, and became a notable hostess among the intelligentsia. She was at the same time an excellent organizer, and played an active part in many facets of public life. A pillar of the St John Ambulance Brigade, she was also a JP, a governor of Godalming Secondary School, of a hospital in the East End of London, and of a borstal for girls.

Another remarkable cookery book was published in 1925, when its author was in her late seventies. This was *Minnie Lady Hindlip's Cookery Book*. According to her great-grandson, Lord Hindlip, Lady Hindlip was by all accounts a remarkable lady, no beauty but very amusing and a wonderful hostess. When she was asked why she liked going to children's parties, she replied: 'My dear, I ask who the little children are and then I think who they really are!'

Also published in the 1920s was *A Book of Scents and Dishes* by Dorothy Allhusen. It was in Mrs Allhusen's charming country house that Jessica Mitford first met her cousin Esmond Romilly, then on sick leave from fighting with the International Brigade in the Spanish Civil War. Over the weekend they fell in love and made plans to elope. A week later they left secretly for Spain, and another of the Mitford legends began to unfold.

Most admired of all the cookery books published in the 1930s was probably *Lady Sysonby's Cook Book*. This is an unusually interesting book, with illustrations by Oliver Messel and an introduction by Osbert Sitwell. Ria Sysonby, whose daughter Loelia married the Duke of Westminster (and later, Sir Martin Lindsay of Dowhill), was married to a courtier. Fritz Ponsonby, later Lord Sysonby, was Private Secretary first to Queen Victoria, and then to Edward VII. The Sysonbys lived in a grace-and-favour apartment in St James's Palace, and, in the country, near Guildford. Unlike most great hostesses, Lady Sysonby was a beauty, and much in demand. Although they were by no means rich, she was always beautifully dressed, and had excellent food. Her daughter Loelia told me: 'Any cook seeking a new situation had only to mention that she had been employed by Lady Sysonby, and she was at once engaged.'

Another esteemed hostess who wrote cookery books was Ruth Lowinsky, whose first book, *Lovely Food*, is a collector's item. Published in 1931 by the Nonesuch Press, it is beautifully produced on hand-made paper, with elegant and idiosyncratic illustrations by her husband, Thomas Lowinsky. Ruth Lowinsky was an heiress. Her father, Leopold Hirsch, was a cultivated banker of German descent who had made a great fortune in gold and diamonds in South Africa in the 1870s. The Hirsches lived in a magnificent house in Kensington Palace Gardens and Ruth was a student at the Slade, where she met her husband-to-be. Thomas Lowinsky was an original and interesting painter, also a discerning collector. In 1990 there was a retrospective exhibition of his work at the Tate Gallery.

Ruth gave up painting on her marriage, and turned her gifts to entertaining. Dumpy and undistinguished in appearance, she was immensely cultivated, sophisticated and amusing. The Lowinskys lived in Kensington Square with their four children. Each summer they were in the habit of taking a large country house; one year they rented Stanway from the Wemysses. (Since many aristocratic families owned several large country houses, it was considered quite normal to rent one or other of them out at certain times of year, when they did not want it themselves.)

Ruth Lowinsky published three cookery books in the 1930s. Her recipes are original, but erratic. Since she did not learn to cook herself until the outbreak of war, she must have relied on information from her Austrian cook. I sometimes wonder what her friend Constance Spry must have made of the Lowinsky oeuvre in this respect, for Mrs Spry was the first cookery writer whose recipes actually worked. But it is for the spirit of her book that Ruth Lowinsky will be remembered. As she says in the introduction to *Lovely Food*, 'Remember that food must above all things be varied, surprising and original.'

There were also other more specialized writers: herbalists like Mrs Leyel, who wrote *The Gentle Art of Cookery* with Miss Olga Hartley in 1925, then went on to found the Society of Herbalists, known today as the Herb Society, and the Culpeper shops. Another herbalist/author was Eleanour Sinclair Rohde, who wrote a number of books about herbs, herb gardens and vegetables in the 1930s.

Another influential publication was *The Week-End Book*, which was edited and published by Francis Meynell, the founder of the Nonesuch Press, and friend and publisher of Ruth Lowinsky. *The Week-End Book* was published annually, with revisions and additions, both in England and the USA, from 1924 until the 1950s. It was rather like a magazine in content, with sections on such disparate subjects as birds, architecture, music and after-dinner games. The cookery section dealt with such things as lists for the weekend store-cupboard, sandwich fillings, picnic food and dishes for the inexperienced cook. It proved immensely successful, and sold more than 50,000 copies in the first four years.

Mrs Simpson did not waste her time writing cookery books, for she had better things to do. Of all the hostesses of her day, she must rate as the most successful, in that her aim was clearly defined. She set out to please and entertain the Prince of Wales, and in this she succeeded beyond her wildest dreams. In social terms she was a brilliant figure, an instigator who enjoyed setting trends, and a perfectionist for whom no detail was too much trouble. She was always immaculately dressed, and proved herself well able to provide a stimulating ambiance, with witty repartee and first-rate food. In his diaries, Cecil Beaton describes going to draw Mrs Simpson shortly before the abdication, in her rented house in Regent's Park. After the session was over, they were joined by the King and Wallis's Aunt Bessy for a quick drink before going on to dine with Emerald Cunard. Even on this informal occasion, a silver tray was handed round with no less than nine different sorts of canapés, eight of them hot, to accompany the cocktails.

## Menus

The English pattern of eating was by no means as hidebound as people pretend. The customary roast on Sunday, followed by a series of dishes of hashed and reheated meat on successive days, was widespread, but only at a certain level of affluence. Below that level, the weekly budget would not rise to a joint, while above that level, in the large country houses for instance, the remains of the joint would have been sent up to the nursery, or served in the servants' hall. In really big houses like Chatsworth, a whole carcass of beef or lamb would be consumed at one time: the prime joints in the dining-room, and the lesser parts in the nursery, schoolroom, housekeeper's room or servants' hall.

There has been a lot of talk, usually tinged with nostalgia, about 'nursery food'. In effect, it was probably less good than people like to recall, for bad relations often existed between nursery and kitchen. In her memoirs, *Astride the Wall*, Ursula Wyndham's memories of nursery food add a sour note: 'greasy mutton, overcooked vegetables wallowing in the water they had been cooked in, burnt rice puddings . . . This prison fare was the unsupervised production of the kitchen maid.'

Like all periods of transition, the two decades between the wars showed a wide variation in patterns of eating. These depended not only on the affluence of the households concerned, which would previously have been the main factor in deciding culinary habits, but also on the position of the family as regards fashionableness. In a household like that of the Mildmays, where Edwardian values were upheld and old ways adhered to, meals were still formal and lengthy. Before a dinner party in their London house in Berkeley Square, for instance, the male guests were informed on arrival who they were to take in to dinner. The guests would assemble in the library and make desultory conversation, without drinks in any form, then they would line up in couples and troop in to dinner.

This would start with a choice of thick or thin soup, followed by a hot fish dish. Then came an entrée, either poultry or game, and a second meat dish. This might be followed by a separate vegetable course, like the celebrated asparagus ice, then a pudding and a savoury. Finally the table was cleared of all extraneous dishes and the fruit plates would be handed round, each one bearing a small lace mat with a glass fingerbowl half filled with water, and a silver gilt knife and fork. A series of dishes of fruit would then be handed round, probably three or four or even five, each one bearing just one sort of fruit which had been sent up from the garden at Flete. These were followed by a silver cream jug and sugar bowl. Then came coffee, after which the ladies would withdraw, leaving the men to their port and brandy.

An unusual pattern can be found in the menus of Mrs Ronnie Greville, at the dinners she held in her house in Charles Street, or at Polesden Lacey. After three hot dishes – soup, fish, and poultry or game – a cold main dish was often served, possibly boeuf en gêlée, or ham mousse, accompanied by a salad.

At Faringdon, where Lord Berners was renowned for his food, the meals were rather idiosyncratic. Lord Berners loved rich food, and judging from the description of his meals, it would seem that his cook indulged him up to the hilt. Lobster was often served – as a first course – for Sunday lunch, followed by a chicken pie, or a roast fillet of beef. Friends spoke fondly of a cold dish of Dover sole, poached fillets lying in a horseradish cream sauce with chives. Sliced chicken was served in aspic, with strips of red pepper set in the jelly. The vegetables were home-grown, very small, and beautifully cooked, and there was always home-made bread baked in a plait. The puddings were very popular with his guests: baked apples stuffed with chopped walnuts in a toffee sauce, summer pudding, strawberry shortcake, and pudding Louise, which was not unlike a Bakewell tart.

One group that broke with tradition in gastronomic matters, as in many others, was the Bloomsbury set. The writers and painters of the 1920s and 30s loved to eat and drink well, but lacked the funds – or the desire – to do it in the traditional ways. Having freed themselves from class distinctions, they ignored current patterns of behaviour in the kitchen and the dining room, and chose to adopt a totally different way of eating, much closer to our own. They were almost without exception badly off, making do with a maid-of-all-work, who also did the cooking. These girls were such modest cooks, usually untrained and inexperienced, that their employers ended up doing much of the cooking themselves. Virginia Woolf used to bake bread, which she enjoyed doing, and Carrington cooked frequently, often preparing food for weekend parties at Ham Spray. In a letter to Lytton Strachey she describes making 'brews of quince cheese which [scent] the whole house'; in another, dated April 1928, she describes making zabaglione: 'I made a Zambal-ione [sic] last night and just as it was finished Henry (Lamb) stepped backwards and knocked the bowl all over the carpet!

But fortunately there were masses of eggs, so I quickly whisked up another one.'

The Bloomsbury set loved to travel, and they did this in a way that is familiar to many of us today, but was very unusual at that time. Whereas the rich and fashionable flitted about from Paris to New York to Cap Ferrat, staying in grand hotels, villas or yachts, the intelligentsia were more adventurous in that they were not afraid of discomfort, although their scope was limited, and rarely stretched beyond France, Italy or Spain. Staying in inns and eating very simply, they became familiar with the local cuisine and the vins du pays in a way that the rich never did, for the food in smart hotels had already become international, much as it is today. In another letter to Lytton Strachey, Carrington describes a meal in France while travelling with Augustus and Dorelia John: 'Lunch was served outside under the planes. Hare pâté, grilled red mullet, a marvellous salad and delicious coffee, and Château des Papes Telegraphes, a whole bottle; our resolution for a cheese and salad lunch faded away!' Carrington's letters are filled with enthusiastic references to food and wine; one in particular refers to having had a very good Nuit Sans (*sic*) George. Spelling was not her strong point.

Back home, meals in the Bloomsbury circle were simple, and very wholesome, most of the time, with the occasional splurge for a special occasion. Frances Partridge wrote: 'Our Ham Spray food between the wars was simple and home-produced. We favoured an almost permanent ham, potted in one of the bathrooms, really wonderful brawn to a recipe by Boris Anrep, and ways of eating every piece of our own pig except the chitterlings, and a wonderful beestings pudding (this was a super-rich bread and butter pudding from a calving cow's first milk, plus sultanas). Home-grown local dishes were jugged hare and perdrix aux choux. We prided ourselves on growing all our own vegetables and fruit; raspberries were splendid, we had fine figs, grapes, peaches and nectarines, average apples and pears. Vegetables simply cooked, though salsify à la crème became a main dish. Seakale, simply boiled with butter, asparagus, celeriac, chicory forced in the woodshed for winter. Cabbages (I did have a splendid way of cooking them very slowly with cinnamon, brown sugar, bacon and sultanas). When we came to London our restaurant meals were most untypical, and a glorious treat – the Basque was a rarity – the Ivy a special favourite. Birthday dinner was often canard sous presse, and crêpes suzette.'

A dinner given by Chips Channon at Moir House, St James's Place, February 1925.

'We began with blinis served with Swedish schnapps, to wash down the caviare. Then soup, followed by salmon, then an elaborate chicken. Then a sweet and a savoury. The candle light was reflected in my gold plate and the conversation was incessant. Eventually Cole Porter was sufficiently intoxicated to play the piano. He played for hours. I got to bed at 4.30 absolutely exhausted.'

A typical day in the life of Siegfried Sassoon, who in the mid-1920s decided to stay in bed all day and work at night. February 1924.

'In bed all day. (As usual.) Haddock and baked apple at 5.30 p.m. Soup, omelette and stewed prunes at the Monico 10.45. It is now 4 a.m. and I've just had some tea and bolted three sponge cakes.'

Luncheon with Lady Cunard, May 1930.

> A poached egg in a baked potato
> A lamb cutlet with six different vegetables
> A silver bowl of tapioca beaten to a froth with cream, served
> cold, with strawberries

A dinner at Buckingham Palace, March 1927.

> Consommé Messaline
> Rosettes de Saumon de Balmoral, Régence
> Cailles Epicurienne
> Filets d'Agneau des Gourmets
> Poulardes Rôties, Salade
> Asperges, Sauce Mousseline
> Soufflé Glacé Daphne
> Paniers de Friandises
> Kisch [*sic*] Lorraine

> One of the guests, Lady Mildmay, commented: 'The dinner
> table was one solid mass of gold plate, and the flowers were
> too lovely, yellow daffodils, blue iris and very golden
> mimosa. Everyone said the dinner was the best they had ever
> eaten, but I do not really agree. There were six things in
> succession, all hot, and the peas were quite uneatable.'

Marcel Boulestin's suggestion for a late supper,
November 1928.

> 'Nothing better, say at 3 o'clock in the morning, than a
> boiling hot soupe au choux and cold meat, with a very fresh,
> crisp salad. And you should drink with this one of those
> little pink or white wines from Anjou or Touraine, which
> have such a pleasant, sharp taste. (This is more suitable,
> though, for Chelsea than Bayswater – unless you happen to
> feel, for once, delightfully Bohemian.)'

Dinner with Mrs Ronald Tree (Nancy Lancaster), in the 1920s.

> Fish Chowder
> Poulets Rôtis au Cresson
> Legumes, Salade
> Mousse à l'Orange – Compote d'Oranges

Dinner (for the Japps) at Ham Spray, September 1925. From a letter to Lytton Strachey from Carrington.

> 'The dinner was indescribably grand. Epoch making; grape-fruit, then a chicken covered with fennel and tomato sauce, a risotto with almonds, onions, and pimentos, followed by sack cream, supported by Café Royal wine, perfectly warmed. (The cradle took Mrs Japp's breath away.)'

A buffet dinner at Lady Mendl's, at the Villa Trianon, Versailles, July 1932, as described in *Vogue*.

> 'Some forty of us dined on the enclosed terrace by candle-light, with the illuminated garden for a background. Of course it was a buffet dinner, as every big dinner is now. Elsie Mendl's menu was hot soup, boeuf braisé with all kinds of vegetables, and ice cream and strawberries. Nothing could be simpler, and nothing better.'

Supper with Frances Partridge, November 1927.

> 'We expected Dadie (Rylands) and Gerald (Brenan) at 41 about ten o'clock, and I had oysters for them, and cold partridges in aspic.'

A summer luncheon, suggested by Quaglino, 1935.

> Caviar de Sterlet, or Crab Cocktail
> Goujons de Sole Frites, Sauce Dugléré
> Noix de Veau en Aspic
> Mousse de Jambon – Salade Niçoise
> Fraises Monte Carlo – Biscuits à la Cuillère
> Canapé Diane

Breakfast served at a ball, 1927, as described in
*Vogue*.

> 'At 2 a.m. tankards of pale and light draught bitters replace
> the champagne, and ordinary roasting tins full of delicious
> little chipolata sausages, still steaming in the medium in
> which they were cooked, oust the more elegant quail. Bacon
> and eggs are still popular, as are kippers.'

Dinner with Mrs Ronnie Greville at Polesden
Lacey, Christmas 1931. (Note the cold main course.)

> Gnocchi à la Suisse
> Faisans Braisés au Céleri
> Viandes Froides – Salade
> Bavarois Vanille – Compote de Mirabelles

A luncheon suggested by Marcel Boulestin, 1928.

> Oeufs à la Gelée
> Pilaf aux Fruits de Mer
> Pintade Farcie, Pommes Pailles & Salade Verte
> Poires au Chocolat

An autumn luncheon, as suggested by Quaglino,
1935.

>Honey Dew Melon – Jambon de Bayonne
>Ravioli au Jus de Veau
>Grouse en Papillote, Pommes Soufflés
>Aubergines Provençales
>Compote de Fruits Frais – Gâteau au Chocolat

Luncheon with Lady Mendl, 1930.

>Cream of Green Pea Soup
>Crayfish Gloucester
>Baked Chicken
>Vanilla Ice with Hot Cherry Sauce

A dinner at Ham Spray, May 1929, from a letter to
Lytton Strachey from Carrington.

>'We had a fine dinner with Moselle and Burgundy, cold
>salmon and tartar sauce, followed by gammon and salad,
>followed by strawberries and kirsch, followed by brandies
>and coffee.'

Dinner for Edward VIII, given by Chips Channon
at 5 Belgrave Square, June 1936.

>'Dinner was perfect, we began with blinis and caviare, then
>sole muscat followed by boeuf provençal. It was served so
>speedily that we had finished before eleven, and then the
>ladies left, curtseying as they got up.'

Luncheon with Madame (Helena) Rubinstein, May
1933, as described in *Vogue*.

> 'At lunch with Madame Rubinstein, you might begin with a
> clear bouillon, then progress to a divine entrée of spinach
> purée rolled up in little crêpes. Then a fish curry (made with
> lobster claws and baby scallops), served with rice and chutney,
> followed by fresh pineapple, or strawberries with kirsch. The
> coffee is black as the ace of spades, in bright red cups.'

A dinner for four at Fort Belvedere, home of the
Prince of Wales, in the 1930s.

> 'It began with oysters in unlimited quantity, followed by a
> mousse of ham and foie gras, and a salad, and ended with a
> dish of very hot cheese fritters.'

A dinner given by Mrs Ronnie Greville at Polesden
Lacey, January 1932. (Note the cold main course.)

> Crème Crécy
> Sole Frite, Sauce Diable
> Soufflé de Jambon à la Parisienne
> Boeuf à la Gelée – Salade
> Poires à la Marquise
> Barquettes de Caviar

Dinner at the Eiffel Tower, now the White Tower,
in October 1929, from a letter to Julia Strachey
from Carrington.

> 'In the evening we had dinner with old Augustus (John) at
> the Eiffel Tour [*sic*]. Rather fun. Very late, at 9.30. Such a
> delicious meal. Snails. Wild duck and orange salad, and real
> iced raspberries with cream and two bottles of Burgundy.'

A dinner given for King George V and Queen
Mary at Chatsworth, July 4th, 1933.

Crème Sarah Bernhardt
Barbue Grimaldi
Caneton à l'Anglaise, Poussins Rôtis, Légumes
Mousse de Jambon, Salade Waldorf
Soufflé Esterhazy, Fraises Romanoff
Chester Cakes

BREAKFAST

It was during this transitional period between the wars that the classic British breakfast took shape. In the large country houses the lavish breakfast of Edwardian days was still the norm. A row of silver dishes on hot plates offered a choice of fried, boiled or scrambled eggs, bacon, sausages, tomatoes, fried bread, devilled kidneys, and a fish dish: either smoked haddock, kippers or kedgeree. On the cold table stood a ham, a tongue, and cold game in season. When there was no game a cold fish dish like soused herrings might take its place. Coffee and tea were served, with copious amounts of toast, butter and marmalade.

In the south, things were already starting to change. According to social historian Arnold Palmer in his book *Moveable Feasts*, a radical change was taking place: 'By 1925 many women had decided to breakfast in bed, at 8.15 or thereabouts, on a glass of orange juice, a piece of toast melba, a cup of coffee unsugared and black, and cigarettes. Their husbands did little better, in fact they often shared the meal.' This was the American influence which was to spread throughout the 1920s and 30s. Canadian Charles Ritchie, writing in his diaries in London just before the outbreak of the Second World War, was struck by 'the new, classless, Americanised English who have grapefruit for breakfast and prefer *The New Yorker* to *Punch*'.

By the end of the 1930s, the most popular breakfast with all classes, except the super sophisticates of Charles Ritchie's world, and the poor who could not afford it, was bacon and eggs, toast and marmalade, and coffee or tea. Even among the very poor, fried bacon was considered the vital ingredient of a proper breakfast, more important even than the eggs. While coffee was the most fashionable drink in

London and the south, tea was still the most widely drunk at all levels of society.

While fruit and fruit juices were starting to become popular on the breakfast table, American cereals had begun to appear in the shops, and were greeted with rapture. Even Lady Jekyll, normally the most sensible of women, writing in her weekly column in Saturday's *Times*, suggested serving 'a few spoonfuls of Puffed Wheat crisped hot in the oven and lying decoratively in small mother-o'-pearl shells', as an inexpensive alternative to salted almonds, for nibbling between courses at dinner parties.

For most people, the hallmark of the British breakfast is marmalade. This had been made in Britain for hundreds of years, with quince and other fruits. In the sixteenth and seventeenth centuries it was usually served sliced, as a dessert or sweetmeat, or as a digestive, or cure for colds. By the eighteenth century it was being made with Seville oranges, and in Scotland it began to be served at breakfast, as a preserve. Until then it had been pounded into a smooth paste; now it appeared in its familiar form, with little bits of peel within it. The first manufactured marmalade was Keiller's Dundee Marmalade, which started in 1797. Two other Scottish firms, Robertson's and Baxters, started selling their products in the 1860s, while the English firms of Cooper's, Wilkins of Tiptree, and Elsenham began production between 1875 and 1890. Jellied marmalade also became popular. Robertson's Golden and Silver Shred were made in late Victorian times, and Rose's Lime Marmalade in the 1930s. There was a wide variety: before the First World War there were twenty-seven varieties of Tiptree marmalade on sale; today there are still at least ten different sorts.

By the eighteenth century Scottish breakfasts were famous, far superior to those in England. Writers like Dr

Johnson, Boswell and Sir Walter Scott refer to a choice of tea, coffee or chocolate; hot porridge served with a mixture of cream and buttermilk; smoked reindeer ham, beef and mutton; smoked salmon and haddock, kippers and fresh herrings; bread, scones and thin cakes of oats and barley, eaten with fresh butter, blueberry jam, currant jelly and marmalade.

Our own breakfasts in Scotland before the last war were much like the traditional English country house breakfast, with a few differences. Whereas in most English houses porridge was only served occasionally, before hunting or shooting for instance, we ate it every day.

Scotsmen like my father ate their porridge standing up, and this seemed to me the most natural thing in the world, despite English mockery. They would help themselves to a dish of porridge from the hotplate, adding a pinch of salt and some cold milk, then instead of carrying it to the table, they would simply wander about the room as they ate it, reading the headlines of the newspapers, or gazing out of the window. In other words, they behaved just as we might with a glass of sherry, before sitting down to lunch.

My grandmother ate the same breakfast every day of her life: porridge, a soused herring, and two oatcakes. Our cook made marvellous oatcakes: triangular, very thin and fragile in the extreme. She claimed to use no fat whatsoever, but I find this hard to believe. With them, we ate butter from the town, which my father perversely preferred to our own farm butter, and Tiptree Orange Marmalade, still in the glass jar it came in. Scones were baked fresh early each morning; these were the Scottish sort, baked on a griddle, thin, soft and triangular in shape. There was always toast as well, but there was never enough. My mother would ring and ask for more, but by the time it came it was too late, and no one wanted it. I remember this as a constant source of friction between my parents.

As well as the array of cooked breakfast dishes, and the cold table, there was an amazing electric contraption in which you boiled your own egg, so that you could have it exactly as you liked, freshly cooked. Even before the war, there was a modicum of self-help in our house which seems unusual in retrospect, at a time when most owners of large houses rang to have a log put on the fire. My father liked to boil his own egg, make the salad dressing, and make up his own packed lunch from the remains of the breakfast table, for a solitary day's shooting.

## Porridge

The porridge at our home in Scotland had a marvellous 'set' quality about it, almost like junket, that I have never been able to repeat; it was probably the result of long, slow cooking, then standing for a while on the hot plate. Nowadays I use a method of my own, a compromise between the old way and the speedy modern version made with Quaker Oats. I no longer eat it for breakfast, but when coming home late at night, tired and hungry, I find it comforting, sustaining and easy to digest.

275ml water
½ teaspoon (or less) sea salt
45g medium oatmeal

Bring the water to the boil in a heavy pan. Add the salt, then sprinkle in the oatmeal, stirring constantly. Boil steadily for 5 minutes, stirring all the time, then transfer to a double boiler and cook gently for 15 minutes, stirring now and then. When the time is up, cover the pan, remove from the heat, and stand until ready to serve. Serves 1–2, with cold milk straight from the fridge. **AB**

# Kedgeree

Originally a breakfast dish, this later became popular as a first course for luncheon, or as a supper dish. In these cases it can be made richer, with the addition of cream and extra butter, but for breakfast it is best made quite simply. It can well be made in advance and reheated.

450g salmon
225g long-grain rice
4 eggs, hard-boiled
55–85g butter
sea salt and black pepper
150ml double cream (optional)
½ tablespoon finely chopped parsley

If cooking the salmon specially (it is also a good way of using up remains of a large fish), put it in a saucepan and cover with cold lightly salted water. Bring slowly to the boil, then simmer gently for 3 minutes. Cover the pan, remove from the heat, and leave until it has completely cooled. Then drain the fish, discard skin and bones, and flake the flesh. Boil the rice as usual and drain well. Assemble in a buttered bowl standing over a large pan of simmering water. Fill with rice and fish in alternate layers, adding roughly chopped hard-boiled eggs, small bits of butter, and lots of sea salt and black pepper. (And cream, if used.) Cover with foil and leave to heat for about 25 minutes, mixing together gently now and then with a wooden spoon. Turn into a serving dish and sprinkle with a little chopped parsley. Serves 4, with a green salad, as a lunch or supper dish, or 5–6 for breakfast. **AB**

# Smoked Haddock with Poached Eggs

Composite breakfast dishes of this sort were not usually served in the big country houses, where the different foods were served separately, so that the guests could combine them, or not, as they pleased. But in the smaller houses this would be a popular breakfast dish, since the combination of smoked haddock and eggs has always been much liked. Nowadays it makes a good light dish for luncheon or supper.

2 smoked haddock, undyed
275ml milk
4 freshly poached eggs
freshly ground black pepper

Cut each haddock in half and wash well. Put the pieces in a broad pan and pour over the milk. Add about the same amount of water, enough to barely cover the fish. Bring to the boil, cover the pan, and simmer gently for 12 minutes. Lift out the pieces of fish with a slotted spoon and drain in a colander, then lay them on a shallow dish. Place a poached egg carefully on each one and sprinkle with black pepper.

Alternatively, the fish can be taken off the bone and flaked, then piled on 4 rounds of hot (thinly) buttered toast. Sprinkle with black pepper, then lay an egg on top of each one. Serves 4. **AB**

## Mrs Anderson's Fish Cakes

Another example of a traditional breakfast dish which makes an excellent light main course for lunch or supper. Mrs Anderson was cook to Kathleen, Duchess of Rutland, before and during the war. She specifies cod or haddock, but I have also used salmon, which was delicious. Her fish cakes are particularly good in that they use a thick béchamel instead of the more usual mashed potato, or breadcrumbs, and the result is very light and moist.

900g cod or haddock fillet
450ml milk
salt and black pepper
55g butter
55g flour
1 tablespoon chopped parsley

2 eggs, beaten
dry white breadcrumbs
sunflower oil, for frying

Poach the fish in lightly salted milk, unless using salmon, which should be cooked in plain water, also lightly salted. When the fish is done, drain it, reserving the milk. Strain it, reserving 275 ml. Melt the butter, add the flour, and cook for 1 minute, stirring. Add the milk and bring to the boil, stirring till blended. Simmer gently for 3–4 minutes, adding salt and pepper to taste. Flake the fish, discarding skin and bone, and stir into the sauce, adding the chopped parsley. (Chop the larger flakes in half.) Chill the mixture for several hours, or overnight, then form into round cakes weighing about 85g each. Shape them on a floured board, then dip first in beaten egg and then in breadcrumbs.

Mrs Anderson's fish cakes were shaped like round balls, but these have to be deep-fried. I prefer to flatten mine, and shallow-fry them in a 1.5cm layer of oil. Drain on kitchen paper before serving. Makes 10–12. If serving for lunch or supper, they can be accompanied by fried parsley (page 155), or a sauce. Iced tomato sauce (page 157), piquant sauce (page 152), sauce tartare (page 157), or egg and parsley sauce (page 153) all go well with them.

They also freeze well, after dipping in egg and breadcrumbs. **Lady John Manners**

## Another Fish Cake

This is a simpler fish cake than the first, better for breakfast. It is less rich than Mrs Anderson's fish cakes, also firmer, therefore better for taking on picnics, or for eating cold, as a snack. The ratio of fish to potato can vary from 50/50 to 25/75, depending on what you have left over, but the higher the proportion of fish the better.

225g cooked fish: cod, haddock, salmon, free from skin and bone
120g freshly mashed potato
15g butter, at room temperature

2 tablespoons chopped parsley
salt and black pepper
1 egg, beaten
dry white breadcrumbs
frying oil

Mix the fish with the mashed potato, beating well with a wooden spoon. Beat in the butter, chopped parsley, and plenty of salt and black pepper. Chill for a few hours, if convenient. Then form into round cakes on a floured board. Dip them first in beaten egg, then in breadcrumbs. Heat a layer of oil about 2.5cm deep in a frying pan, then fry the fish cakes until golden on both sides. Makes 4 large fish cakes. They freeze well, before frying.

Note: If using equal quantities of fish and potato, double the butter.
**Adapted from *A Year's Dinners*, by May Little**

## Herrings in Oatmeal

This used to be a popular breakfast dish; now it makes a good lunch or supper dish. The herrings were usually fried, but I prefer to grill them. Herrings are not much eaten these days, which is a pity, for they are probably the best value for money, in terms of nutrition, to be found.

4 herrings, filleted and skinned
6 tablespoons milk
approx. 120g coarse oatmeal
45g butter

Rinse the herrings and pat them dry. Take out any stray bones, then dip each fillet first in milk and then in coarse oatmeal, patting it on well. Heat the grill, then lay the herrings on the rack, plump side uppermost. Dot them with butter and grill for 3 minutes, then turn and grill for another 3 minutes. Serve on hot plates. Serves 4. If to be eaten as a main course, they can be served with a mustard sauce, and some buttered leeks. **AB**

# Soused Herrings

Although usually served as a first course at lunchtime, in my grandparents' house in Scotland these were a regular feature of the cold table at breakfast, together with a ham, tongue and cold game in season. Unlike rollmops, which are salted, and pickled, these are freshly cooked in a marinade, then eaten within a day or two of cooking. I use a mixture of white wine and vinegar for the marinade, but water can be substituted for the wine. (In this case, malt vinegar should be used.)

250ml dry white wine
250ml white wine vinegar
1 small onion, cut in rings
1 carrot, thinly sliced
3 stalks of parsley
2 bay leaves
1 sprig of thyme
½ tablespoon sea salt
8 black peppercorns
3 cloves
6 herrings, filleted, without their roes

GARNISH
1 small carrot
½ small onion, cut in thin semi-circular slices
1 tablespoon finely chopped parsley

Put the wine and vinegar in a pan with the sliced onion and carrot, herbs and seasonings. Bring slowly to the boil and simmer for 20 minutes, half covered. Leave to cool.

Later, have the herring fillets lying in a rectangular dish. Pour the cooled marinade over them, cover loosely with foil, and bake for 10 minutes at 180°C/gas 4. Remove from the oven and leave to cool. These may be served after cooling, or kept for 2–3 days in the refrigerator, in their marinade.

Before serving, prepare the garnish. Make grooves in the side of the carrot with a canelle knife and cut in thin slices. Put them in a small strainer, lower into a pan of boiling water, and cook for 2 minutes, then drain and rinse briefly under the cold tap. Divide the onion slices into single semi-circular rings. Lift the fillets out of the marinade and lay them on a flat dish. Moisten with a little of the marinade, and scatter the flower-shaped carrot slices, onion rings and chopped parsley over all. These are good served with thinly sliced rye bread and butter, or pumpernickel, and small glasses of neat vodka, but not at breakfast! **AB**

## Irish Potato Cakes

Potato dishes of this sort were often served for breakfast, with fried bacon, eggs, tomatoes, etc. Nowadays they come in useful as part of a simple supper or lunch dish, good with ham and eggs, or grilled tomatoes and bacon. They are also good served with roast or grilled meat, as part of a more formal meal.

30g butter
2 tablespoons milk
¾ teaspoon salt
680g hot mashed potatoes (allow 900g raw potatoes)
55g flour
¾ teaspoon baking powder

Melt the butter in the milk and add it and the salt to the potatoes. Mix the flour and baking powder together. Add them. Knead lightly and roll out till the paste is about 1cm thick. Cut out into scone-shaped [*triangular*] pieces. [*Or take egg-sized pieces and roll into a ball, then flatten.*] Bake on a greased and heated griddle, or cook in butter in a frying pan. [*Makes about 10–12; serves 5–6.*] **Vegetable Cookery, by Elizabeth Lucas**

## A Breakfast Dish

This recipe comes from a little book called *Tempting Dishes for Small Incomes,* which was published in 1872. Yet it is still relevant to the 1920s and 30s, for more modest households that could not run to the lavish display of different dishes on offer in the great houses often cooked mixed dishes of

this sort for breakfast. Another, called chasse, included potatoes and grated cheese, as well as eggs, tomatoes and ham,
but I prefer this simpler one. Nowadays, when I can only
face an oatcake at breakfast, I would make this for a light
supper, with a green salad.

3 tomatoes, skinned and sliced, seeded and drained
30g butter
85g chopped ham, fat removed
salt and black pepper
2 eggs, lightly beaten
4 slices of thick toast, buttered
1 tablespoon chopped parsley

Take three tomatoes, slice them and put them in a stewpan with a little
butter, a little finely chopped ham, pepper and salt, and let them cook
for a few minutes; then add 2 raw eggs and stir all together for a few
minutes till the eggs set, then serve on buttered toast with a little finely
chopped parsley sprinkled over the top. [*Serve immediately. Serves 4 on toast,
or 2 with a dish of boiled rice, and a green salad.*] **Tempting Dishes for Small
Incomes, by Mrs de Salis**

## Marmalade

Although excellent marmalades were already being made
commercially – Keiller's Dundee Marmalade was the first,
in 1797 – many cooks preferred to make their own, just as
they do today. This is an unusual recipe in that the fruit is
boiled whole. The results are excellent: quite the best I
know. Seville oranges are only in season for a few short
weeks after Christmas, in January and February.

1.85kg Seville oranges, washed
1 lemon, washed
2 litres water
3kg preserving sugar
1½ tablespoons brandy

Put the whole oranges and lemon in a deep pan with the water. Cover and cook gently for 2 hours, till very soft. Remove the oranges and lemon, leaving the liquid in the pan. Cut the fruit in half and scoop out the insides into a sieve placed over the pan they cooked in. Sieve all the pulp back into the pan, then cut the rind into strips, as thick or thin as you like, and add to the pan also. Bring back to the boil, then remove from the heat and stir in the sugar. (Preserving sugar gives a clearer jelly, but granulated sugar will do perfectly well.) Stir until all the sugar has dissolved, then put the pan back over the heat. Bring to the boil, then simmer, uncovered, for 30–40 minutes, or until it sets when tested on a saucer. Spoon into hot sterilized jars, dividing the strips of peel evenly between the jars, and leave to cool overnight, covered with a light cloth. Next day, cover with rounds of greaseproof paper dipped in brandy, and screw down the lids tightly, or cover with larger rounds of greaseproof paper secured with elastic bands. Makes 4.5 kg. **Sarah Stuart**

## Oatcakes

These were very popular at breakfast, especially in Scotland. They are not easy to make, and demand some practice. To be really good, they should be very thin indeed, crisp and fragile: impossible to butter without breaking.

55g coarse oatmeal
225g medium oatmeal
¼ teaspoon bicarbonate of soda
15g lard
150ml boiling water
approx. 15g fine oatmeal

Mix coarse and medium oatmeal together with bicarbonate of soda. Melt the lard and add it to the mixture. Mix it well, and pour on the boiling water. Mix with enough fine oatmeal to give a fairly moist consistency. Divide into 3 or 4 pieces. Roll each one out very thinly, in a circle; cut each circle in quarters or 'farls'. Lay them on greased baking sheets and bake for 20 minutes, or until crisp and lightly coloured, at 170°C/gas 3, turning them over halfway through. Makes about 14. **Katie Colquhoun**

FIRST COURSES

# FIRST COURSES

Although by the 1920s meals had become shorter and simpler, they still conformed to a fairly rigid pattern. Certain dishes were considered suitable for one meal, but not for another. Egg dishes, for example, were often served for lunch, but never at dinner, while soup, which was the usual start to the evening meal, was never served in the middle of the day, except en gelée.

Soups came for the most part in two categories: thick and thin. At a formal dinner there was often a choice, and the footman would enquire which you preferred. Roughly speaking, the more elegant the occasion, the smoother, or clearer, the soup. A consommé was considered the ultimate test of a good cook, and the ideal start to an exquisite meal. It might be served quite plain, or with some small garnish floating in it: small vegetable dice, a few grains of rice, or minuscule soup pasta. In a less conventional household a more elaborate garnish might be served separately: round croutons piled high with whipped cream, or a bowl of saffron-flavoured rice, or even a jug of beetroot juice for adding, with cream, to a consommé made with duck and beef stock. This practice of handing round separately a number of elaborate garnishes amused the English. Part of its appeal was that by enabling the guests to assemble their own dishes it pandered to their distrust of what they described as 'mucky food'. In practice it must have been quite tedious, in that the conversation was constantly being interrupted.

The place that soup held at the dinner table was taken by egg dishes at lunchtime. It amazes us today to realize just how many eggs people ate: in breakfast and lunch dishes, snacks and sandwiches, custards and mayonnaise, cakes and puddings, soufflés and ice cream. Many of the first-course dishes were based on hard-boiled eggs. Hot, they were sliced and served in sauces flavoured with boiled onions, or cheese, or curry. They were chopped and made into croquettes, often called egg cutlets, coated with more egg and bread-crumbs and deep-fried, then served with a spicy tomato sauce. Whole eggs were coated with a thick white sauce, then egg and breadcrumbs, before frying. Cold hard-boiled eggs were masked with mayonnaise, or with aspic, or with a curry-flavoured sauce, à l'Indienne. Poached eggs were concealed within a soufflé, or hidden inside a baked potato. Cold baked eggs were covered with a layer of mayonnaise, then with shelled shrimps.

In London, where hearty breakfasts were on the decline, popular breakfast dishes were often served as the first course for lunch: poached eggs on smoked haddock, kedgeree, and scrambled eggs with grilled mushrooms, or chipolatas. Soufflés were popular as first courses; these were usually made with fresh or smoked fish. Vegetable soufflés were more often served as a separate course after the main dish, while a cheese soufflé was treated as a savoury.

Vegetables did not feature much as first courses, apart from the obvious things like asparagus and artichokes, unless combined with another food like pastry, cheese or eggs. Plovers' eggs, and those of the black-backed gull which we used to gather from a nearby loch, were highly prized during their short season in late May and early June. They were served cold, as a first course at lunchtime: hard-boiled, unshelled, with celery salt and cayenne pepper, brown bread and butter.

Fish dishes were popular at both lunch and dinner. At lunch-time cold fish dishes, often uncooked, were served: smoked salmon or eel, dressed crab, or potted shrimps, while hot fish dishes were served at dinner. Whole whiting were fried in breadcrumbs and served with their tails in their mouths, while fried sprats and whitebait were also popular, especially with the men. One fish that has vanished without trace is the smelt, called éperlan in France. These were supposed to smell of cucumbers when very fresh, and were esteemed for their delicacy of flavour. They were served like whiting, simply fried, and my father loved them dearly.

Dover sole was prized for its versatility. Yet it too was often served simply, fried in breadcrumbs, either as whole fillets or cut in strips called goujons. It was garnished with fried parsley, or served with a contrasting sauce, usually cold, sometimes even semi-frozen, like a small sorbet. The fillets were served in literally hundreds of different ways: one of the best was Dugléré, a speciality of the Savoy. Another good dish that has been forgotten is a souchet of slips: a soup and fish dish combined. Baby soles were poached and served whole, each in a soup plate, with a delicately flavoured fish consommé spooned over them.

## Consommé

This delicious consommé does not need clarifying but is best made over two days. It may be used as the basis for any of the consommés that follow, or for beef broth with cabbage toasts (see page 20), or it may be served as it stands. It can also be made in advance and frozen, although it loses something in the process. The original recipe calls for 7.2 litres of water, but few of us have pans that large. I use half that amount, filling up the pan from time to time with more cold water.

1 large chicken
1.15kg shin of beef, cubed
2 large carrots, thickly sliced

2 onions, thickly sliced
2 leeks, thickly sliced
3 stalks of parsley
3 sprigs of thyme
1 large clove of garlic, peeled
salt and black pepper
2 cloves

[*Start a day in advance.*] Wash a chicken carefully, put it in a large soup pot, add the shin of beef and cover well with 3.6 litres of cold water. Let stand for half an hour, then put on the fire and bring slowly to the boil. Remove the scum, add 1/2 a glass [*120ml*] of cold water and bring to the boil again. Repeat this process twice. Simmer very slowly for an hour, then add 2 large carrots, 2 white onions, 2 leeks, some parsley and thyme, 1 clove of garlic, salt and pepper, and 2 cloves. Let simmer for seven hours. Strain through a fine sieve and then through a wet cheesecloth. When cold [*after chilling overnight*], carefully remove grease. [*Makes 2.75–3.6 litres, serves 12.*] **June Platt, in** *Vogue*

# Beef Broth with Cabbage Toasts

A comforting soup for a supper party on a winter night.

1 green cabbage, tender leaves only
salt and pepper
8 bread rolls, 1 day old
55g butter
120g freshly grated Parmesan
2.25 litres beef stock, or consommé
1½ tablespoons finely chopped parsley

Shred the tender part of a green cabbage very finely. Boil some water and add the washed, shredded cabbage and salt to taste. Cook for 5 minutes, then drain thoroughly. The cabbage should be tender and green, not soft and mushy.

Slice the rolls thinly and toast them to a delicate brown. Butter them well, pile a little cabbage neatly on each and sprinkle liberally with cheese.

Put a tiny piece of butter on top of each one and set under the grill until the cheese and butter have melted together to a light brown. In the meantime, heat the beef broth to boiling point. Season to taste with salt and pepper. Pour it into a hot tureen and sprinkle with a little parsley. Place the tureen in front of the hostess and bring the cabbage toasts piping hot on a separate dish. The hostess then places 2 or 3 of the cabbage toasts in each soup plate and pours over them a ladleful of the hot bouillon. Serves 8. [*This dish really needs large old-fashioned soup plates, broad enough to hold 2 or 3 of the toasts. If you only have bowls, allow 1 toast per person, making them slightly more substantial.*] **June Platt, in** *Vogue*

## Consommé à l'Estragon

Lady Jekyll recommends this soup, with its 'clean and delicate flavour', for those who are trying to lose weight. Yet it is unusual and elegant enough for a dinner party. Like all the clear soups, it demands a good home-made stock, or, better still, a consommé (see page 19).

1.5 litres chicken, veal or vegetable stock, or consommé
8 sprigs of tarragon
2 egg whites
salt and black pepper

Make the required quantity of clear vegetable stock in the usual way, or use a chicken carcase or some veal, if convenient, with some ordinary stock. For garnish pick some 6d worth [*8 sprigs*] of tarragon, letting half simmer for 30 minutes in the consommé. About 10 minutes before dinner, whisk the whites of 2 eggs stiffly with salt and pepper, adding the rest of the tarragon leaves finely chopped [*about 1 tablespoon*]; take a heaped dessertspoon of the whipped whites and drop each to the required number [*six*] into a frying pan of boiling water to poach for 3 minutes [*turning them over halfway through*]; pour the boiling soup into a hot tureen [*or into cups*], drain each poached white, and let them float like snow islands on the top, serving one to each person. [*Serves 6.*] **Kitchen Essays, by Lady Jekyll**

# Consommé à l'Indienne

A curry-flavoured consommé, usually served with some rice and/or chicken in it, was a popular dish, ideal for an after-the-theatre supper. This one is simply made, and very good. The garnishes may be served separately if preferred.

1.2 litres chicken stock, flavoured with carrot, leek and celery
2 medium onions, sliced
1 large Bramley apple, cored and sliced
1 tablespoon desiccated coconut
½ tablespoon curry powder
chicken or game bones (if available)

> GARNISH
> 1 raw chicken breast
> 45g long-grain rice

1.2 litres of good stock. Slice into it two onions, one large cooking apple, and add one tablespoonful of desiccated coconut, one dessertspoonful curry powder (or more if liked hot) and bones of roast chicken or game. Simmer one hour, strain, reboil; serve pieces of game or chicken and a little plain boiled rice. [*Poach the whole chicken breast in the soup during the last 15 minutes, then chop in neat dice. Boil the rice as usual and drain. Serve 1 tablespoon of chopped chicken and 1 tablespoon of rice in each bowl of soup. Serves 4.*] **Lovely Food**, by **Ruth Lowinsky**

# Garden Nectar

This beautiful ruby-coloured soup is an elegant variation of borscht. It can be served hot, chilled, or jellied. It looks best served in thin white china cups; sour cream may be served with it.

6 medium beetroots, coarsely chopped
4 carrots, coarsely chopped
2 stalks of celery, coarsely chopped
900g tomatoes, fresh or tinned, coarsely chopped

1 clove of garlic, coarsely chopped
1 teaspoon chopped chives
1 medium onion, coarsely chopped
2 egg whites, lightly beaten
2 egg shells, crushed
1 teaspoon sugar
1 small bay leaf
3 cloves
5 black peppercorns
salt to taste

Scrub the beets and top them. Put them in a saucepan with the carrots and celery and cover with 1.75 litres of water. Bring to the boil and cook till tender [*about 45 minutes*]. Strain off the liquid. In a separate pot put the tomatoes [*if fresh, add 150ml of water*], the garlic, the chives, the onion, the egg whites and shells, the sugar, a bay leaf, a few cloves and peppercorns, and salt to taste. Mash all together and cook over a slow fire for about ½ an hour, then strain through cheesecloth and add to the beet juice. [*Serves 8. If to be served cold, make a day in advance and chill overnight. If to be served en gelée, add 15g of gelatine to every 570ml of liquid and chill overnight, then break up the jelly with a palette knife to serve in small cups or bowls. Sour cream may be served with the hot or chilled version, and lemon quarters with the jellied soup.*] **Vogue's Cookery Book, edited by Hilda Powell**

## Celery Soup

Rarely seen nowadays except in a few good restaurants like Bibendum, celery soup was very popular before the war. It needs a generous sprinkling of chopped herbs to offset its pallor. It is always in season, and freezes well.

1 large bunch of celery, inner stalks and leaves only, weighed after trimming, chopped (about 450g)
45g butter
450g potatoes, peeled and chopped

1.2 litres light chicken stock
salt and black pepper
150ml single cream
1½ tablespoons each finely chopped parsley and chives

Cook some finely cut hearts of celery in butter for 5 minutes, add same quantity of finely cut potatoes and braise [*covered*] for 10 minutes – cover well with stock and cook for 45 minutes – finish off with cream [*and herbs*]. [*Serves 6.*] **The Complete Hostess, by Quaglino**

## Green Pea Soup

This exquisite soup is made from the recipe for jugged peas on page 95. At its best for a few short weeks in June and July, this strictly seasonal soup should on no account be overlooked.

approx. 340g jugged peas, freshly cooked (see page 95)
570ml light chicken stock
4 tablespoons double cream

Discard the mint and put the jugged peas in the food processor with the chicken stock and cream, then process until blended. Taste for seasoning and adjust as required. Serve in small cups, white china for preference, hot or chilled. Serves 4. **AB**

## Bouillon de Poisson

This is a good example of Marcel Boulestin's recipes: delicious, healthy and inexpensive, yet simple enough to fall within the ability of the most modest cook. It can be served as thick or thin as you like – in fact it is also good without being sieved at all – by passing through a coarse, medium or fine food mill, or through a sieve for a true bouillon. I don't bother with croutons, unless I have some rouille or grated Parmesan to top them with.

1½ tablespoons olive oil
30g butter
1 carrot, chopped
1 small onion, chopped
1 stalk of celery, chopped
2 shallots, chopped
2 tomatoes, chopped
1 clove of garlic, chopped
1 leek, chopped
1 sprig of parsley
1 small bay leaf
1 sprig of thyme
1 small sprig of rosemary
450–680g mixed white fish: cod, whiting, conger eel, etc.
a few small crabs, when available
sea salt and black pepper
½ teaspoon curry powder
175ml dry white wine

Melt a small quantity of olive oil and butter mixed and fry in it one carrot, one onion, a piece of celery, two shallots, two tomatoes, one clove of garlic and one leek, all then cut in smallish pieces. Add a bouquet of parsley, bay leaf, thyme and rosemary, then add your fish also cut up in pieces, salt and pepper and a pinch of curry powder. Cook two minutes, then add a glass of dry white wine and 825ml boiling water, allowing for reduction. Bring to the boil and let it simmer for one hour, when it will be reduced by one-third.

Pass through a colander [*or food mill, or sieve*], pounding well the fish and vegetables against the sides, and serve the bouillon very hot, well spiced and with fried croutons. [*Makes 825ml–1.2 litres, depending on the mill or sieve; serves 4–5.*] **What Shall We Have To Drink?, by X. Marcel Boulestin**

## Goujons of Sole with Fried Parsley

This was a favourite first course: small strips of sole, coated in egg and breadcrumbs, and deep-fried. They were often served with deep-fried parsley, crisp and emerald green, or with a fresh tomato sauce. The sauce was often cold, even semi-frozen. The piquant sauce on page 152 is a good example.

2 Dover sole, skinned and filleted
2 egg yolks
2 tablespoons light olive oil
2 tablespoons water
dry white breadcrumbs
frying oil

GARNISH
10 large sprigs of parsley

Cut the fillets into strips diagonally, about 1.5cm wide. Beat the egg yolks with the olive oil and water. Dip the strips of fish in this, then in the crumbs. Heat the oil to about 180°C. Drop the goujons in, being careful not to crowd them, and cook for about 1½ minutes on each side, turning once. When they are golden brown and crisp, lift them out with a slotted spoon. Drain on kitchen paper, then transfer to a dish and keep warm. Allow the oil to come back to the desired temperature before putting in the next batch, then proceed as above. When all are done, lower the temperature of the oil slightly, to about 160°C, and drop in the sprigs of parsley, a few at a time. Cook them for about 30 seconds on each side, just long enough to become crisp and brittle, rather like the fried seaweed you get in Chinese restaurants. Drain on soft paper, then lay over and around the goujons. Serve immediately. Serves 4. **AB**


## Souchet of Slips

Lady Jekyll suggests this for supper before the theatre, since it combines soup and fish in one dish. It is quite delicious, and surprisingly exotic for an English dish, oddly reminiscent of Japanese food. (I tend to add a dash of soy sauce at the table, instead of the horseradish cream.) I make it whenever I can find slips in the market, which is rare, alas. Dabs or other small flat fish can be used instead of sole, but do not have the same delicacy.

4 slips (baby soles), heads, tails and side fins removed, and skinned
some fish bones, preferably sole, plus the trimmings of the slips
1 large onion, halved
1 large carrot, halved
1 large leek, halved
2 stalks of celery, halved
5 sprigs of parsley
1 bay leaf
½ tablespoon sea salt and 6 black peppercorns
150ml dry white wine

GARNISH

½ carrot, cut in thin strips, 2.5cm x 5mm x 5mm
½ leek, cut in thin strips as above
horseradish cream (optional) (see page 28)

Make a fish stock with the fish bones and trimmings: put them in a large
pan, adding the halved vegetables, herbs and seasonings. Pour on about
1.5 litres of water, adding a drop of white wine, or as much as you have
handy. Bring slowly to the boil. Simmer gently for 30 minutes, then
strain through a colander which you have lined with a cloth wrung out
in hot water. Measure it; you will need just under 1.2 litres for four
people. If you have more, reduce it by fast boiling, but do this after straining, not before. Then set aside.

Shortly before serving, bring a broad pan of salted water to the
boil and reheat the fish stock in a separate pan. When the salted water
boils, lower the heat and drop in the slips. Poach them gently for 5
minutes. While they are cooking, make the julienne garnish. When
the fish stock reaches boiling point, drop in the strips of carrot and
cook for 1 minute, then add the leeks and cook for another minute.
When the slips have finished poaching, lift each one into a large soup
plate, then ladle the fish consommé with its vegetable garnish over it.
Serve at once, with the horseradish cream in a small dish, and brown
bread and butter. Serves 4. **Adapted from *Kitchen Essays*, by Lady
Jekyll**

# Horseradish Cream

150ml double cream, lightly whipped
1½ tablespoons grated (fresh) horseradish, or Kochs Grated Horseradish

Stir the grated horseradish into the lightly whipped cream, and serve in a small dish, with the souchet. **AB**

# Délices de Sole Murat

An unusual combination of ingredients, this excellent dish is rarely, if ever, seen nowadays. Once popular as a first course, it is equally good today as a light main dish, needing no extra vegetable. It must be made with Dover sole, as lemon sole is not firm enough.

1 medium potato, peeled
2 artichokes
1 Dover sole, skinned and filleted
seasoned flour
30g butter
2 teaspoons lemon juice
1½ tablespoons finely chopped parsley

OPTIONAL GARNISH
2 tomatoes, thickly sliced
1½ tablespoons olive oil

Boil the potato until tender; drain, then cut into 1cm dice. Boil the artichokes, drain, then trim down to the bottoms and cut in cubes slightly smaller than the potato ones. Cut the fillets of sole into strips about 3.5cm by 1cm, roll them in seasoned flour, and fry in butter, adding a little lemon juice. Add the cubed potato and artichoke and cook all together for a few minutes, stirring gently. Serve on a round dish, sprinkled with chopped parsley. The dish may be garnished with a border of tomato slices which have been fried in olive oil. Serves 2. **Adapted from *Vogue's Cookery Book*, edited by Hilda Powell**

# Filets de Sole Pochés

This utterly simple and exquisite dish should only be made with the very freshest of fish. It is very good served alone, after a surfeit of rich food, or as Boulestin suggests with melted butter or sauce mousseline (see page 155), or with sauce Dugléré (see page 152).

150ml dry white wine
sea salt and a few black peppercorns, roughly crushed
1 stalk of parsley
1 bay leaf
1 mushroom, sliced
1 Dover sole, filleted, plus bones

A plain poached sole is not to be despised. It has flavour and delicacy, and is a very useful dish to serve as a contrast to 'rich' dishes. Put in a saucepan a glass [*150 ml*] of water, a glass [*150 ml*] of dry white wine, salt, coarsely broken peppercorns, parsley, bay leaf, one mushroom cut in slices and the bones of the sole. Bring to the boil and cook ten minutes, by which time the court bouillon is well flavoured. Put in the fillets of sole when boiling and let them poach for five to six minutes on a slow fire. When they are white and firm remove them, drain them well and serve at once with melted butter or sauce mousseline. [*Serves 1, but may be multiplied at will.*] **What Shall We Have Today?, by X. Marcel Boulestin**

# Fillets of Sole with Horseradish Sauce

A favourite dish of Lord Berners, this came originally from the cold table at the Ritz. At Faringdon, it was served as a first course, at luncheon.

Make the poached fillets of sole above, using 2 large Dover sole for 4 people. After cooking, allow them to cool to room temperature, then lay them on a shallow dish and cover with the cold horseradish sauce on page 103. Chill for a couple of hours, then bring back to room

temperature and sprinkle with 2 tablespoons of chopped chives before serving. Serves 4 as a first course, or 2 as a main dish. If serving as a main course, it may be accompanied by steamed or boiled new potatoes, served warm, and two salads: one of lettuce and one of sliced tomato.
**Lady Harrod**

## Sole Dugléré

This was a speciality of the Savoy Hotel, served cold. It is still sometimes on their menu in the summer.

2 Dover sole, lemon sole, or plaice, skinned and filleted, with skin and bones

VEGETABLE TRIMMINGS
½ small onion, sliced
½ small carrot, sliced
ends of leek and celery
½ bay leaf
1 stalk of parsley
salt and 6 black peppercorns
15g butter
1 small onion, finely chopped
2 tomatoes, skinned, seeded and finely chopped
½ tablespoon finely chopped parsley
freshly ground black pepper
4 tablespoons dry white wine
½ tablespoon flour
2 tablespoons double cream

Put the fish bones, skins, etc. in a pan with the vegetable trimmings, bay leaf, parsley, salt and pepper. Just cover with water, bring to the boil, and simmer for 20 minutes. You only need 4 tablespoons, but keep the rest for another fish dish. Cut the fillets in half diagonally, so you have 16 pieces of fish. Melt the butter and cook the chopped onion until it softens and starts to colour, then add the chopped tomatoes and the parsley. Cook for 1 minute, adding salt and black pepper, then lay the fillets of fish on top of the tomatoes and spoon over them 4 tablespoons of fish stock and 4 tablespoons of dry white wine. Cover and simmer for 5–6 minutes, until they are cooked. Then transfer them to a shallow serving dish. Stir the flour into the cream and add to the pan, beating in well. Stir for 3 minutes over a low heat, then pour over the fish and serve, either as a first course, or with boiled rice and a green salad as a light main dish. Serves 3 as a first course, or 2 as a main dish. To serve cold, cool the sauce quickly before pouring over the fish. (Stand it in a sink half full of cold water and stir to prevent a skin forming.) Serve at room temperature; do not chill. **AB**

## Fish Mayonnaise

This was usually served as a first course for a summer luncheon; today it would serve equally well as a main course. When crabs are not available, use twice the quantity of prawns. I sometimes lighten the mayonnaise by adding a little yoghurt, but this would not have been done then.

570g haddock fillet (450g after flaking)
340g salmon steak, or tail end (225g after flaking)
1 small crab, white meat only
225g prawns
½ cucumber, peeled and diced
salt and white pepper
lemon juice, to taste
6–8 feathery sprigs of chervil, or 1½ tablespoons chopped chives

MAYONNAISE
2 egg yolks
275ml light olive oil
5 tablespoons yoghurt (optional)

For six you need enough home-made mayonnaise [*see page 155*] to coat 450g of fresh white poached fillet, 225g of flaked salmon, the flesh of one crab, a dozen large unshelled prawns for decoration, and a diced, well-drained cucumber. Mix all together carefully [*adding salt and pepper and lemon juice to taste*], arrange on a long white dish and garnish with snipped chives [*or sprigs of chervil. I keep back some of the cucumber dice and shelled prawns to scatter over the top, and lay the chervil, or chopped chives, over all. Serves 6 as a first course or 4 as a main dish*]. ***Eat at Pleasure: Drink by Measure*, compiled by Olof Wijk**

## Smoked Salmon and Cream Cheese

This is a useful way of using up a small amount of smoked salmon. It is good for canapés, or as part of a mixed hors d'oeuvre. I have made it less rich by using a low-fat cream cheese, and substituting yoghurt for half the cream.

225g low-fat cream cheese
2 tablespoons double cream
2 tablespoons yoghurt
1 tablespoon chopped chives or gherkins
6 slices of pumpernickel
225g smoked salmon
freshly ground black pepper
1 teaspoon lemon juice

Beat up some cream cheese with some double cream [*and yoghurt*] until it is fluffy and only just firm. Add chopped chives or finely chopped gherkins and spread it thickly on slices of pumpernickel [*cut in half for canapés*]. On the top of each slice, pile minced smoked salmon, sprinkle with a little black pepper and lemon juice. The mincing not only gives the smoked salmon a lightness and attractive appearance, but makes it go twice as far. [*Serves 6.*] ***Eat at Pleasure: Drink by Measure*, compiled by Olof Wijk**

## Salt Herrings

Pickled herrings were very popular, especially with the men. They exist in various forms – rollmops, soused herrings, etc. – and may be made with either fresh or salt herrings. These can be bought already prepared, in glass jars, but I prefer to make them myself.

4 herrings, split and boned
1 bay leaf, crumbled
45g coarse salt

Get the fishmonger to prepare the herrings for you. When you get them home, wash them well and pick out any bones that remain. Cut each one in half so that you have 8 fillets, trimming the edges neatly. Lay them in a rectangular dish and scatter the crumbled bay leaf over them. Put the salt in a heatproof jug and dissolve in a little very hot water. Then make up to 450ml with cold water and pour over the herrings. Place low down in the refrigerator for 24 hours, laying a small dish on the fish to keep them below the surface of the salt water. Next day, drain them and pat dry. They may be skinned or not, as desired. (The skins were left on for dishes of rollmops or Bismarck herrings.) **AB**

## *Rollmops*

Rollmops are uncooked herring fillets which have been salted, then left for a few days in a marinade. In the big houses these were usually laid out on the cold table at lunchtime, together with other cold dishes. In a more modest house, they would have been served as a first course, also at lunchtime. Bismarck herrings are made in exactly the same way, without being rolled up.

8 salt herring fillets, bought or home-made (see above)
½ medium onion, halved and thinly sliced
½ small pickled cucumber, or 1 dill pickle, cut in thin strips
3 bay leaves, crumbled
1 teaspoon mustard seed
8 black peppercorns
4 dried chillies
6 cloves
white wine (or malt) vinegar

If using bought salt herrings, soak them overnight in a mixture of milk and water to get rid of excess salt. If using home-made ones, simply rinse them and pat dry. Lay the fillets out flats, and put an onion slice and a strip of pickled cucumber on each one. Then roll them and pack tightly into a stoneware crock, or glass preserving jar, scattering the rest of the mixed seasoning over and among them. Using a mixture of vinegar and water, fill the crock (or jar) to the brim. If using wine vinegar, use two-thirds vinegar to one-third water; if using malt vinegar, use equal amounts of vinegar and water. Store in a cool larder, or at the bottom of the refrigerator, for at least 3 days, or up to 2 weeks. Serves 4. **AB**

## Cold Baked Eggs with Shrimps

This was a popular dish in the men's clubs, as a first course for lunch on a summer's day.

7g butter
4 large eggs
salt and black pepper
4 tablespoons home-made mayonnaise (see page 155)
40 shrimps, peeled

Butter 4 ramekins (or oeuf en cocotte dishes) and break an egg into each one. Sprinkle with salt and pepper, stand them in a roasting tin half full of water, and bake for about 15 minutes at 170°C/gas 3, or until the whites are just set. Err on the shorter time, as the eggs will go on cooking slightly as they cool. Take them out of the roasting tin and leave to cool. Then spread 1 tablespoon of mayonnaise over each one, and lay the shrimps over the top. Serve at room temperature; do not chill. Serves 4 as a first course. **AB**

## Shrimp Paste

This lovely old-fashioned recipe should be made with small brown shrimps, although a simpler version can be made with prawns. It would have been served as a first course at lunch, or in sandwiches for picnics or tea. Today it serves equally well for dinner.

450g brown shrimps, unshelled
570g white fish fillet, e.g. haddock
sea salt and black pepper
ground mace
cayenne pepper
a dash of anchovy essence, or Tabasco
approx. 225g butter

Shell the shrimps, and put heads and tails to boil in enough water to cover [*for 20 minutes*]. Drain, remove the heads and shells, and now cook the white fish in this shrimp water till soft. [*About 8 minutes, then drain.*] Let cool, and pound to a smooth paste [*or blend in a food processor*], with a careful seasoning of [*salt and pepper*], powdered mace, cayenne and one single spot of anchovy essence [*or a dash of Tabasco*]. Now measure, and add half as much butter. When smooth, stir in all the whole shrimps. Press into pots and flood with melted butter on top. The effect was a solid potful of shrimps, cemented together with a soft, delicately seasoned pink butter. It was a great delicacy and always served in fine white china. [*Makes about 570g; serves 6, with hot toast and lemon quarters. Once sealed with melted butter, the pots will keep for 2–3 weeks under refrigeration.*] **Food in England**, by Dorothy Hartley

## Eggs Benedict

This was an American dish which became very popular in England between the wars. It made an ideal dish for a late supper, eaten after the theatre, often in a nightclub. It was also popular with the sophisticated hostesses as a luncheon dish. Muffins were easily obtainable then; Elizabeth David (in *English Bread and Yeast Cookery*) writes of hearing the muffin-man ringing his bell on Primrose Hill in the 1930s; apparently he made his rounds at weekends, mid-afternoon, just in time for tea. For many years they were almost impossible to buy, and quite a lot of work to make at home, but today they can be found in several of the big supermarkets. A recipe for making them can be found in *English Bread and Yeast Cookery*.

4 muffins, bought, or 2 home-made muffins, split in half
30g butter
4 small slices of ham, not too thin
4 eggs, freshly poached and drained
Hollandaise sauce (see page 154)

Toast the muffins under the grill, and butter the split (holey) side. Lay a slice of ham on each and trim to fit. Then lay a poached egg on the ham, and cover with a large spoonful of hollandaise sauce. Serve immediately. At whatever time of day this delicious dish is served, it needs no accompaniment, but may be followed by a green salad if desired. Serves 4. **AB**

## Egg Croquettes

Egg croquettes, sometimes called egg cutlets, were a popular first course for luncheon. They were usually served with a spicy tomato sauce, like the piquant sauce on page 152, or with fried parsley (see page 155). They are best made a day in advance and left overnight in the refrigerator to firm up.

3 hard-boiled eggs
salt and black pepper
1 tablespoon chopped parsley
1 egg, beaten
dry white breadcrumbs

PANADA
30g butter
30g flour
150ml milk

FOR FRYING
30g butter
1½ tablespoons sunflower oil

Chop the hard-boiled eggs, make a panada [*thick white sauce*] with the butter, flour, and milk, add the eggs, season with salt and pepper, mix well [*adding the chopped parsley*], place on a wet plate [*and chill in the refrigerator overnight. Next day*], divide into equal portions, form into cork shapes, coat with egg and breadcrumbs, fry a golden brown in hot [*butter and oil*]. Serve on a hot dish, garnish with fried parsley. Enough to make eight croquettes. [*Serves 3.*] **A Year's Dinners, by May Little**

## Oeufs Cendrillon

This was a speciality of the Travellers' Club, and it comes courtesy of the late Robin McDouall, who was Secretary of the Travellers' Club for twenty-nine years. Before the war, this would have been served as a first course, but nowadays it seems more like a light main dish, or even a meal in its own right.

4 large floury potatoes
4 eggs

SAUCE MORNAY
275ml milk
½ bay leaf
a pinch of mace
1 thick slice of onion
2 cloves
salt and black pepper
30g butter
2 tablespoons flour
55g freshly grated Parmesan
POTATO PURÉE
15g butter
4 tablespoons milk
salt and pepper

Bake the potatoes for 1½ hours at 200°C/gas 6, until soft. While they are baking, make the sauce. Put the milk in a small pan with the bay leaf, mace, onion, cloves, and salt and pepper. Bring slowly to the boil, then remove from the heat and stand, covered, for 20 minutes. Then strain and reheat. In a clean pan, melt the butter, add the flour, and cook for 1 minute, stirring. Then add the reheated milk and bring back to the boil, stirring till smooth. Simmer for 3 minutes, adding salt and pepper to taste. Stir in the grated cheese, keeping back 15g. Set aside.

When the potatoes are ready, cut a slice off the top of each and scoop out the flesh. Purée about two-thirds of it, adding a scrap of butter, a little hot milk, and salt and pepper to taste. Pile back into the skins, making generous hollows to hold the eggs. Keep warm while you poach the eggs. Drain them, then slip one into each potato. Spoon the sauce over them, sprinkle with the reserved Parmesan, and brown quickly under the grill. Serves 4. **Adapted from *Clubland Cooking*, by Robin McDouall**

## Oeufs Mollets à l'Indienne

A dish of cold curried eggs: just the sort of thing you might be offered as the first course for a summer lunch. The eggs may be hard-boiled if preferred.

4 large eggs
1 teaspoon curry powder
1 onion, finely chopped
1 tablespoon oil
5 tablespoons pulped tomatoes, fresh or preserved
5 tablespoons dry white wine
sea salt and black pepper
2 teaspoons lemon juice
1½ tablespoons sieved apricot jam
2 tablespoons thick (or lightly whipped) cream
140g rice, boiled and drained
paprika

MAYONNAISE
1 egg yolk
salt and pepper
a little dry mustard
150ml oil
1 teaspoon white wine vinegar
1 teaspoon lemon juice
2 tablespoons lightly whipped cream

First prepare the mayonnaise [*see page 155*], adding a little whipped cream. Place the eggs in boiling water and boil for 5 minutes from the time the water comes back to boiling point. Put immediately into cold water and leave 7–8 minutes, then peel carefully and slip into fresh cold water until wanted. Meanwhile, cook the curry and onion in the oil until soft, add the tomato pulp, wine, seasonings, and lemon; continue cooking for a few minutes and then strain. Add the curry sauce and apricot jam to the mayonnaise to taste, adding cream to mellow the flavour. Arrange the rice down the centre of a serving dish, dry the eggs and place on this. Spoon over the curry cream and garnish with a dusting of paprika. [*Serves 4.*] **The Constance Spry Cookery Book, by Constance Spry and Rosemary Hume**

## Mimosa Eggs

Egg dishes were very popular, especially as first courses for luncheon parties. This is one of the best: light, pretty and quickly made.

6 large eggs
45g butter
3 tablespoons flour
450ml milk, heated
3 tablespoons freshly grated Parmesan
sea salt and black pepper

Hard-boil the number of eggs required. When done, put them under the cold water tap for a few minutes. Shell them, remove the yolks, slice the whites into thin slices, and put in a [*shallow*] fireproof dish. [*A white porcelain quiche dish works well.*] While the eggs are cooking, make a thick white sauce with the butter, flour and hot milk, working into a perfectly smooth cream with a wooden spoon, then add the grated cheese, and salt and pepper. Pour the sauce over the whites of egg, rub the yolks through a coarse sieve [*or Moulinex cheese grater*] over this and put in the oven for 3 minutes. [*At 190°C/gas 5. Or prepare in advance and reheat, loosely covered with foil, for 30 minutes at 170°C/gas 3. Sprinkle with a little finely*] *chopped parsley before serving. Serves 4–5 as a first course, or 3 as a light main dish, with a green salad.*] **Lightning Cookery, by Countess Morphy**

## Egg Mousse

Most egg mousses – and there were many – were bland and slightly boring, but this one is superior, partly because the eggs are roughly chopped instead of being sieved, and partly because it is served with a sharp sauce of uncooked tomatoes. I have added some grated horseradish and substituted Tabasco for the anchovy essence.

6 hard-boiled eggs
1 tablespoon gelatine
200ml thick mayonnaise (home-made) (see page 155)
salt, pepper, cayenne
a dash of anchovy essence, or Tabasco
1–2 tablespoons grated horseradish (optional)
2 tablespoons lightly whipped cream
  GARNISH (OPTIONAL)
  ½ bunch of watercress, tender ends only

Chop the eggs coarsely and set aside. Dissolve the gelatine in 4 tablespoons of very hot water and while still hot add to the mayonnaise. Whisk well while cooling. Season highly, add the eggs [*and horseradish, if used*], and lastly the whipped cream. Turn into a plain mould or soufflé dish. Leave to set. [*2–3 hours, or overnight, in the refrigerator.*]

 Turn out and garnish. [*Or serve in its dish, which precludes a garnish. Serve with the piquant sauce on page 152, in a sauceboat. Serves 3 as a first course, or 2 as a light main dish, with a green salad.*] **Party Food and Drink, by Rosemary Hume**

## Oeufs Pochés Surprises

A slightly more substantial version of oeufs en gelée, these need some oval metal moulds, or small china dishes, and some really good chicken stock. Given that, they are simple and inexpensive to make, yet elegant and appetizing in appearance. They were a popular first course for summer luncheons, both in restaurants and at home. Today they may be served as a light main course, allowing two eggs per person.

570ml chicken stock
2 large sprigs of tarragon, plus 6 large leaves
6 eggs
15g gelatine
6 large thin slices of ham

GARNISH
a few sprigs of watercress, or rocket, or small lettuce
leaves

Put the chicken stock, strained and free from all fat, in a pan with the sprigs of tarragon, reserving 6 perfect leaves for the garnish. Bring slowly to the boil, then remove from the heat and stand for 30 minutes, covered. While it rests, poach the eggs and drain on a cloth. (Or, if you prefer, boil them for exactly 5 minutes, then drop into cold water and leave to cool before shelling.) When the stock has finished infusing, strain it and reheat 5 or 6 tablespoons. Dissolve the gelatine in this, then mix it with the rest of the stock. Pour enough to make a thin layer into each of 6 oval moulds, or dishes – the shape is important. Lay a tarragon leaf on each, then chill until the jelly has set. Trim 12 oval pieces of ham to fit the moulds, then lay one in each. Place a poached or soft-boiled egg in each mould, and cover with another piece of ham. Then pour over enough stock to cover, and chill for a few hours, or overnight. To serve, turn out on to a flat dish and garnish with sprigs of watercress, or rocket, or tiny lettuce leaves. Serves 6 as a first course, or 3–4 as a light main dish. **Adapted from Lady Sysonby's Cook Book**

## A Summer First-Course Dish

This is a delightfully simple dish, just the thing for a summer luncheon, or for an elegant picnic. I serve it in crisp lettuce leaves.

5 hard-boiled eggs, cooled and shelled
340g shelled shrimps or prawns

    MAYONNAISE
    1 egg yolk
    150ml olive oil
    1–2 teaspoons lemon juice
    4 tablespoons whipping cream
    GARNISH
    thinly sliced brown bread
    unsalted butter
    mustard and cress
    small lettuce leaves, e.g. Little Gem

Take hard-boiled eggs, cut in small pieces, and same quantity of shelled shrimps [*or prawns*]. Mix up with a good cream mayonnaise sauce [*see page 155*]. Make very cold [*chill for 2–3 hours*] and serve with sandwiches of brown bread and mustard and cress. [*I usually pile the mixture into small lettuce leaves and lay on a platter. If small lettuces are not available, line small bowls with larger leaves and fill with the shellfish and eggs. Serves 3–4 as a first course.*] **Food for the Greedy**, by Nancy Shaw

## Tomato Jelly Ring

A chilled tomato jelly was originally an American dish which became popular in London about this time. Ideal as the first course for a summer luncheon, the ring can be filled with warm scrambled egg, as suggested here, or with a number of alternative fillings, based on shellfish, rice, avocados or cucumbers. The jelly is especially good when made with freshly squeezed tomatoes, but for this you need a vegetable juice extractor.

570ml tomato juice, freshly made if possible
salt and pepper
celery salt to taste
paprika to taste

1 tablespoon lemon juice

1 teaspoon sugar

1 teaspoon tomato ketchup, or ½ teaspoon Tabasco

15g gelatine (1 packet)

A tomato jelly is a very nice garniture for a mixed salad, and it can also be used as the basis for a number of summer luncheon dishes. To make it, add seasonings of salt, pepper, celery salt, paprika, lemon juice, sugar, and tomato ketchup [*or Tabasco*] to 570ml of tomato juice. [*Made at home for best results, in a juice extractor.*] Melt the gelatine in a little of the mixture made hot, pour into the rest of the juice, and stir well. Set in a ring mould. The centre can be filled with hot scrambled eggs, a combination of hot and cold that is surprisingly good. [*Serves 4.*] **Vogue's Cookery Book, edited by Hilda Powell**

## Fillings for Tomato Jelly Ring

*I. Warm scrambled eggs*

4 large eggs

sea salt and black pepper

15g butter

2 teaspoons chopped chives

GARNISH (OPTIONAL)

1 bunch of thin asparagus, tips only

About 30 minutes before serving, cook the asparagus tips, if used. Beat the eggs lightly, adding sea salt and black pepper, and warm the butter in a shallow pan. Scramble the eggs as usual, then set aside for about 15 minutes before serving. Just before taking to the table, spoon the eggs into the centre of the ring and scatter the chopped chives over them. Arrange the asparagus tips around the ring and serve. **AB**

*II. Sliced avocados in oil and lemon*

2 avocados

2 tablespoons olive oil

1 tablespoon lemon juice

sea salt and black pepper

½ bunch of spring onions, bulbs only, sliced
2 tablespoons chopped chives

Shortly before serving, prepare the avocados. After stoning and peeling, cut them in quarters, then in small thick slices. Mix gently with the oil and lemon juice, sea salt and black pepper. Stir in the spring onions, then spoon into the centre of the ring. Scatter the chopped chives over and serve soon after making. **AB**


## Macaroni Cheese

This was a very popular luncheon dish, both in the nursery and for simple meals in the dining-room.

225g macaroni, cooked and drained
120g grated cheese: Cheddar, Gruyère, or Emmenthal
15g butter

WHITE SAUCE
55g butter
4 tablespoons flour
570ml full cream milk
salt and black pepper

[*Cook the macaroni. Drain it well. Meanwhile prepare a white sauce. The sauce must be kept to a consistency of thin cream.*] Take a [*buttered*] fireproof dish. Pour in a thin coat of the sauce. Sprinkle two [*heaped*] tablespoons of grated cheese. Then make a bed with a third of the macaroni. Flatten it with a fork, pour some of the sauce over it and sprinkle two [*heaped*] tablespoons of grated cheese. Go on until all the macaroni is in. Pour over it what you have kept of the sauce, which ought to be almost half of the whole quantity. Sprinkle with two more [*heaped*] tablespoons of grated cheese. Place here and there some small dabs of butter, and put into a medium oven until the surface is a good golden colour [*40 minutes at 180°C/gas 4*], and the dish of macaroni is very hot and swollen. Serve in the dish. [*Serves 5–6, with a green salad.*] **Be Your Own Chef, by Lucie Marion**

# Cauliflower Gratin

A dish which seems to have graduated from the nursery to the dining-room, at least for simple meals like lunch or supper. It could be found equally well as a first course, before cold meat and salad, for instance, or as a light main dish.

2 small cauliflowers
salt
70g butter
3 tablespoons flour
275ml chicken stock
150ml single cream
pepper
30g coarse breadcrumbs
15g freshly grated Parmesan

OPTIONAL EXTRAS
120g chopped ham
120g rice

Cook the cauliflowers in lightly salted boiling water, either whole, or divided into florets. Drain well in a colander. If cooked whole, divide into fat sprigs after cooking, and cut the stalks into chunks. Lay them in a shallow dish which you have buttered well. To make the sauce, melt 55g of butter, add the flour, and cook for 1 minute, stirring. Heat the stock and cream together and pour on, stirring till blended. Simmer for 3 minutes, adding salt and pepper to taste. Pour the sauce over the cauliflower. Toss the breadcrumbs for a moment or two in 7g of butter in a non-stick frying pan; stop as soon as they are light golden and crisp. Mix with the grated Parmesan and scatter over the surface of the dish. Reheat for 15 minutes at 180°C/gas 4, then brown quickly under the grill. Alternatively, make in advance and then cook for 30 minutes at the same temperature. Serves 4 as a first course, or 2–3 as a light main dish.

If serving as a main dish, you may like to add one (or both) of the following: some chopped ham, scattered over and among the sprigs of cauliflower, before pouring on the sauce; some long-grain rice, freshly boiled and well drained, laid in the bottom of the dish, underneath the cauliflower. In either of these cases, it will serve 4 as a main dish. **AB**

## Vermicelli Soufflé

This sort of dish was popular at the time as a luncheon dish, either as a substantial first course with some cold meat and salad to follow, or as a light main dish. I have had the recipe for many years but alas have forgotten the source.

120g vermicelli
225g tomatoes, skinned and chopped
55g butter
2 tablespoons flour
200ml milk, heated
85g grated Parmesan
salt and black pepper
3 egg yolks, beaten
4 egg whites
paprika

Cook the vermicelli in boiling salted water and drain well. Cook the tomatoes for a few moments in half the butter, then mix with the vermicelli. Put in the bottom of a buttered soufflé dish. Make a sauce with the remaining butter, flour, and heated milk. Stir in the grated cheese and season well with salt and black pepper. Add the beaten egg yolks off the heat. Beat the egg whites until stiff and fold in. Pour half the soufflé mixture over the vermicelli and mix lightly. Pour the rest on top and sprinkle with paprika. Cook for 25 minutes at 180°C/gas 4. Serve immediately. Serves 5–6 as a first course, or 4 as a main dish. **AB**

MAIN COURSES

# MAIN COURSES

Main courses differed, depending on the environment and the time of day. In London, the main dish at lunchtime would probably be poultry, game, or fish, while in the country it was usually what was termed 'butcher's meat', or game. These would not have been roasts, but simple dishes like Irish stew or Lancashire hotpot, braised oxtail or beef olives: all the traditional meat dishes which were considered too heavy to serve in the evening.

For dinner, either in London or the country, meat or game was almost always served, usually plainly roasted. In the great Catholic houses, fish was always served on Fridays and fast days, but it was often very luxurious; lobster hardly seems a penance to our way of thinking.

Although the dishes themselves were simple, the manner of their serving had become more sophisticated, and this applied to the simplest dish as well as the grandest. A Lancashire hotpot was rarely cooked in its traditional lidded earthenware pot any more, except perhaps in Lancashire. Further south, meat and potatoes were layered in a broad shallow dish, thus presenting a neater appearance for serving at table, and facilitating the service. For a dinner party, a saddle of lamb was carved in the kitchen, the resulting caviry filled with a purée of turnips, and the strips of meat laid across it. Joints of meat were only carved at the table for family meals; for a dinner party they were always carved in the kitchen, and the slices of meat laid on a large dish, surrounded with piles of different vegetables.

Garnishes were carefully considered and rated of importance, but they differed widely from those of today. For garnishing was done with restraint, using materials intrinsic to the dish. Leeks and celery might be cut in julienne strips for laying over a dish of braised oxtail, while carrots and mushrooms were cut in flower shapes for garnishing a game casserole. A whole poached fish might be surrounded with a border of semi-circular slices of lemon alternating with sprigs of parsley; the effect was light, colourful, and pleasing.

While most of the dishes are traditional, therefore familiar, one or two strike us as echoes of another age. The grilled rack of lamb, for instance, is a survival from Edwardian times that was still served in one or two houses. This was a twice-cooked dish, like the French range of dishes called Sainte-Ménéhould, where pigs' feet and breast of lamb are braised ahead of time, then coated with breadcrumbs and grilled, for serving with a piquant sauce. This sort of dish is calculated to appeal to the Englishman's palate: clean, crisp and dry, served with a separate, contrasting sauce or garnish. There is something rather delicious about well-cooked meat when it has been done intentionally, and braising is a better medium for this than roasting, since the meat stays moist and juicy. Roast beef was always served medium rare, and the large joints then customary gave a nice range of doneness, stretching from the well-done outer crust to the pinkness in the centre. Mutton and lamb were always well cooked, as were pork and veal. Game, on the other hand, was served very rare, and well hung. When in prime condition, it was almost always roasted, except in the case of partridge, which was sometimes boiled, wrapped in a vine leaf, for serving cold, at breakfast or supper. When past their prime, game birds were slowly stewed in pies and casseroles, terrines and soups.

In old-fashioned houses, few fish dishes were served as a main course, except on fast days. The exceptions were those that incorporated pastry or potatoes, like fish pie, or rice, like fish curry. The same applied to salmon, and to boiled cod with egg or parsley sauce, which was often served for lunch on Friday. A whole Dover sole might be considered suitable as a main luncheon dish, but the endless dishes of sole fillets in sauce, or fried, were more often served as first courses. Inevitably, such things varied from house to house, according to personal tastes; Lord Berners, for instance, used to have lobster as a first course for Sunday lunch, often followed by chicken pie, and a cream pudding.

Some of the more sophisticated London hostesses started serving main courses of pasta and vegetables at luncheon, but this did not always appeal to the men, who still expected to eat meat at every meal. In ways like these, the country trailed several years, if not decades, behind the city. I remember the dismay on our country landlord's face when presented with kedgeree as a main course one evening in my mother's holiday cottage. This was in the early 1950s, when we were both learning to cook, but we had been living in London since the war, and had lost touch with the country-man's tastes.

## Fish Pie

This is a uniquely English dish, since it does not exist in quite the same form in any other country. It is just this sort of bland, comforting food that the English miss when living abroad.

680g haddock or cod fillet
275ml milk
20g butter
1 tablespoon flour
sea salt and black pepper
2 tablespoons chopped parsley
3 large hard-boiled eggs, coarsely chopped
340g tomatoes, skinned and thickly sliced (optional)

POTATO PURÉE
680g floury potatoes
150ml milk
55g butter, cut in bits
sea salt and black pepper

Put the fish in a broad pan and pour over the milk. Add enough cold water to barely cover the fish. Bring to the boil, cover and simmer for about 8 minutes, or until the fish is cooked. While it cooks, start boiling the potatoes for the potato purée. When the fish is ready, lift it out and strain the cooking liquor. Measure 200ml and set aside. Flake the fish, chopping the large flakes in half, and discard all skin and bone. Make a sauce as usual with the butter, flour and measured fish liquor. Season well with sea salt and black pepper, then fold in the flaked fish and chopped parsley. When all is well mixed, turn into a soufflé dish which it fills by slightly more than half. Cover with the coarsely chopped eggs, and the sliced tomatoes, if used. Finish making the potato purée and spread it over the tomatoes so that all is covered. Reheat for 15 minutes at 170°C/gas 3. Alternatively, make in advance and reheat for 40 minutes at the same temperature, standing in a roasting tin half full of water. Do not overheat, or the sauce will boil and merge with the potato purée. Serves 4, with a green salad. **AB**

## Baked Cod

An excellent way of cooking a large piece of cod, an alternative to boiled cod with parsley sauce for Good Friday.

1.15kg cod, on the bone
120g butter
juice of 1 large lemon
salt and black pepper
4–6 tablespoons dry breadcrumbs

Lay the fish in a buttered fireproof dish and surround it with the butter, cut in pieces. Pour the lemon juice over the fish, season with salt and pepper, and cover with a buttered piece of foil. Bake for 30 minutes at

180°C/gas 4. Take out of the oven and peel away the top layer of skin. Scatter the breadcrumbs over the top surface of the fish, making a thick layer. Baste with the butter and lemon juice in the dish, and return to the oven for a further 30 minutes, uncovered, or until the fish comes away from the bone easily. Baste once or twice during the second half of the cooking. Serve in the same dish, with boiled (or steamed) potatoes. Serves 4–6. **AB**

## Curried Cod

A simple dish for family meals, but good none the less.

680g cod
55g butter
1 medium onion, chopped
225g tomatoes, skinned and crushed to a pulp
1 tablespoon curry powder
sea salt and black pepper
juice of ½ lemon

Boil the cod in salted water for about 15 to 20 minutes, till tender. Place in a colander and drain well. While the cod is cooking make the following sauce: melt 55g butter in a frying pan. When hot, put in the chopped onion, and cook till slightly brown, then add the pulp of 225g tomatoes, stir in 1 tablespoon of curry powder, salt and pepper. Cook this, stirring occasionally, while the cod is boiling. [*When it is cooked, drain it, then break into large chunks free from skin and bone.*] Place the fish, well drained of all water, on a hot dish, pour the sauce over it, and add the juice of ½ a lemon. [*Serves 4, with rice.*] **Lightning Cookery, by Countess Morphy**

## Sole Colbert

This is the best ever way of cooking Dover sole, in my opinion. Once a standby of Wheeler's Fish Restaurant – the original Wheeler's was an oyster bar in Old Compton Street, which opened in 1929 – the correct presentation does demand a degree of expertise, but even if the removal of the backbone is omitted, it still tastes just as good.

1 x 400g Dover sole per person, minus head and skinned
seasoned flour
1 egg, beaten
dry white breadcrumbs
sunflower oil

MAÎTRE D'HÔTEL BUTTER (ENOUGH FOR TWO)
15g butter
1 teaspoon chopped parsley
½ teaspoon lemon juice

Make an incision down the centre of the thick side, between the two fillets, and cut through a section of the backbone about 5cm long. Dip in seasoned flour and coat with egg and breadcrumbs. Fry till golden brown in sunflower oil, then part the fillets where they have been cut, and remove the section of bone. Have maître d'hôtel butter made in advance and chilled: mash the butter with the back of a wooden spoon, work in the chopped parsley and lemon juice, and chill until firm. Put a lump of the butter in the opening and serve straight away. Serves 1. Alternatively, for a simpler version, omit the cutting and removal of the backbone and serve the whole fish with a slice of maître d'hôtel butter lying on it. **Adapted from *A Year's Dinners*, by May Little**

## Haddock Monte Carlo

One of the few fish dishes substantial enough to rate as a main course, this would probably have been served at a ladies' lunch, or for a light supper. Alternatively, it could have been served as a first course, with some cold meat and salad to follow.

2 large smoked haddock, undyed, or 900g smoked haddock fillet
275ml milk
4 tomatoes, sliced

150ml single cream
freshly ground black pepper
4 eggs, lightly poached

Cook the haddock in the milk [*mixed with an equal amount of water*] for about 10 minutes. Take the flesh from the bones, keeping it as far as possible in four large fillets and discarding the skin with the bones. Arrange the fillets in a buttered fireproof dish, slice the tomatoes over the top, season [*with freshly ground black pepper*]. Reduce the fish-flavoured milk [*by half*] by fast boiling, and add cream. Pour over the fish and tomatoes and finish quickly in the oven [*15 minutes at 190°C/gas 5*]. Arrange lightly poached eggs on top. [*Serves 4, with a lettuce salad.*] ***Wheeler's Fish Cookery Book*, by Macdonald Hastings and Carole Walsh**

## Poached Salmon

The classic method for poaching salmon to eat cold is both simple and foolproof, providing you have a fish kettle that roughly fits the fish. Simply cover the fish with cold water, add salt, bring to the boil, turn off the heat and leave, covered, until it has cooled. Whatever its size, the fish will be perfectly cooked. (The only time this will not work is if the pan is much too big for the fish, or if the fish fits it too tightly, without leaving enough space for an adequate quantity of water.) Cold salmon was invariably served with mayonnaise, hot (or warm) new potatoes, and a cucumber salad. The fish was served simply, with its top skin removed, and garnished with thinly sliced cucumber, sprigs of parsley, and/or lemon slices.

Hot poached salmon is treated in much the same way. (Salmon is never cooked in a court bouillon, at least in Britain.) Cover the fish with lightly salted cold water and bring to the boil. Calculate the cooking time; this depends on the thickness of the fish rather than its weight, and will probably be from 15 to 25 minutes. Time it from the moment the water boils. When the time is up, drain it and transfer to a serving dish. Lift off the top skin; hot salmon is not garnished. Serve with hollandaise, new potatoes and green peas, or asparagus. **AB**

# Corn Meal Soufflé

This shows the relaxed American influence prevalent at the time, in some circles at least, and is a good example of the new style of entertaining. It is not a true soufflé, rising only an inch or so, and is equally good after it has sunk back. Mrs Lancaster suggests serving it with cold ham; it is also good with Parmesan bacon (see page 213), or bacon crisps (see page 213). A lettuce salad is almost obligatory.

480ml milk
85g corn meal, or polenta
15g butter
3–4 tablespoons freshly grated Parmesan
1 teaspoon sea salt
¼ teaspoon paprika
a few grains of cayenne
3 eggs, separated

This is an excellent luncheon dish combined with cold ham and a green salad. Heat the milk to boiling point, then stir in the white or yellow corn meal and 1 tablespoon [15g] butter. Reduce the heat and stir in 3 tablespoons, or more, grated cheese. Cook these ingredients to the consistency of mush [5 *minutes*]. Season with 1 teaspoon salt, ¼ teaspoon paprika, a few grains of cayenne. Add 3 beaten egg yolks. Cook and stir for a minute longer to permit the egg yolks to thicken. Cook these ingredients, whip until stiff, then fold in 3 [*stiffly beaten*] egg whites. Bake the soufflé in an ungreased 18cm baking dish [*it does not need to be more than 5cm deep*], in a moderate oven [*180°C/gas 4*] until it is slightly crusty, about 30–35 minutes. Serves 3. **Mrs Nancy Lancaster**

# Baked Chicken with Noodles

A useful dish for a party in that it can be prepared in advance, and needs nothing more than a green salad as accompaniment.

1.8kg roasting chicken
340g noodles
sea salt and black pepper
55g grated Gruyère or Emmenthal
15g grated Parmesan
7g butter

FLAVOURING VEGETABLES
1 onion, halved
1 leek, halved
1 carrot, halved
2 stalks of celery, halved
1 bay leaf
3 stalks of parsley
salt and 8 black peppercorns

CREAM SAUCE
30g butter
2½ tablespoons flour
275ml chicken stock (from poaching chicken)
150ml single cream
2 egg yolks

GARNISH
30g grated Gruyère or Emmenthal

Boil a good, tender chicken [*about 1 ¼ hours, with flavouring vegetables, herbs and seasonings*]. Boil noodles in 1.2 litres of boiling salted water for fifteen minutes [*or less*]. Drain and season with salt, pepper, grated Swiss and grated Parmesan cheese. Butter a round baking dish and fill to three-quarters of its depth with the noodles. Place on top of the noodles the chicken, from which you have previously removed the skin, and cut into pieces about 5–7.5cm long and 2.5cm wide. Make a rich cream sauce with the bouillon of the chicken, and thick fresh cream. [*Melt the butter, add the flour and cook for 1 minute, stirring. Then add the heated stock and bring to the boil, adding salt and pepper to taste. Stir in the cream and simmer gently for 4 minutes, stirring often.*] Thicken well with the yolks of eggs. [*Remove from the heat and allow to cool slightly, before stirring in the beaten egg yolks. Replace over the fire and stir over very gentle heat for 3 minutes, without allowing it to boil.*]

Pour this sauce over the chicken and noodles. Sprinkle over the top a good covering of grated Swiss cheese and brown in a hot oven. [*Or under the grill. Or make in advance and reheat for 30–35 minutes at 180°C/gas 4. Serves 6.*] **Elsie de Wolfe's Recipes for Successful Dining**

## Pulled and Grilled Chicken

This is a fairly complex dish which was popular in grand households between the wars. This recipe comes from Polesden Lacey, Mrs Greville's house near Guildford.

1.8kg chicken
45g dry white breadcrumbs
7g butter

VELOUTÉ SAUCE
30g butter
2 tablespoons flour
200ml chicken stock
75ml single cream
sea salt and white pepper

DEVIL MIXTURE
3 tablespoons chutney, not too sweet
2 teaspoons English (made) mustard
2 teaspoons Dijon mustard
1 tablespoon Worcestershire sauce

Boil or roast the chicken as usual, then remove the white meat from the breast and wings and pull it into coarse shreds, using two forks. Make the velouté sauce, using some of the chicken stock if you have boiled the chicken. (If you choose to roast it, make a little stock in advance from the neck, wing tips, etc. You only need 200ml.) Keep warm, while you devil the brown meat. Carve the legs into 4 neat joints. Make the devil mixture: mix the chutney with the two mustards and the Worcestershire sauce. Make small slits in the outside of the joints, through the skin, and rub all over with the devil mixture, then coat with crumbs. Dot with tiny bits of butter and grill until golden brown, turning to colour evenly.

To serve, stir the pulled chicken into the velouté sauce and reheat gently. Pour into the centre of a shallow dish and lay the grilled joints around the edge. Serves 4. **Adapted from *English Country House Cooking*, by Fortune Stanley**

# Roast Chicken in Cream

This was one of Lord Berners' recipes, typical of the period; it also works well with roast pheasant. Lord Berners was inordinately fond of rich food, and liked to have cream in every course. This caused one of his friends and travelling companions, Siegfried Sassoon, much suffering, for *his* preferred diet was fried sole and milk puddings, eaten late at night, for he, like Proust, liked to work all night and spend the days in bed. I substitute Chambéry vermouth for the sherry.

2–3 onions, sliced
55g butter
1.8kg roasting chicken
sea salt and black pepper
150ml double cream
3 tablespoons dry sherry or Madeira (or medium dry vermouth)
1 tablespoon lemon juice

Cook the sliced onions slowly in the butter, allowing about 15 minutes for them to soften. Then add the chicken, sprinkle with salt and black pepper, and turn to brown on all sides. Then cover the casserole and cook for 1¼ hours at 170°C/gas 3. Lay the chicken on its side for the first ½ hour, then on the other side for ½ an hour, then turn it right side up for the last 15 minutes. Test to make sure it is done before removing to a carving platter; keep warm while you make the sauce. Strain the juices into a clean pan; skim off most of the fat, discard the sliced onions. Heat slowly, adding the cream, vermouth and lemon juice. Boil steadily for 2–3 minutes. Adjust seasoning to taste. Carve the chicken, lay on a shallow dish, and pour over a little of the sauce; serve the rest separately, in a sauceboat. Accompany the chicken with rice or noodles, and a green vegetable. Serves 4. For pheasant, allow 1 hour in the oven; the sauce will be plenty for a brace of pheasants. Serves 5–6. **Adapted from** *The Alice B. Toklas Cook Book*

## Roast Duck

One of the most classic of English dishes, served with new potatoes, green peas and apple sauce.

1 duck, 1.8–2.3kg dressed weight
1 tablespoon sea salt

Prick the skin here and there with a sharp fork and rub with sea salt. Lay the bird upside down in a roasting rack, in a tin. Roast for 45 minutes at 200°C/gas 6, then turn the bird right side up and pour off the fat in the tin. Turn down the oven to 180°C/gas 4, and roast the bird for another 45 minutes. (Or 18–20 minutes per 450g.) Transfer to a serving platter to serve, with the apple sauce with sage on page 146, and young vegetables simply boiled. Serves 3–4. **AB**

## Roman Pie

Roman pie was a popular dish which has completely disappeared. Formerly much in evidence at country luncheons, shooting parties, and other simple meals, it existed in various different forms. Usually made with chicken or rabbit, with additions of tongue or bacon, it was sometimes covered with pastry. A cold version was made with aspic instead of the cream sauce. This version is an amalgam of contemporary recipes.

1.8kg roasting chicken
1 onion, halved
1 leek, halved
1 carrot, halved

2 stalks of celery, halved

1 bay leaf

3 stalks of parsley

salt and 10 black peppercorns

180g sliced tongue or cooked ham, or thick rashers of green streaky
bacon

285g macaroni

30g grated Parmesan

SAUCE

55g butter

4 tablespoons flour

450ml chicken stock (from poaching bird)

275ml single cream

salt and pepper

Start a day in advance. Poach the chicken as usual, with flavouring vegetables, herbs and seasonings. It will take about 1¼ hours. Then remove the
flesh from the bones, put the carcase back in the pot, and boil for another 2
hours to make a good stock. Strain and cool, then chill overnight.

Next day, remove the fat, reduce if still weak in flavour, and measure
450ml. Cut the chicken in neat pieces about 5 x 1cm. Cut the cooked
tongue or ham in 2.5cm squares. If using bacon, remove the rind, then
fry until crisp. Drain on soft paper, then cut or break into 2.5cm squares.
Cook the macaroni for 14 minutes, or until tender, in lightly salted boiling water, then drain. While it cooks, make the sauce. Melt the butter,
add the flour and cook 1 minute, stirring. Then add the heated stock and
the cream, with salt and pepper to taste, and stir till blended. Simmer for
3 minutes, then set aside.

Choose a shallow baking dish holding about 1.75 litres and rub with
butter. Divide each of the three main ingredients into three parts, and
make alternate layers of chicken, tongue (or ham, or bacon), and macaroni, with a layer of sauce over the chicken and tongue (or ham, etc.) and
over the macaroni. Season each layer of chicken and macaroni with salt
and pepper; not too much salt because of the bacon. Finish with a thick
layer of sauce and sprinkle the grated cheese over it. Bake for 40 minutes
at 180°C/gas 4. Serves 6, with a green salad. **AB**

# Roast Squab

Squab are pigeons that have been specially reared, or farmed as we would say nowadays. They have long been popular in the USA and have been raised in this country at different times. At present, they are imported from France; the French pigeons de Bresse are particularly delicious. Squab are much more tender than wild pigeon, and more delicate in flavour.

55g butter
1 carrot, sliced
1 onion, sliced
sea salt and black pepper
4 squab (1 per person)
150ml good stock: veal, game or chicken
8–10 sprigs of watercress
2 tablespoons olive oil
1 tablespoon lemon juice

Melt plenty of butter [*30g*] in a roasting pan and sprinkle on the bottom [*sliced*] carrot and onion. Salt and pepper the birds and spread a little butter [*30g*] on the breasts. Put them in the roasting pan and place in a hot oven [*200°C/gas 6*] to roast to a golden brown. When brown [*or after 10 minutes*], turn down the heat [*to 180°C/gas 4*], and let them cook slowly for [*about*] half an hour [*35–40 minutes in all, basting carefully with the concentrated stock*]. Drain off all the juice in the pan, strain and reduce to a glaze by simmering. Pour over the birds and decorate them with watercress, which has been lightly mixed at the last minute with a little olive oil, salt and pepper, and lemon juice. [*Instead of reducing to a glaze, the pan juices may simply be served in a small jug, as gravy. Serves 4.*] **June Platt's Party Cook Book**

# Roast Grouse (and other game birds)

Smear the grouse all over with softened butter and sprinkle with sea salt and freshly ground black pepper. Lay them on a roasting rack, or directly on the oven rack with a roasting tin on the shelf beneath. Roast for 25 minutes at 200°C/gas 6, turning them right way up halfway through. Move them to a warm place to rest for 5–10 minutes before serving, with bread sauce (see page 148), browned breadcrumbs (see page 160), game chips (see page 97), and a green vegetable like Brussels sprouts. Cut in half to serve: one bird will serve 2.

For roast pheasant, allow 45–60 minutes, depending on size. For partridge, allow 20 minutes. For snipe and woodcock, allow 15 minutes. A hen pheasant will serve 2; a cock serves 3. Partridge, snipe and woodcock serve 1 each. **AB**

## Cold Quails with Grape Salad

This was the sort of dish you might expect to find for a late supper after the theatre, or halfway through a ball.

4 quails
570ml veal or chicken stock
225g white grapes, halved and seeded
2 small, crisp lettuces

SAUCE
150ml mayonnaise
75ml double cream, lightly whipped
2 small onions, peeled and halved
1½ tablespoons chopped parsley
1½ tablespoons chopped chervil

Cook the quails lightly in veal [or chicken] stock. [Drop them into the simmering stock and poach for 9 minutes.] Let them get quite cool in it. Then drain and arrange neatly on a flat dish. Serve with a grape salad arranged on lettuce leaves, and the following sauce. Mix mayonnaise with some cream. Add small onions cut in halves. These should remain in for an hour only just for flavouring. After they have been removed, the sauce must be mixed again and sprinkled with chopped parsley and chervil. This sauce should be thick and very light. [Serves 2–4.] **June Platt, in Vogue**

# Grouse Salad

This makes an elegant supper dish. An excellent way of using up cold grouse, it is even better when the birds have been cooked especially and are still warm. It is also good as a simple salad, without the grouse. Simply increase the eggs, beetroot and rocket, and serve with a lettuce and cucumber salad.

3–4 hard-boiled eggs, thickly sliced
3–4 small beetroot, freshly cooked and sliced
2 cooked grouse, cut in quarters (or remains of cold grouse)
12 sprigs of rocket, or watercress

SAUCE
2 shallots, finely chopped
1½ tablespoons chopped tarragon
1½ tablespoons chopped chervil
¼ teaspoon caster sugar
2 egg yolks
sea salt and black pepper
a pinch of cayenne
175ml olive oil
4 tablespoons white wine vinegar
2–3 dashes of Tabasco
150ml double cream, lightly whipped

Mix the chopped shallots with the chopped herbs, sugar, egg yolks and seasonings. Add the oil very gradually, almost as if making mayonnaise. Then stir in the vinegar, also slowly, adding a few dashes of Tabasco. Fold in the whipped cream, then pour into a bowl to serve. Make a border of sliced eggs and beetroot round the edges of a dish and pile the pieces of grouse in the centre. Decorate with rocket, or watercress. Serves 4.
**Adapted from *The Gentle Art of Cookery*, by Mrs C. F. Leyel and Miss Olga Hartley**

# Roast Haunch of Venison

Rarely seen nowadays, this is a wonderful dish, especially when made with the tender roe, or fallow, deer. It must be started 1–2 days in advance.

2.3–3kg] haunch of roe (or fallow) deer
6 tablespoons olive oil
1 teaspoon flour
150ml sour cream
approx. 150ml chicken stock
sea salt and black pepper

MARINADE
1 medium onion, sliced
2 shallots, sliced
2 cloves of garlic, sliced
1 large carrot, sliced
1 stalk of celery, sliced
3 tablespoons olive oil
1 bottle of red wine
3 large sprigs of parsley
½ tablespoon sea salt
8 black peppercorns
8 juniper berries
2 bay leaves

Make the marinade 1–2 days beforehand. While young roe deer may not actually *need* marinating, in this case the marinade becomes part of the dish, and forms the basis of the sauce. Cook the sliced onion, shallots, garlic, carrot and celery in the oil for 5 minutes, stirring now and then. Add the red wine, with parsley, sea salt, peppercorns, juniper berries and bay leaves. Bring to the boil, cover, and simmer for 45 minutes, then leave to cool. Lay the haunch in a large dish and pour the (unstrained) marinade over it. Leave for 1–2 days in a cool place, turning it over twice a day.

When ready to cook, drain the haunch and pat dry with soft paper. Lift the sliced vegetables out of the marinade with a slotted spoon (discard the herbs), and lay them in the bottom of a roasting tin. Rub the haunch all over with 2 tablespoons of olive oil then lay it on the sliced vegetables. Roast for 20 minutes at 220°C/gas 7, then reduce the heat to 180°C/gas 4 and roast for 20 minutes per 450g in all. Once the meat has gone into the oven, measure 150ml of the strained marinade and warm it in a small pan with 4 tablespoons of olive oil. Once the oven heat has been reduced, start to baste the meat with this mixture. When the meat has finished cooking, transfer it to a serving dish and cover loosely with foil and a thick towel. Rest for 15–20 minutes before carving.

Now make the sauce. Stir the flour into the sour cream and beat till amalgamated smoothly. Put the vegetables (except any that are burnt) from the roasting tin into the processor, adding the juices in the tin and about 150ml of chicken stock – enough to make up to about 275ml. Process, then add the sour cream and flour and process again. Pour through a coarse strainer into a pan and reheat, adding salt and pepper to taste, and stirring constantly. Simmer gently for 3–4 minutes, then pour into a heated jug and serve with the venison. Serves 8, with a purée of mixed root vegetables (potatoes, celeriac, turnips or swedes), and Brussels sprouts. **AB**

## Roast Ribs of Beef

This is adapted from a recipe by June Platt that appeared in *Vogue* in the 1930s. She specifies a three-rib roast, on the bone; this may be fore ribs, wing ribs or sirloin. I tend to buy the same cuts already boned, and ask the butcher to include the rib bones – plus one or two others if he has them. If the ribs are still joined together, you can use them as a roasting rack; otherwise lay them in the roasting tin and put the beef on them.

1.7kg boned and rolled fore ribs, wing ribs or sirloin, plus bones
150ml red wine

Heat the oven to 220°C/gas 7. While it heats, weigh the joint and calculate the cooking time. I allow 20 minutes per 450g for medium-rare beef, subtracting 10 minutes for rare beef, and adding on 10 minutes for reasonably well-done meat. Or, as June Platt says: 'Cook it in all 18 to 20 minutes per 450g for rare meat, 22 to 25 for medium-done – but please don't like it any more cooked than that.'

If using the joined ribs as a roasting rack, tie the beef on to them with string. Or, lay it in the roasting tin, fat side up, with the single ribs lying beneath it. Roast for 20 minutes at high heat – even hotter than the above temperature, if you can bear it, then reduce the oven heat to 180°C/gas 4. During the remainder of the cooking time, baste every 15–20 minutes with the fat in the pan. When the time is up, transfer the meat to a carving dish and cover loosely with foil and a thick towel. Pour off the fat in the tin, leaving the juices. Add the wine and bubble away over a moderate flame, scraping all the bits of sediment together. When it has reduced a little, pour through a strainer into a small pan and set aside. When ready to serve – the meat must be allowed to rest for at least 20 minutes before carving – pour the juices that have accumulated on the carving dish into the pan, and reheat. Serve with the beef, with horseradish cream (see page 28), and a good mustard. Don't carve the beef too thin. Serves 8. (If roasting a joint to eat cold, subtract 5 minutes from the roasting time.)
**Adapted from June Platt, in *Vogue***

## Beef Olives

One of the best of the old dishes, rarely seen today. This would have been served for Saturday lunch in a country house.

6 thin slices of buttock steak or topside
55g shredded suet
30g soft white breadcrumbs
2 rashers of streaky bacon, chopped
½ teaspoon grated orange rind
1 tablespoon chopped parsley
½ teaspoon fresh thyme, or ¼ teaspoon dried thyme
salt and black pepper
1 egg, beaten

45g butter
1 onion, thinly sliced
1 carrot, thinly sliced
1 leek, thinly sliced
1 stalk of celery, thinly sliced
½ tablespoon flour
275ml beef or chicken stock

Lay the slices of beef on a sheet of cling film and cover with another sheet. Beat them out until very thin. Trim the edges to make a roughly rectangular shape; chop the trimmings and put them in a basin with the suet and breadcrumbs. Add the bacon, orange rind, parsley, thyme, salt and pepper. Mix well, adding the beaten egg, then divide the stuffing between the 6 slices of beef. Roll each one up and tie with string.

Melt the butter in a casserole and brown the sliced vegetables quickly, stirring constantly. When they have coloured, take them out and put in the beef olives. Brown them on all sides, then remove them also. Shake the flour into the casserole and blend with the butter. Cook for 1 minute, stirring, then add the heated stock and stir till blended, adding salt and pepper to taste. Put the vegetables back into the pan, and lay the olives on them. Cover and cook gently for 1½ hours, either on top of the stove or in a low oven, 170°C/gas 3.

To serve, remove the string and lay the olives on a bed of mashed potato. Spoon the vegetables over the top, moistening with the sauce. Serves 6. **AB**

## Cottage Pie, or Shepherd's Pie

At a time when so many roast joints of meat were being consumed, dishes like these were constantly being made to use up the remains. In the big houses they were more likely to appear in the nursery than in the dining-room. Strangely enough, I don't remember them often in my own home, where we used to eat up rare roast beef, cold, without ever tiring of it. When made with beef, this is called cottage pie; when made with mutton or lamb, it becomes shepherd's pie.

180–225g carrots, thinly sliced
285–340g cold cooked beef, mutton or lamb
1 small onion, chopped
15g butter
2 teaspoons flour
salt and black pepper

POTATO PURÉE
680g potatoes
4 tablespoons milk
30g butter

Cook the sliced carrots for 5 minutes in very lightly salted boiling water, then drain, reserving the water. Have the meat trimmed of all fat and neatly chopped by hand. Fry the chopped onion in the butter for 5 minutes, then add the meat and cook for a further minute or two, stirring. Then add the flour and cook for 1 minute, stirring to blend with the fat. Measure 150ml of the carrot water, substituting any meat gravy or good stock you happen to have, and add to the pan, stirring until it has blended. Simmer gently for 4 minutes, adding salt and pepper to taste. Then turn the contents of the pan into a greased pie dish, or soufflé dish. Lay the sliced carrots over the meat. Make a potato purée as usual, but be careful not to make it too moist or it will merge with the meat below. Make rough ridges in the surface and bake until nicely browned, 30–35 minutes at 190°C/gas 5. Serves 4, with a green vegetable. This can also be made with raw meat, minced or finely chopped in a food processor. Simply allow an extra 5 minutes initial frying with the onion, then proceed as above. **AB**


## Sea Pie

I love this simple version of steak pudding, where the suet crust is merely laid on top of the meat for cooking, instead of all around it.

900g best stewing steak
salt and black pepper

2 medium carrots
2 small onions

SUET PASTE
120g shredded suet
225g self-raising flour
approx. 120ml water

Cut the steak into thin slices about 7.5cm square, put them into a shallow stewpan, season with salt and pepper, barely cover the slices with boiling water, put on the lid and simmer gently. Slice the carrots thinly, cut the onions into small pieces, and add them to the meat. Make the suet paste [*according to the directions on the packet*], roll into a round rather less than the top of the stewpan [*using the lid as a guide*]. Lay the paste on top of the meat when it has simmered for about ½ an hour, replace the lid and continue the cooking for about 1½ hours longer. When the pie is done, cut the paste into 4 pieces, and remove them carefully from the stewpan to a plate; arrange the meat and vegetables neatly on a hot dish, and place the crust on top. Sufficient for 4 persons. **Mrs Beeton's All About Cookery**

## Boiled Silverside

One of the best of the traditional dishes, not often seen nowadays. You may have to order the salt beef from your butcher a few days in advance. The French also love boiled beef, but their bouilli is made with fresh beef.

1.5–1.8kg salted silverside
680g large carrots
2 leeks, halved
2 onions, halved
4 cloves
2 bay leaves
4 stalks of parsley
10 black peppercorns

Put the beef in a large pan and surround it with 2 of the carrots cut in half, the leeks, onions stuck with cloves, bay leaves, parsley and peppercorns. Cover generously with cold water and start to bring slowly to the boil. As it approaches boiling point, skim carefully, removing all the grey scum that rises to the surface. When only a light white foam remains, cover and cook steadily for 1½–2 hours, or 30 minutes per 450g. Towards the end of the time, cook the remaining carrots separately; they may be left whole, or, if very large, cut in halves or quarters lengthwise. When the meat is ready, lift on to a serving platter and carve in fairly thick slices. Taste the stock to make sure it is not too salty, then use some to moisten the slices. Lay on a platter, surrounded with the carrots. Serve with a bowl of boiled potatoes sprinkled with chopped parsley. Serves 6. **AB**

## Spiced Beef

Cold spiced beef (it can also be eaten hot, but rarely was at that time) was a popular joint for the sideboard, also for shooting and picnic lunches, and for summer holidays. Since saltpetre, which was used in the pickling mixture, is now unobtainable by law, I have had to go back to a Victorian recipe for spicing beef with common (or sea) salt and spices. I have doubled the quantity of salt to be on the safe side. The cooking instructions are based on those of Elizabeth David, as given to Harrods' meat department in 1958, when they first started selling spiced beef according to Mrs David's recipe. (They still do, for Christmas.)

2.3–3kg beef: topside, round, silverside or brisket, boned and rolled
1 teaspoon ground mace
1 teaspoon coarsely ground black pepper
30g juniper berries, roughly crushed
2 teaspoons ground cloves
½ small nutmeg, grated
⅛ teaspoon cayenne
100g dark-brown muscovado sugar
225g Maldon sea salt

Mix all the spices and seasonings except the salt and rub the beef all over. Lay it in an earthenware crock with a lid (I use a bread crock, unless it is a long sausage-shaped joint when I use an oval earthenware dish covered with foil). Leave it for 3 days, then add half the salt. Rub it well with the spice and salt mixture and put back in the crock, or dish. Rub it or turn it every day for 12 days, adding half the remaining sea salt on the 4th day, and the remainder on the 8th day.

When the time is up, wipe off the spices, rinsing the meat briefly if necessary, but on no account soak it. Put it in a casserole that fits it as closely as possible and add 275ml of water. Cover with 2 sheets of foil and the lid and cook for 45–50 minutes per 450g in the bottom of a low oven – 140°C/gas 1. When it is cooked, unless you are going to eat it hot, take it out of the oven and leave to cool for 2–3 hours in its pot. Then lift out the meat and lay it on a flat surface. Weigh down with a board with 3 x 1kg weights standing upon it, and leave overnight. Next day, wrap in foil and keep in the refrigerator. It should keep for 10–14 days, replaced in the refrigerator after use. To serve, carve in thin slices and serve with baked potatoes and a mixed salad. **Adapted from *Modern Cookery*, by Eliza Acton**

## Beef Stew

This recipe has evolved over the years in my kitchen, based originally on recipes of the period.

1.15kg chuck steak or topside, thickly sliced
1 large onion, sliced
30g butter
4 tablespoons olive oil
2 large carrots, cut in thick strips
½ celeriac, or 3 stalks of celery, cut in thick strips
1 large parsnip, cut in thick strips
2 large cloves of garlic, crushed
about 1½ tablespoons seasoned flour
275ml beef or chicken stock
275ml red wine

1 tablespoon tomato purée
juice of 1 orange
1 strip of orange peel, 5 x 1cm
1 large bay leaf
3 shakes of Tabasco
sea salt and black pepper
3 tablespoons coarsely chopped parsley

Trim the beef, cutting away all gristle and membrane, then cut it in neat rectangles. Cook the sliced onion gently in the butter and half the olive oil, for about 3 minutes, then add the root vegetables which you have cut in strips like thick matchsticks about 3.5cm x 7.5mm. (In spring and summer, substitute fennel for the celeriac, and green pepper for the parsnip.) Cook all together gently for about 5 minutes, adding the crushed garlic halfway through. Then lift out the vegetables with a slotted spoon, add the remaining 2 tablespoons of oil, and put in the sliced beef which you have coated lightly with flour at the last minute. Brown the meat on both sides, doing it in 2 or 3 batches. Then remove it and put the vegetables back in the pan. Heat the stock and wine together and pour on to the vegetables, stirring to blend with the flour. When all is smooth, put back the meat and add the tomato purée, orange juice and peel, bay leaf and Tabasco. Add sea salt and black pepper, bring to the boil, then cover the pan and cook for 1 hour in a low oven, 150°C/gas 2. Then remove the lid and cook for another hour, basting the surface of the stew 2 or 3 times with the juice. This produces a really excellent dish, for the reduction of the sauce increases the flavour, at the same time causing the surface of the casserole to become almost caramelized. It must be transferred to a clean dish for serving, however, for the evaporation of the meat juices will have discoloured the casserole. Sprinkle with parsley and serve with a purée of potatoes and a boiled vegetable, or a green salad. Serves 6. **AB**

## Braised Oxtail

A wonderful winter dish, sustaining without being too expensive. It takes two days to make properly.

1ST DAY

2 oxtails, cut in 5cm sections

2½ tablespoons flour

salt and black pepper

2 tablespoons olive oil

30g butter

2 cloves of garlic, crushed

2 tablespoons tomato purée

1 large onion, halved

1 large carrot, halved

1 stalk of celery, halved

1 bay leaf

3 stalks of parsley

720ml beef stock

150ml red wine

2ND DAY

30g butter

1 tablespoon olive oil

1 leek, cut in thick strips

2 medium carrots, cut in thick strips

2 small turnips, cut in thick strips

2 stalks of celery, cut in thick strips

1 parsnip, cut in thick strips

2 tablespoons coarsely chopped parsley

Start 1 day in advance. Trim excess fat off the oxtail. Season the flour with salt and pepper and shake over the meat, turning so that it is lightly and evenly coated. Heat the oil and butter in a heavy casserole and brown the oxtail on all sides, lifting them out as they are done. Put the garlic and tomato purée in the pot and replace the meat, adding the halved vegetables and herbs. Heat the stock and wine together and add to the pan. Bring to the boil slowly, adding more salt and pepper, then cover and cook for 4 hours in the oven, at 150°C/gas 2. Remove and leave to cool overnight.

Next day remove the fat from the surface and transfer the pieces of meat to a shallow earthenware dish. Discard the flavouring vegetables and herbs. Heat fresh butter and oil in a sauté pan; put in the vegetable strips and fry gently for 8 minutes, then add 275ml of the oxtail stock taken from the stew, and simmer gently for 15 minutes. Then lift out the vegetable strips with a slotted spoon and scatter them over the surface of the oxtail. Pour their stock, and the rest of the oxtail stock, over them, and cook for 1 hour at 180°C/gas 4, basting from time to time. When the time is up, they should have acquired a slightly crisp, caramelized exterior from the evaporation of the meat juices. Sprinkle with coarsely chopped parsley and serve in the same dish, with boiled or baked potatoes, and a green salad. Serves 6. **AB**

## Roast Rack of Lamb

This is a good, simple dish, typical of the best cooking of the time. I have adapted it from contemporary recipes.

1 x 8-bone rack of lamb, trimmed for roasting, with chine bone
    removed
15g butter
1 small onion, thinly sliced
1 carrot, thinly sliced
175ml meat stock, heated

Rub a piece of foil with half the butter and lay over the rack of lamb. Rub the rest of the butter over the bottom of a roasting tin and lay the sliced onion and carrot in it. Stand the lamb in the tin, on a rack if you have one, and roast for 15 minutes at 190°C/gas 5. Then remove the foil and baste with some of the heated stock. Continue to roast for 25 minutes (40 minutes in all), basting two or three times, then rest in a warm place for 10 minutes before carving into cutlets. While it rests, lay the roasting tin over a low flame and stir up the juices. Let them bubble all together for a few minutes, adding a drop more stock if you have it, or a drop of red wine, then strain into a sauceboat. Serves 3. For two people, buy a 5-bone rack of lamb and cook for 35 minutes. These times will give you meat that is slightly pink; add an extra 5 minutes, if you must, for well-done meat. **AB**

# Roast Saddle of Lamb

Rarely seen nowadays except at Guildhall dinners, this is one of the glories of the English kitchen. In pre-war days it would often have been a saddle of mutton, which has a character all of its own. But a saddle of well-reared lamb is also a marvellous dish. It is carved in long rectangular strips, quite thick and slightly wedge-shaped, which look very good on the plate. Allow roughly 450g per person.

1 saddle of British lamb, approx. 3kg
3 tablespoons best olive oil
1 tablespoon lemon juice
freshly ground black pepper
6 branches of tarragon (optional)
8 branches of chervil (optional)
275ml lamb, beef, veal or chicken stock

Virtually nothing needs to be done to this joint, except paying for it, before putting it in the oven. In spring and summer, when the lamb is young, I merely rub a little virgin oil all over it, sprinkle over a few drops of lemon juice and some freshly ground black pepper, and lay branches of tarragon and chervil all over. In winter, when the lambs are older and fresh herbs hard to come by, I merely rub it with oil, lemon juice and pepper. Lay on a roasting rack and cook for 1¼–1½ hours, whatever its weight, at 180°C/ gas 4. (The weight merely extends its length, while the cooking time should be calculated according to its thickness.) It doesn't need basting, since it is completely covered with its own fat. When the time is up, move on to a carving platter and cover loosely with foil and a heavy cloth. Stand in a warm place for 15–20 minutes to rest before carving; this is very important. While the meat rests, make the gravy. Heat the stock in a small pan and pour off the fat in the roasting tin. Stand the tin over a moderate flame. Add the hot stock to the tin, scraping and stirring with a wooden spoon until all the caramelized meat juices amalgamate with the stock. Let it all bubble away and reduce for a few minutes, then pour through a strainer into a sauceboat. Although the saddle is a good-looking joint, it is perhaps easiest to carve it in the kitchen. It must be cut parallel to the bone, in long strips, about 5mm thick on the outside, tapering slightly as they meet the bone. If too long, they may be cut in half to serve. Sometimes the whole saddle is slightly concave, making it very hard to carve. In this case, cut the whole joint across in half with a strong knife, then carve as above, in shorter strips. Serves 6. This is good served with the grilled slices of potatoes on page 96, mint sauce and/or redcurrant jelly, or the sauce soubise on page 154, and as many simple vegetables as you can manage. **AB**

## Grilled Rack of Lamb

This was a favourite dish of Edward VII, still popular between the wars. Twice-cooked meat can be very good, when done with that end in view. The little cutlets are very tender, and are also good cold, for eating in your fingers: perfect picnic food. The caper sauce is optional, certainly not for taking on a picnic. Allow 2–3 cutlets per person, remembering that the end ones will not be so perfect in shape as the others. Start a day in advance.

1.8-bone rack of lamb, in one piece, chined
approx. 1.2 litres light beef or chicken stock
1 leek (or onion), thickly sliced
1 carrot, thickly sliced
1 stalk of celery, thickly sliced
sea salt and 6 black peppercorns
¼ bay leaf
30g butter, melted
dry white breadcrumbs

CAPER SAUCE (OPTIONAL)
275ml reduced stock (see above)
1 tablespoon capers, chopped
1 tablespoon chopped pickled gherkins

Put the rack of lamb in an oval pan and add enough stock to almost cover it. Remove the meat and put in the sliced vegetables, salt and peppercorns, and bay leaf. Bring slowly to the boil, then replace the meat. Bring back to the boil then simmer gently, covered, for 1 hour. Remove the meat and leave to cool overnight. Continue to boil up the stock, uncovered, until reduced to a good flavour. (You only need just over 275ml.) Strain and cool, then chill overnight.

Next day, divide the meat into cutlets and trim off most of the fat. Dip each one in melted butter, then in breadcrumbs. To make the sauce, remove the fat from the surface of the reduced stock. Heat the stock in a small pan, adding roughly chopped capers (if small, they can be left whole) and gherkins. Grill the cutlets for about 4 minutes on each side, just until nicely browned. (They are already cooked and only need warming through.) Serve them on a flat dish, with the caper and gherkin sauce, if used, in a sauceboat. If serving without a sauce, they may be garnished with a few capers and thinly sliced gherkins. Serves 3. **Adapted from Kitchen Essays, by Lady Jekyll**

## Pâté Don Pedro

This oddly named dish is one of my favourites, and typical of its genre. Its essence lies in its simplicity: a style of cooking where nursery and dining-room meet.

12 lamb cutlets, middle end of neck, trimmed
sea salt and black pepper
1 medium carrot, thinly sliced
1 medium onion, thinly sliced
2 stalks of parsley
½ small bay leaf
570ml beef or chicken stock

POTATO CRUST
680g floury potatoes, peeled and halved
6 tablespoons milk
15g butter
sea salt and black pepper

Trim 1 dozen cutlets as for Irish stew, place in circular order in a stewpan. Season with salt, pepper, carrot, onion, and herbs, and 570ml of good stock. Cook by the side of the stove fire till tender [*about 1 hour on top of the stove*]. Remove cutlets into pie dish, skim all grease from gravy, reduce it [*to 175ml*], and pour over the cutlets, cover with a potato crust [*mash the freshly boiled and drained potatoes with the milk and butter, which have been heated together, with plenty of sea salt and black pepper*], brown, and serve hot. [*Serves 4–5.*] **Lady Sysonby's Cook Book**

## Côtelettes Soubises

An appetizing dish of lamb cutlets masked with a thick onion sauce under a coating of egg and breadcrumbs. Also good cold, this makes an elegant dish for a picnic.

8 lamb cutlets, trimmed of excess fat

SAUCE SOUBISE

180g onions, thinly sliced

15g butter

½ tablespoon flour

150ml veal or chicken stock

sea salt and black pepper

WHITE SAUCE

20g butter

1 tablespoon flour

150ml milk

4 tablespoons thick cream

a pinch each of ground cloves and mace

¼ bay leaf

sea salt and black pepper

COATING

1 large egg, beaten

1 tablespoon milk

approx. 55g dry white breadcrumbs

30g butter, melted

Cook [*grill*] your cutlets lightly [*4 minutes*] the side on which the sauce is to be. Then press them flat between two plates to get cold. Prepare a sauce half soubise, half white sauce. [*Cook the sliced onions gently in the butter in a non-stick pan for 5 minutes, stirring now and then, and stir in the flour. Add the heated stock, salt and black pepper, and simmer gently, covered, for 10 minutes, stirring occasionally. Set aside. In another pan make the white sauce. Melt the butter, stir in the flour, and cook for 1 minute, stirring. Then add the heated milk and bring to the boil, stirring. Add the cream, ground cloves, mace, bay leaf, salt and pepper and simmer for 4 minutes, stirring often. Then mix the two sauces together and set aside to cool. If you prefer a smooth purée, they can be put briefly in the food processor. Once cool, chill in the refrigerator for an hour or two.*] Then spread thickly over the cooked side of the cutlets, egg and breadcrumb them both sides, and finish cooking in a hot oven. [*Lay them on a greased baking tray and dribble the melted butter over them. Bake for 25 minutes at 190°C/gas 5, then brown briefly under the grill. Serves 4.*] **Lady Sysonby's Cook Book**

## Boiled Leg of Mutton with Caper Sauce

Before the war, lamb was a seasonal dish, only to be had in the spring. For the rest of the year they ate mutton, and this was one of the best ways of cooking it. Mutton is beginning to regain its popularity, especially in the West Country.

1 leg of mutton, trimmed of excess fat
1.5–1.75 litres light meat or chicken stock
1 stalk of celery
1 medium onion, halved
3 carrots
20 black peppercorns

Start 1 day in advance. Place the leg in a large saucepan or casserole. Cover with the stock [*add the vegetables and peppercorns*] and bring slowly to the boil. Simmer for 2 hours, then leave to cool overnight.

Next day, remove any excess fat from the top of the pan and discard the vegetables. Bring slowly back to the boil and simmer for another hour. You can add some fresh root vegetables to the pan for the last half hour. Any mutton left over can be kept in the juice in a cool place overnight. Reheat thoroughly just before serving. Serves 6–8, depending on the breed of sheep. [*Serve with the caper sauce, below.*] **Caroline Blackburn**

## Caper Sauce

30g butter
20g flour
½ teaspoon dry mustard
150ml mutton stock (see above)
salt and black pepper
2 tablespoons capers, drained
½ tablespoon caper juice
1 tablespoon double cream

Melt the butter in a pan, add the flour and mustard, and mix well. Add 150ml of stock from the mutton, and season well with salt and pepper. Simmer for 2 to 3 minutes. Add a good quantity of capers to taste, plus 1 dessertspoon of their juice. Simmer a few moments more, and add a tablespoon of cream just before serving. **Caroline Blackburn**

## Cold Roast Loin of Pork

This is a combination of two recipes of June Platt's, published in *Vogue* in 1938. Like many young American women living in England then, she was ahead of her time, and was constantly urging her readers to be more adventurous and to break with the conventions. She starts her recipe by saying: 'Try serving a well-cooked roast of pork cold, accompanied by a big bowl of mayonnaise and a delicious French bean salad with French dressing.'

1.8kg loin of pork, on the bone
1 tablespoon sunflower oil
sea salt and black pepper

Preheat the oven to its maximum. Rub the crackling lightly with oil, and sprinkle with salt and pepper. Lay it on a rack in a roasting pan. If there are bone ends, cover each one with a twist of foil. Roast 15 minutes in a very hot oven, then turn down the heat to 190°C/gas 5, and cook more slowly, basting now and then, for 1 hour 50 minutes, 2 hours 5 minutes in all. Or, 28 minutes per 450g plus the initial 15 minutes. If it starts to get too brown, lay a piece of foil loosely over it. When it is done, take out of the oven and leave to cool. Pour off the juices in the pan and reserve for another dish. Leave the joint in a cool place overnight – preferably not in the refrigerator. Next day, cut out the bone carefully; with a small sharp knife this is not hard to do, and makes carving very much easier. Then remove the crackling in one piece, and discard most of the fat between the crackling and the meat. Carve the meat in neat slices, not too thin, and lay them on a serving dish. Break the crackling into strips and lay around the meat. Serves 6–8, with an apple sauce, or mayonnaise, or a cherry salad (see page 149); a new potato salad, and another of string beans. **Adapted from June Platt, in _Vogue_**

## Escalopes de Veau aux Concombres

A typical dinner-party dish, this also works well on a small scale, for two – or even one.

½ cucumber, peeled and cut in oval lozenges about 2.5cm long
55g butter
4 thin veal escalopes
275ml double cream
salt and pepper
a pinch of paprika

Drop the cucumber lozenges into lightly salted boiling water and cook for 2 minutes, then drain and refresh under the cold tap. Keep warm while you cook the veal. Heat half the butter in a broad frying pan. When very hot, put in 2 escalopes and cook until nicely coloured, about 2 minutes on each side. Remove them as they are done and keep warm while you fry the others. When all four are done, add the cucumber lozenges to the dish and make the sauce. Pour the cream into the frying pan, scraping all the juices and caramelized bits of sediment together. Let it boil briskly for a few minutes to reduce, adding salt and pepper and a pinch of paprika. Then swirl in the remaining 30g butter, cut in small bits. Once it has melted, pour the sauce over the veal and cucumber and serve at once. Serves 4, with noodles, or new potatoes, and a green salad. **Adapted from *What Shall We Have Today?*, by X. Marcel Boulestin**

VEGETABLES

One of the great culinary advances during this period was in the treatment of vegetables. As Mrs Martineau recalls in the introduction to her book *Caviare to Candy*, published in 1927: 'My own mother gave each of her daughters a recipe book on their marriage, and though filled with many good dishes, there is not a single vegetable dish nor salad therein.' This illustrates clearly the cook's priorities before the First World War. Once that war was over, however, the vegetable began to grow in favour. This was due in part to the American influence which was spreading among sophisticated London folk, but not entirely. An old family friend recalled going to lunch with King George V and Queen Mary, and being struck by the meal, for a dish of green peas was served on its own, after the main course, and the old King remarked how much he liked to eat vegetables in this way.

Many households, even the most conservative and old-fashioned, took to serving a vegetable dish alone, usually after the main course. Mrs Martineau describes the vegetable soufflés made by Lady Wilton's chef at Melton: 'a soufflé of small Brussels sprouts, boiled very soft with well-beaten eggs and cream one night, the next a soufflé of white (Jerusalem) artichokes or asparagus, and the third night one of spinach which, boiled with cream and whipped up with eggs was a delicate green colour with a brown top'.

In 1931 a whole book devoted to the subject of vegetables appeared, something that would have been unthinkable before the First World War. This was *Vegetable Cookery* by Elizabeth Lucas, who speaks with authority, as her strictures on butter show: 'One thing is essential – the use of good butter. Delicious butter with a faintly nutty flavour is rarely to be found in private houses. To use too much is as great a crime as to use none. Vegetables swimming in butter are nauseating. They should be turned over in it at the last moment (enrober is the good French word) and be eaten before it has lost its freshness.'

As the 20s and 30s progressed, the enthusiasm for vegetables continued to grow. 'Get as many vegetables as you can,' wrote Lady Sysonby, 'and a simple dinner will at once become elegant if you have a vegetable served as a separate course.' An alternative use of vegetables was serving as many as four or five, each cooked separately, with a simple meat dish, like grilled chicken, or lamb cutlets. This custom can be traced back to the United States, where it had long been popular with elegant hostesses. Lady Cunard took it to extremes, sometimes serving as many as six different vegetables at one meal, while Englishwomen like Lady Aberconway, then Mrs Henry MacLaren, followed suit.

Few people today realize just how strong the American influence was at that time. One dish that displays this trend was the composite salad, which had not appeared until then on English menus, where 'a salad' was always made with green leaves. The American salad is well described in *Vogue* in 1927, in an article on current trends in suppers, as served at balls. (Despite the fact that the guests had all been included in dinner parties beforehand, it was thought necessary to provide both supper and breakfast at the ball itself.) 'American salads are a good deal served. These are salads in which lettuce, fruit finely cut up, and sliced nuts are delicately mixed with some variety of mayonnaise, hollandaise or tartare sauce, and put in the same bowl as the straw-sliced chicken, tongue, ham or shredded lobster or prawn, or whatever the principal ingredient may be.'

The new fashion for serving vegetables very small – another American idea – provoked running battles between cooks and gardeners, who were outraged at being asked to pick their produce before it had reached its prime, regarding it as infanticide. The head gardener was vital to the cook, for he provided all the vegetables for the house, and most of the fruit, except for a few exotic things like bananas.

In her book *Cottesbrooke*, Susan Campbell has provided us with a valuable document in the history of kitchen gardens. Cottesbrooke belonged to the Macdonald-Buchanans, and until Lady Macdonald-Buchanan's death in 1987, the three-acre kitchen garden was still run on precisely the same lines as it had been since the family acquired it in 1935. The author describes a typical garden of this sort: 'The traditional garden would be enclosed by high walls, with possibly an orchard alongside. It would have hothouses capable of supplying its owner with figs, grapes, peaches, melons, and nectarines, as well as forced vegetables and exotic pot plants. It would have potting sheds, vegetable and fruit stores, and a work-force big enough to keep a fair-sized household in fruit, cut flowers, vegetables and indoor plants all the year round. Gardens like this were the rule, rather than the exception in all proper country establishments before the Second World War.'

One of the nicest things about having your own garden was that it enabled you to have special varieties of fruit and vegetables on your table. At our home in Scotland, I remember yellow tomatoes, and yellow raspberries; one of the specialities at Cottesbrooke was white carrots.

## Broad Beans with Artichoke Bottoms

This is an utterly delicious dish, quite capable of standing alone. It would probably have been served on its own, after the main course, but it works well today as a first course.

450g shelled broad beans (allow 1.5–1.8kg in their pods)
3 artichokes
30g butter
150ml chicken, veal or vegetable stock
sea salt and black pepper
1½ tablespoons chopped chervil (optional)

Cook the two vegetables separately in salted water. [*Cook the beans as usual. Boil the whole artichokes for 40–45 minutes, then drain well. Discard the leaves and choke.*] Cut up the artichoke bottoms into small dice. Melt 30g butter in a pan. Add the vegetables. Cook for a moment or two, then add a very little [*150 ml*] good stock, and seasoning. Simmer for ten minutes [*covered*], shaking the pan from time to time. Do not stir the contents, or you will break the beans. [*Turn into a serving dish, sprinkle with chopped chervil when available, and serve as soon as possible. Serves 4 as a first course or vegetable accompaniment, or 3 as a light main dish, with rice.*] **Vegetable Cookery, by Elizabeth Lucas**

## Endives au Jus

Our chicory is called endive in French, and vice versa, which is very confusing. I love cooked chicory, which is seldom seen in this country, and this recipe is quite exceptional.

680g chicory
30g butter
1 tablespoon flour
250ml good veal or chicken stock
salt and black pepper
½ teaspoon sugar
2 tablespoons double cream

Blanch the chicory by throwing them, whole, into a pan of fast-boiling water. Cook for 6 minutes then drain in a colander. Run the cold tap over them, then drain again and squeeze out the moisture between the hands. Chop by hand, then tie in a cloth and squeeze out once more. Melt half the butter in a sauté pan that can go in the oven, or a deep frying pan with lid. Cook the chopped chicory for 5 minutes over a gentle heat, stirring often. Then add the flour and stir for 1 minute. Pour on the heated stock and stir till blended. Add salt and black pepper and sugar, then cover closely with a buttered piece of foil and the lid, and cook in the oven for 1 hour at 150°C/gas 2.

When the time is up, take out of the oven and pour off the remaining liquid through a strainer into a small bowl. Put the pan over a gentle heat and stir in the cream, and the remaining butter, and 2 tablespoons of the cooking juices. Add more salt and pepper as required, and simmer gently for 3–4 minutes, then tip into a serving dish. Serves 4. This delicious dish goes well with dry dishes of roast or grilled chicken, game, veal, lamb cutlets, or grilled steak. **Adapted from** *Vegetable Cookery*, **by Elizabeth Lucas**

## New Carrots with Curry

This is a surprisingly modern dish in that it can be served either with a meat dish, or alone, or with other vegetable dishes, as part of a vegetarian meal (if vegetable stock is used).

340g new carrots, cut in 5mm slices
275ml chicken stock
30g butter
½ small bay leaf
2 stalks of parsley
1 sprig of thyme
salt and black pepper
a pinch of sugar
1 onion, finely chopped
1 tablespoon curry powder
½ teaspoon flour
250ml milk
180g rice
1½ tablespoons chopped coriander or parsley (optional)

Scrape the carrots and cut them across. Put them in a pan with 275ml stock, a little [15g] butter, a bouquet [bay leaf, parsley and thyme], salt, pepper and a pinch of sugar. [Cook till the carrots are tender, then drain, reserving the liquid for soup.]

Chop a large onion and fry it in [the remaining 15g] butter and when it is pleasingly browned, add a tablespoonful of curry powder and a big pinch of flour. Continue to fry the onion gently for two or three minutes. Then add a little [250ml] milk. Put it through a sieve [or medium food mill] and back into the pan. Add the drained carrots. Simmer for five or six minutes and serve in a border of rice. [Boil the rice as usual and drain well, then pack into a greased 570ml ring mould and stand in a very low oven for 10–15 minutes. When the carrots are done, unmould the rice on to a flat dish and tip the carrots into the centre. Sprinkle the chopped coriander or parsley over all. Serves 3–4.] **Vegetable Cookery, by Elizabeth Lucas**

## Savoury Lentils with Rice

An unusually modern dish, except that in the original recipe the lentils were sieved before adding to the rice. This is a useful vegetarian dish, good for serving with other vegetables, like grilled tomatoes, or alone, with a dash of soy sauce.

140g green or brown lentils
140g long-grain rice
180g onions, chopped
30g butter
sea salt and black pepper

Boil the lentils as usual; drain. Cook the rice as usual, and drain well. Fry the chopped onions in the butter until they are brown; about 12 minutes. Then add the lentils and rice to the onions and stir well. Cook gently until all is well mixed and hot, adding sea salt and black pepper to taste. Serves 4. **Adapted from The Gentle Art of Cookery, by Mrs C. F. Leyel and Miss Olga Hartley**

# Glazed Onions

The delicious sweetness of these little onions makes a wonderful accompaniment to a grilled steak of beef or lamb, or a joint of roast meat.

450g very small onions, or pickling onions, trimmed and wiped
55g butter
1 teaspoon caster sugar
175–250ml veal, beef, or chicken stock

Prepare a number of small onions as directed. Let them be all the same size. Melt some butter in a pan and when it is hot, add the onions and sprinkle them with a teaspoonful of caster sugar. Cook very gently in a covered pan, shaking them occasionally, for ten minutes, by which time they should be evenly coloured. Add enough stock to cover the onions and cook them, still with the lid on, until the liquid is reduced to a glaze. [*About 20 minutes. Serves 4.*] **Vegetable Cookery, by Elizabeth Lucas**

# Onions au Gratin

This is a useful supper dish which can be served as an adjunct to cold meat, or on its own.

680g onions, peeled
salt
55g coarse breadcrumbs
30g butter
55g grated Parmesan
freshly ground black pepper
      CREAM SAUCE
      275ml milk
      ¼ bay leaf
      2 cloves
      a pinch of mace, or nutmeg
      30g butter

2 tablespoons flour
4 tablespoons double cream
salt and pepper

Put the whole onions in a pan and cover with cold water. Bring to the boil, then throw away the water. Cover the onions with fresh cold water, add salt, and bring to the boil. Cook steadily till the onions are very tender, 20–30 minutes. While they are cooking, toss the breadcrumbs in butter until light golden, then set aside. When the onions are cooked, drain them well, then slice thickly. Butter a shallow gratin dish and make a layer of half the onions, covered with half the breadcrumbs and one-third of the grated cheese. Fill up the dish with alternate layers of onions, breadcrumbs and Parmesan, keeping back one-third of the Parmesan. Season the onion layers with salt and black pepper.

To make the sauce, heat the milk in a small pan with the bay leaf, cloves and mace (or nutmeg). When it reaches boiling point, remove from the heat and stand, covered, for 20 minutes. Then strain the milk and reheat. Melt the butter, stir in the flour, and make your sauce as usual, using the flavoured milk and cream, salt and pepper. Pour over the dish, scatter the reserved cheese over the top, and bake for 20 minutes at 200°C/gas 6, or until the top has browned. Alternatively, make in advance, leaving the sauce still in its pan. Then reheat the sauce at the last moment, pour over the dish, and bake for 30 minutes at 180°C/gas 4. Serves 4. Serve with hot or cold roast lamb, or vegetarian dishes, or as a dish in its own right, with a green salad. **Adapted from *Cantaloup to Cabbage*, by Mrs Philip Martineau**

## Onion Rings

Deep-fried onion rings were perhaps more American than English, but they appeared in the pages of English *Vogue* during the 1930s. Extremely delicious, they are equally good served with meat or other vegetables.

2 large Spanish onions
1 egg white, lightly beaten

1 generous tablespoon flour
½ teaspoon salt
frying oil

Peel the onions, cut into 1cm slices and separate into rings. Place in a bowl of ice water for 1 hour. Make a batter by mixing the egg white with the flour and ½ teaspoon salt. Dip the rings in the batter, fry them in deep fat [*or oil*] until brown and crisp, drain on crumpled paper, and serve. These rings are excellent with beefsteak or with lamb chops. [*Serves 6.*] ***Vogue's Cookery Book*, edited by Hilda Powell**

## *Jugged Peas*

'Jugging' was once a common method of cooking in England, as in jugged hare. This also makes the base for a superb green pea soup (see page 24).

1.5kg green peas
15g butter
¼ teaspoon sea salt
¼ teaspoon sugar
12 small leaves of mint
black pepper

Shell your green peas and put them into a jar or bottle with a screw lid or anything with a closely-fitting top. [*I use a Kilner jar.*] Put in with the peas a tablespoonful of butter, a saltspoonful of salt, ¼ teaspoonful of powdered sugar, a dozen mint leaves, and a very little black pepper. Cover the vessel tightly and put in a saucepan of boiling water to reach halfway up the jar. Put the saucepan on the fire and boil quickly for half an hour. If the peas are old they may take more than half an hour to cook. Take out the mint leaves before serving. Lettuce leaves and young onions may be used for flavouring instead of mint if preferred. These should be tied together and removed when the peas are dished up. [*Makes about 340g; serves 4.*] ***The Gentle Art of Cookery*, by Mrs C. F. Leyel and Miss Olga Hartley**

# Mousse of Green Peas

This is a wonderful summer dish, good for serving alone, as a first course, or with other cold dishes. When served on its own, it is improved by a fresh tomato sauce. Also good made with broad beans, for serving with a cold roast leg of lamb.

570ml shelled green peas (about 900g unshelled)
1 Little Gem lettuce, or heart of round lettuce
1 teaspoon chopped onion
sea salt and black pepper
a pinch of sugar (optional)
15g gelatine
150ml double cream, lightly whipped

BÉCHAMEL SAUCE
15g butter
1 tablespoon flour
150ml chicken or veal stock

Cook the freshly shelled peas, 570ml or so, in salted boiling water, together with the heart of a lettuce [*roughly chopped*] and a teaspoonful of chopped onion. When they are tender, strain off the water [*reserving the liquid*] and put the vegetables through a sieve. [*Or purée in a food processor with the béchamel sauce.*] Mix the purée, to which you have added seasoning and a very little sugar, with 150ml of béchamel sauce made with chicken or veal stock. Melt some aspic jelly or a jelly made from a veal knuckle bone. [*Or, melt 15g of gelatine in 4 tablespoons of the reserved pea stock.*] Strain it into the purée. Pour the mixture into a bowl. Whisk it [*over ice*] till it begins to cool. Then add a small cupful of whipped cream. Season and beat together until it begins to set. Pour into a mould or bowl. Serve very cold. [*Serves 4. If making with broad beans, allow 1.15kg unshelled.*] **Vegetable Cookery, by Elizabeth Lucas**


# Grilled Slices of Potatoes

This unusual recipe is quite delicious, when made with firm, waxy potatoes. It is also very practical for a dinner party, in that most of the cooking is done in advance. An excellent dry potato dish for serving with grilled or roast meat or game.

4 large waxy potatoes, weighing about 180g each, freshly cooked and
   cut in 5mm slices
6 tablespoons olive oil
1 small onion, finely chopped
30g butter
sea salt and black pepper

Slices of cooked potatoes can be marinated for half an hour [*or longer*] in oil with a little chopped onion. They should then be drained [*leaving most of the chopped onion*]. Put a tiny piece of butter with pepper and salt on each slice and grill. [*For 8–10 minutes, lying on a baking sheet. Serves 4.*]
***Vegetable Cookery*, by Elizabeth Lucas**

## Game Chips

The traditional accompaniment to roast game, together with bread sauce and browned breadcrumbs. It is worth making your own game chips now and then, instead of buying them, for the cost is minimal and they do not take long. I like King Edwards best for frying, and I prefer them left unsalted.

4 medium potatoes, peeled and very thinly sliced
frying oil
salt (optional)

Slice the peeled potatoes as thinly as possible, either by hand or with a mandoline. Rinse well in cold water, then dry them very thoroughly between two layers of cloth. Heat the oil to 190°C, as for chips, then lower in the potatoes carefully, about a quarter of the total at a time. Cook them for 2–2½ minutes, until they are light golden. There is no need to turn them, but they should be moved about from time to time. When they have reached a perfect shade, lift them out and drain on soft paper. Allow the oil to come back to the correct temperature before lowering in the next batch, then transfer the first lot to a warm dish and keep hot. A pinch of salt may be sprinkled over them at this stage if you wish. They are at their best eaten soon after frying, but they can be kept hot for an hour or two without losing their crispness. Serves 4. **AB**

## Roast Potatoes

Roast potatoes are usually cooked in the same tin as the joint they are to accompany, but I prefer to cook them separately, while the joint 'rests'.

680–900g potatoes, preferably King Edwards
3–4 tablespoons (45–55g) dripping, fat or olive oil
sea salt

Peel the potatoes and cut in halves or quarters, depending on size. Put them in a pan, cover with lightly salted cold water and bring to the boil. Cook for 5 minutes, uncovered, then drain in a colander. When cool enough to handle, dry them in a cloth and rough up the cut surfaces with a fork. If a joint is already cooking, take some of the fat from the tin and put in a shallow baking dish. Heat this in the oven for 5 minutes, then lay the potatoes in it, turning them to coat with fat. (If no joint is cooking, use goose or duck fat, beef dripping or olive oil.) Roast them uncovered, for 35–40 minutes, turning frequently, at 220°C/gas 7. When golden brown and crusty all over, drain them on soft paper and sprinkle with sea salt. Serves 4–6. **AB**

## Steamed Spring Vegetable Pie

Lord Berners was well known for the excellence of his food at Faringdon, and this is an adaptation of one of his recipes. It was probably served as a first course, or as a separate vegetable dish, but today it makes a good main dish for a light meal. I have substituted shortcrust for the puff pastry in the original, as I find it almost impossible to fasten the unbaked lattice on to the fragile shell which has already been baked.

PASTRY

225g flour

a pinch of salt

120g butter

a little iced water

FILLING

85–140g of any 4 or 5 of the following:

    baby carrots

    leeks

    small courgettes

    pickling onions, or shallots, or large spring onions

    asparagus tips

    shelled broad beans or peas

    cherry tomatoes

30g butter, melted, or 2 tablespoons virgin olive oil

sea salt and black pepper

GLAZE

1 egg yolk, beaten

Make the pastry as usual. Chill for 20 minutes, then roll out and use two-thirds of it to line a 23cm pie tin. Prick with a fork and weigh down with foil and dried beans, then bake for 8 minutes at 190°C/gas 5. Remove the foil and beans and bake for another 5 minutes at 180°C/gas 4. While the tart is baking, prepare the vegetables. If the carrots are really tiny, leave them whole, otherwise cut across into 2.5cm chunks. Cut the leeks and the unpeeled courgettes in like-sized pieces. Peel the pickling onions or shallots, leaving them whole, or trim the spring onions to within 2.5cm of the bulbs. Trim the asparagus to about 3.5cm of the tender tips; leave the broad beans, peas and cherry tomatoes whole, unpeeled. Steam them (except for the tomatoes) in separate groups until just tender; allow about 10 minutes for the carrots and 5 minutes for the rest. Leave the tomatoes raw.

When the shell is baked, lay the steamed vegetables in it in little clumps, and lay the cherry tomatoes over them. Pour the melted butter over all, and sprinkle with sea salt and black pepper. Cut the remaining pastry into long strips about 5mm thick. Brush the edges of the pie with beaten egg, then lay the strips of pastry over the vegetables to form a lattice, pressing the ends firmly on to the sides of the pastry case. Then brush the lattice with egg yolk and bake for about 10 minutes at 180°C/gas 4, until the lattice is nicely browned. Serve as soon as possible, as a first course or light main dish. Serves 5–6 as a first course or 3–4 as a main dish. No other accompaniment is needed. **Adapted from *The Alice B. Toklas Cook Book***

## Vegetable Soufflés

In some houses, a vegetable soufflé was served after the main course, as a dish on its own. Nowadays it is more likely to be served as a first course.

225g vegetables, weighed after trimming: broccoli, shelled broad
   beans, carrots, cauliflower, celery, onions, spinach or tomatoes
2 shallots, finely chopped
15g butter

THICK WHITE SAUCE
30g butter
30g flour
150ml milk
salt and pepper
mace, or nutmeg (with spinach or onions)
3 eggs

Cook the vegetables as usual. Broccoli, broad beans, carrots, cauliflower and spinach should be cooked quickly in lightly salted boiling water, then drained thoroughly. Celery cut in chunks, or roughly chopped, skinned tomatoes, should be softened in 2 tablespoons of butter or olive oil for 10 minutes, while onions should be quartered and blanched for 5 minutes in boiling water, then drained and chopped, and stewed gently in 30g of butter for 10 minutes.

After draining well, the cooked vegetables should be roughly puréed in a food processor, or by pushing through a coarse food mill, together with the shallots, which have been softened in butter. Make a thick white sauce with the butter, flour and heated milk, season carefully with salt and pepper, and mace, or nutmeg, in the case of spinach and onions. Then weigh 120g of the vegetable purée and mix it with the sauce, stirring over a low heat till amalgamated. Remove from the fire and stir in 2 egg yolks, one at a time, then 1 whole egg. Cool for a little, then fold in 2 stiffly beaten egg whites. Turn into a greased 825ml–1.2 litre soufflé dish and bake for 20 minutes at 200°C/gas 6. Serve alone, after the main course, or as a first course. (The onion soufflé makes a good accompaniment to roast or grilled lamb.) Serves 3 on its own, or 4 as a vegetable accompaniment to a meat dish. **Adapted from *Vegetable Cultivation and Cookery*, by Eleanour Sinclair Rohde**

## Tomato and Rice Pie

A surprisingly modern dish, this would probably have been served as a vegetable accompaniment to a meat dish, at a simple family meal. Nowadays, it could serve as a light main dish, together with one or more other vegetables.

140g rice
1 medium onion, sliced
30g butter
2 tablespoons chopped mixed herbs: basil or tarragon, parsley, etc.
salt and black pepper
340g tomatoes, skinned and sliced
4–6 tablespoons dry white breadcrumbs
1½ tablespoons freshly grated Parmesan

Boil the rice as usual and drain well. Fry the sliced onion in half the butter. Mix with the rice, adding the chopped herbs and salt and pepper to taste. In a buttered gratin dish, make alternate layers of rice and sliced tomatoes, seasoning the tomatoes with salt and pepper. Make two layers of each, finishing with tomatoes. Mix the breadcrumbs and Parmesan; the amount you need will depend on the shape of the dish. Scatter them over the tomatoes and dot with the rest of the butter, cut in tiny bits. Bake for 40 minutes at 180°C/gas 4. Serves 4. **Adapted from *Vegetable Cultivation and Cookery*, by Eleanour Sinclair Rohde**

# Fried Tomatoes in Cream

This is good made with large ripe tomatoes, and served with rice, or with other vegetable dishes, or with bacon, gammon, or ham.

6 large, ripe tomatoes, unskinned, cut in 1cm slices
sea salt and black pepper
a pinch of sugar
2 tablespoons flour, sifted
30g butter
2 tablespoons bacon fat, melted (or 4–5 rashers of fatty bacon)
120ml double cream
1 tablespoon chopped chervil, parsley or chives

Pat the sliced tomatoes with kitchen paper, then sprinkle them on both sides with sea salt, black pepper and sugar. Dip them in the flour, shaking off the excess. Heat the butter and bacon fat in a broad frying pan. (If you don't have any bacon fat, cook a few fatty bacon rashers very slowly beforehand, turning them until they have given out all their fat.) When the fat is hot, put in as many of the sliced tomatoes as the pan will hold in one layer and cook briskly, until lightly browned and soft. Turn them and cook the second side, then remove to a hot dish while you cook the rest. When all are done, pour the cream into the pan and swirl around. Let the juices and the cream bubble together for a couple of minutes, then pour over the tomatoes and sprinkle with chopped chervil, parsley, or chives. Serves 4. **Adapted from *Vogue's Cookery Book*, edited by Hilda Powell**

# Iced Tomatoes and Horseradish Sauce

This has become my favourite dish for serving with a cold roast of beef or lamb, or a cold roast duck. (It is also wonderful with cold boeuf en gelée.) When I can get them, I use a mixture of red and yellow cherry tomatoes; I always prefer to use small ones, rather than the large ones specified in the original recipe.

450g small tomatoes, skinned
>
> HORSERADISH SAUCE
>
> 150ml mayonnaise
>
> 150ml double cream, lightly whipped
>
> 2–3 tablespoons grated horseradish
>
> 1–2 tablespoons milk

Very good to serve as a salad on a hot summer day are large tomatoes, skinned and put in the ice chest [*or refrigerator*] till very cold, and at the last moment some good creamy horseradish sauce poured over them. The sauce to be just slightly iced. With a joint of cold lamb this is excellent. The best horseradish sauce to use is made by grating some horseradish into a mayonnaise to which has been added some cream. [*At the last moment, thin the sauce with a drop of milk to achieve a spooning consistency. Serves 6.*] **Food for the Greedy, by Nancy Shaw**

## Salade aux Truffes

> An interesting example of the comestibles that were available at the time, for those that could afford them. This recipe was published by X. Marcel Boulestin in *Vogue* in 1926, when he was their regular food writer. It is a wonderful dish, one of the best ways of appreciating a small fresh truffle, or a tin of truffle peelings. It is also good without the truffle. Truffle oil may be used as a flavouring, or omitted altogether.

120g thinly sliced celery heart
340g new potatoes, freshly boiled in their skins
4 tablespoons extra virgin olive oil
½ tablespoon white wine vinegar
sea salt and black pepper
1 black truffle, fresh or tinned, cut in thin strips (or peelings)

This salad is prepared with celery cut very thinly, slices of boiled potatoes [*skinned after boiling, while still hot*], and a sprinkling of fresh truffles cut en julienne. Quite plain seasoning, and not too much vinegar.

I would, once more, remind my reader that for this, as well as for all salads, the olive oil must be the very best, and the vinegar wine vinegar, either made with red or white wine. [*Best eaten within the hour, while the potatoes are still warm. Serves 3–4, as a separate course. Or, without the truffle, served with other dishes of cold meat or vegetables.*] **Vogue's Cookery Book, edited by Hilda Powell**

## Mimosa Salad

A simple and delicious salad, good for serving with a meat or chicken dish, or as a course on its own.

2 Little Gem lettuces

DRESSING

sea salt and black pepper

¼ teaspoon Dijon mustard

a pinch of sugar

3 tablespoons olive oil

1½ tablespoons white wine vinegar

2 hard-boiled egg yolks, chopped

1 heaped tablespoon chervil leaves

Season crisp lettuce salad with a vinegar and oil sauce. Sprinkle thickly over it, before serving, chopped yolks of hard-boiled eggs, and leaves of chervil. [*Serves 4.*] **Elsie de Wolfe's Recipes for Successful Dining**

## Watercress Salad

This is a truly delicious dish, and quite unusual. I serve it alone, as a first course, or as part of a spread of salads.

680g waxy (or new) potatoes, freshly boiled

120ml single cream

sea salt and black pepper

450g tomatoes, skinned and sliced

2 tablespoons chopped parsley (optional)

½ large bunch of watercress, tender sprigs only
2 tablespoons best olive oil
1 tablespoon white wine vinegar

Dice [*or slice thickly*] even, waxy new potatoes and drop into a very little salted cream. Cover the bottom of a flat dish with sliced tomatoes. Take a small bunch of parsley and shred finely over the tomatoes. On this green bed lay a layer of the white potatoes, and finally cover the whole with watercress sprigs. [*Season each layer well with sea salt and freshly ground black pepper, except for the watercress which needs no seasoning. Mix the olive oil and vinegar and spoon over all. Serves 3–4.*] **Food in England, by Dorothy Hartley**

# PUDDINGS

# PUDDINGS

English puddings have been famous for hundreds of years, and rightly so. Both at home and abroad, they are acknowledged as excellent and uniquely English. There are an immense number of them, falling within a relatively limited range. Within each group a few examples still survive, while many more have been forgotten. Probably the most typical are the hot steamed and baked puddings that only exist in this country. These are made with varying combinations of suet, flour and, sometimes, breadcrumbs. Some are made with fresh fruit, usually apples, while others contain dried fruit. Many are flavoured with jam, marmalade, syrup, treacle, or ginger. They may be steamed, boiled or baked; those containing suet are always cooked in steam, or water. Nowadays, these are made in pudding basins standing within a large covered saucepan half filled with boiling water. Until Victorian times, however, these same puddings were simply wrapped in a cloth and submerged in boiling water. This explains the traditional 'cannon-ball' shape of plum puddings in old prints. In some parts of the country, people continue to boil their puddings in the old way, maintaining that they taste better.

Puddings made with fat instead of suet may be baked or steamed according to taste. Baking gives a light, crisp pudding, rather like a hot cake, while steaming produces a softer, moister texture. Most of these puddings were served with a custard sauce, or with cream, or both. Some had sauces relating to their fillings. A canary pudding was accompanied by a hot jam sauce, sometimes laced with brandy, while castle puddings were served with a sauce of golden syrup warmed and sharpened with a dash of lemon juice.

Then we come to the sweet pastry dishes, the fruit pies and tarts. Unlike the Continental and American fruit pies, which were made with two crusts, the English version was made in a deep china or glass dish filled with sweetened fruit, usually sliced apples or whole gooseberries, and covered with a pastry lid. Even the traditional apple pie was capable of variation, as in Lady Portarlington's version, where a dollop of Devonshire cream was slipped under the lid before serving. Another remarkable pastry dish was Bakewell tart; this was an old Derbyshire dish not far removed from the almond tart often seen today in fashionable restaurants. Bakewell tart is especially good when made with fresh raspberries, instead of jam, and served with clotted cream.

English apple puddings are legion. Indeed, we are the only country to grow cooking apples commercially; Continental dishes like the French tarte aux pommes and the Viennese apfelstrudel are made with dessert apples. And for these sorts of dishes the dessert apple is best, but for others where a soft fluffy mass is desired, only the Bramley will do. Apples were often combined with pastry; with suet, as in apple hat; with bread, as in apple Charlotte and brown Betty; with sponge, as in Eve's pudding; or on their own, as in baked apples, compotes and purées. The combination of crisp fried bread, caramelized sugar, and tart, juicy apples is unbeatable; a good example is Elsie de Wolfe's caramel apples.

Also very English are the bread puddings. Two are still much in evidence: summer pudding and bread and butter pudding. Both had many variations which have been long forgotten: paradise pudding, made with alternate layers of bread soaked in milk, and soft fruit; and satisfaction pudding, made like bread and butter pudding, with jam added, and a meringue topping. Best of all is probably Constance Spry's toffee pudding, whereby fingers of white bread are soaked in milk, then dipped in toffee sauce and served hot, with cream.

With few exceptions, milk puddings are viewed askance today, by grown-ups and children alike. Yet before the Second World War they were very popular indeed, at all levels of society. Most favoured by the upper classes, especially the men, were the steamed and baked puddings, also rice pudding. The Bath Club's speciality was a cold rice pudding set almost solid with a little gelatine, and cut in slices like a cake. An elaborate form of creamed rice was tête de nègre: set inside a round mould, encased within a chocolate shell, and topped with a turban of whipped cream. Milk puddings were most popular lower down the social scale, but these too were enjoyed at all levels, in a slightly more elaborate form. Lady Cunard used to serve tapioca beaten up with cream at her luncheon parties, while Lady Mendl offered a blancmange with orange sauce, or semolina with currant sauce.

Fortunately, the English love for custard survived the invention of Bird's Custard Powder (which was already in existence by 1920), at least in the upper-middle classes. In working-class homes, Bird's Custard soon ousted the real thing in popularity, and was much used in trifles, or with tinned fruit. But there is nothing quite so good with hot fruit puddings as a true boiled custard, sometimes called sauce à la vanille. Often it would be served with cream as well, or with a proportion of whipped cream incorporated within it. Sometimes it formed part of the dish, in combinations of custard and meringue, like floating island and bombe favorite. Variations of the former are still found on the dessert trolleys in old-fashioned hotels and restaurants; a modern innovation is the golden thread of caramel dribbled over the meringue.

Lastly come the ices, on which the country houses prided themselves. With superlative fruit grown to order in their greenhouses, cream from the home farm, and obliging kitchen maids to crank the churn, these set few problems, and the results were often exquisite. They were always freshly made, since domestic freezers did not exist. Refrigerators appeared in 1925, but by 1939 only one house in fifty had one. Yet ice was not a problem. Most of the big country houses had their own ice house, where great blocks of ice were stored all year round. In the big towns, the ice-cart would deliver two or three times a week. The ice came in a huge block and was stored in a chest; pieces were hacked off and used as required.

In the grand houses, the pudding was followed by cheese at lunchtime, and a savoury at dinner. After the cheese, or savoury, the table was cleared and dishes of fresh fruit were handed round. It was very carefully arranged, each variety kept separate, piled high on sets of matching porcelain dessert dishes, often Sèvres or Meissen. There would be four or even five to choose from, at certain times of year: figs, peaches, nectarines, melons, grapes, apricots, strawberries, raspberries and giant dessert gooseberries, as well as apples and pears. All were grown in the garden, and came under the jurisdiction of the head gardener, rather than the cook. In some houses, he would indicate which pear was to be eaten next. The hothouse muscat grapes were often a special source of pride. At Cottesbrooke, the Macdonald-Buchanans' garden, it took a gardener up to twenty minutes to thin a bunch of grapes, so that each individual grape could grow extra large.

## Apple Charlotte

A classic English pudding, and one of the very best.

900g cooking apples, peeled, cored and thickly sliced
120g granulated sugar
120g butter
4 tablespoons water

juice of ½ lemon
2 tablespoons apricot jam
approx. 8 thin slices of dry white bread, crusts removed

Put the sliced apples in a heavy pan with the sugar, 30g of butter and 4 tablespoons of water. Cook gently, covered, until soft. Then uncover the pan and continue to cook, uncovered, over a low heat until you have a thick purée. Stir in the lemon juice and apricot jam; set aside.

Cut the bread to fit a mould or soufflé dish about 7.5cm deep. Melt the remaining 85g of butter and dip the pieces of bread in it so that they are coated on both sides, then replace them in the dish. Fill the lined dish with the apple purée and cover with a lid of more bread dipped in butter, cut to fit neatly into the top of the dish. Bake for 35–40 minutes at 180°C/gas 4, or until the top layer of bread is crisp and golden brown. Turn out on to a flat dish to serve, fairly hot but not scalding, with a jug of thick cream, or creamy custard sauce (see page 161). Serves 4–6. **Adapted from Come Into the Garden, Cook, by Constance Spry**

## Apple Hat

Suet and apples go together like bread and cheese, but for this great English dish I prefer to use crisp dessert apples, like Granny Smiths, rather than Bramleys. Custard sauce is almost obligatory with this pudding, or thick cream.

45g butter
225g self-raising flour
a pinch of salt
120g shredded suet
4 Granny Smiths, or other crisp apple, peeled, cored and sliced
4 tablespoons brown sugar
grated rind of 1 lemon

Grease a 1.2 litre pudding basin with some of the butter. Sift the flour with the salt and cut in the suet with the blade of a knife; mix lightly. Stir in enough cold water to make a firm dough, and cut in 2 pieces, one larger than the other (75/25). Roll out the larger piece to line the greased bowl. Put the apples in it, sprinkling with brown sugar and lemon rind. Roll out the remaining suet and lay over the bowl. Damp the edges, press together to seal and trim. Cover with a piece of buttered foil, doming it slightly to allow for expansion. Tie with string around the rim of the bowl. Steam over (or in) boiling water for 2 hours. Serves 5–6. Serve with creamy custard sauce (page 161), or cream. **AB**

## *Lady Portarlington's Apple Tart*

This is an unusual two-crust apple pie, with a generous dollop of whipped (or clotted) cream slipped under the lid before serving. Lady Portarlington served it 'iced'; I assume this meant chilled, but I prefer to serve it warm.

PASTRY
340g flour, sifted
1½ teaspoons caster sugar
180g butter, cut in bits
1 egg yolk
about 6 tablespoons iced water

FILLING
3–4 crisp dessert apples, Cox or Granny Smith, peeled,
    cored and sliced
2 teaspoons caster sugar
1 tablespoon lemon juice

GLAZE
1 egg yolk
1 tablespoon milk

GARNISH
275ml double cream, lightly whipped, or clotted cream
icing sugar, sifted

Make the pastry as usual and chill for 20–30 minutes. Divide it in 2 pieces, one slightly larger than the other. Roll out the larger one and line a 23cm pie tin. Weigh down with foil and dried beans and bake blind for 8 minutes at 190°C/gas 5, then remove the foil and beans and bake for another 5 minutes. Remove from the oven and leave to cool.

Lay the sliced apples in the pastry case, sprinkling with sugar and lemon juice. Brush the edges of the pastry case with the egg yolk beaten with the milk, then roll out the remaining pastry and lay over the base. Trim the edges and seal. Decorate with some pastry leaves, then brush all over with the egg glaze. Bake for 10 minutes at 190°C/gas 5, then for a further 30 minutes at 180°C/gas 4. Remove from the oven and leave to cool for 30–60 minutes. Just before serving, cut round the edge carefully and lift off the lid. Do not worry if it breaks into 2 or 3 pieces. Spread the lightly whipped cream over the surface of the apples and replace the lid. Sprinkle very lightly with icing sugar and serve straight away. Serves 6. **Adapted from Lady Portarlington, in** *Vogue*

## Caramel Apples

The combination of tart apples, crisp fried bread and thick cream is unbeatable.

3 Granny Smith dessert apples, peeled, cored and thickly sliced
70g butter
approx. 85g caster sugar
4 tablespoons apricot jam, warmed and sieved
4 slices of dry white bread, 7.5mm thick, crusts removed

Fry the sliced apples in half the butter. Do them in batches, in a broad frying pan. As each batch is done, transfer them to a shallow (or flat) serving dish and sprinkle each layer with 1 tablespoon caster sugar and brush with the sieved apricot jam. Keep in a warm place while you fry the rest of the apples, piling them in a level mound.

Then prepare the bread. Cut each slice in 3.5cm squares, then cut each square into 2 triangles. Fry these in the remaining butter until lightly coloured, then drain on soft paper and lay on a baking sheet. Sprinkle them with half the remaining sugar, then place under the grill just until the sugar has melted and lightly coloured. Then remove from the grill, turn the bread over, sprinkle with the remaining sugar and replace under the grill. When lightly browned on both sides lay them over the apples and serve, hot, with a jug of thick cream. Serves 6. **Adapted from *Elsie de Wolfe's Recipes for Successful Dining***

## Bread and Butter Pudding

This is my own recipe for an old favourite among puddings, and one that is fairly typical of the period. A delicious accompaniment, although not authentic, is home-made vanilla ice cream. Between the wars this pudding would have been served with a jug of cream, or, for a simple meal, alone.

85g dry white bread, crusts removed, sliced
approx. 30g unsalted butter
20g raisins
275ml milk
150ml single cream
3 eggs
85g vanilla sugar, or caster sugar

Butter the slices of bread, cut each one in half diagonally, and lay them in a buttered china dish holding 570ml. Scatter the raisins between each layer of bread and over the top. Heat the milk with the cream in a small pan. Beat the eggs with the sugar, using an electric hand-beater or wire whisk. When the milk is about to boil, pour it on to the eggs, continuing to beat. Then pour on to the bread through a strainer. Bake for 40–45 minutes at 170°C/gas 3, until the custard has set and the top has become crisp and golden brown. Serves 4. This pudding is best served warm, about 45 minutes after taking out of the oven. Accompany it with a jug of thick cream, or some vanilla ice cream. **AB**

## Bakewell Tart

Jam puddings of this sort are once again fashionable, I am glad to say. I make this with short pastry instead of puff, as stated in the original recipe.

120g flour

70g unsalted butter

½ teaspoon caster sugar

a little iced water

FILLING

4 tablespoons each strawberry and apricot jam

2 tablespoons ground almonds

85g unsalted butter

55g caster sugar

3 egg yolks

1 large lemon

70g soft white breadcrumbs

1 egg white

a pinch of salt

Line a round tin with pastry, roll out the bottom quite thin, put on it a layer of two sorts of jam, strawberry and apricot, sprinkle on it a thin layer of ground almonds. Beat to a cream 85g of real butter and add to it 55g of caster sugar. Then add the yolks of three fresh eggs, the grated rind and juice of 1 large lemon, 70g of fine breadcrumbs, and the white of one egg well beaten with a pinch of salt. Pour on this mixture [*into the pastry case*] and bake carefully [*for about 40 minutes, or until set, at 180°C/gas 4*]. The mixture *must* set and the jam must *not* boil up and show. Eaten as a rule cold. [*Even better warm.*] Enough for six people. **Lovely Food, by Ruth Lowinsky**

## Castle Puddings

These little individual puddings like tiny sandcastles are made in dariole moulds. They may be either baked or steamed, and are usually served with a golden syrup sauce. If you don't have dariole moulds, make one big pudding in a bowl and steam it. In this case it is called canary pudding, and is usually served with a hot jam sauce.

120g unsalted butter

120g caster sugar

120g self-raising flour, sifted

2 large eggs, lightly beaten

1 teaspoon grated lemon rind

2 tablespoons milk, or as needed

SAUCE

6 tablespoons golden syrup

2 tablespoons lemon juice

The sponge mixture may be made in a food processor or mixed by hand. Cream the butter and sugar, then mix in the sifted flour and beaten eggs alternately, a little at a time. Add the lemon rind and, lastly, enough milk to give a soft dropping consistency. Pour into small dariole moulds which have been well buttered. Do not fill them more than ¾ full. They may be baked for 20 minutes at 180°C/gas 4, or steamed over boiling water for 30 minutes.

When the time is up, make the sauce. Warm the syrup in a small pan, adding the lemon juice, and pour into a small jug or sauceboat. Turn out the puddings to serve, cutting a slice off the top of each one to make a level base. Serve with the warm sauce and a jug of thick cream. Serves 6. **AB**

## Canary Pudding

This is made with exactly the same mixture as castle puddings, but instead of using individual moulds the mixture is turned into a greased pudding basin holding about 825ml. (If to be served with a jam sauce, 2 tablespoons of the same jam may be put in the bottom of the bowl before adding the sponge mixture.) The bowl is covered with foil and tied as usual, then steamed for 2 hours. If made with jam, serve with the apricot jam sauce on page 160 or the mixed jam sauce on page 163. Alternatively, make without jam and serve with the golden syrup sauce above. Serves 5–6. **AB**

# Seven-Cup Pudding

My mother was given this receipt by her Scottish mother-in-law when she married. It is an old favourite: like a simpler version of plum pudding, made on the 'cup' principle instead of using scales. On a cold grey day it is very good indeed, served with a creamy custard sauce (see page 161), or lemon and vanilla sauce (see page 162). Use a teacup holding 175ml as your measure.

1 teacupful soft white breadcrumbs
1 teacupful shredded suet
1 teacupful sultanas
1 teacupful currants
1 teacupful caster sugar
1 teacupful plain flour
55g chopped mixed peel
55g coarsely chopped almonds
2 teaspoons ground ginger
1 teaspoon ground cinnamon
1 teaspoon mixed spice, or allspice
a pinch of salt
1 egg
approx. 150ml milk
1 teaspoon bicarbonate of soda
1 teaspoon wine vinegar

Mix all the ingredients together except for the egg, milk, bicarbonate of soda and vinegar. Break the egg into a measuring jug and make up to 175ml with milk. Stir into the mixture. Dissolve the bicarbonate of soda in the vinegar for a few moments, then stir in also. Mix all together very well, then turn into a buttered pudding basin and steam for 4–6 hours. Turn out to serve, with creamy custard sauce (page 161), lemon and vanilla sauce (page 162), plain custard, or cream. Serves 6–8. **Lady Moray**

# Christmas Pudding

Everyone has their own recipe for plum pudding; this is a good one, less rich than some, but light and full of flavour. In the old days, the puddings were kept from one year to the next, or made months ahead of time. The old houses had cool airy larders in which to store them, however, and anyone who tries to keep a plum pudding for long in a centrally heated flat is in for a nasty surprise, as it is sure to grow a coating of mould. Ideally, I would make the Christmas puddings about six weeks in advance.

680g seedless raisins
225g cut mixed peel
225g glacé cherries, halved
120g coarsely chopped almonds
340g shredded suet
340g soft white breadcrumbs
8 eggs, beaten
150ml Guinness
6 tablespoons brandy

Mix the raisins, peel, cherries, almonds, suet and breadcrumbs in a large bowl. Stir in the beaten eggs, Guinness and brandy. Leave for a few hours at this stage, or even overnight if convenient, for the flavours to develop. When ready to cook, pack the mixture into three 825ml pudding basins which have been well buttered. (If adding charms, put them in now, and remember to indicate which bowl has the charms.) Do not fill them too full; there should be at least 2.5cm left empty at the top. Cover with a buttered piece of foil, doming it slightly to allow extra room for the pudding to swell. Then wrap in a square piece of clean linen – part of an old sheet will do – knotting the four corners over the top to form a handle, useful for lowering the pudding in and out of the water. Have a very large pan ready with boiling water to come halfway up the side of the bowls. Lay each bowl on an upturned saucer or small cake tin, and cover the pan. Boil steadily for 6 hours, adding more boiling water from time to time, as needed. When the time is up, lift out the puddings and leave to cool; one can be eaten straightaway if you like. The others should be stored in a cool place. If giving one or two as presents, wrap them in clean cloth after cooling.

Before serving, they should be boiled again in the same way, for 4–6 hours. To serve on Christmas Day itself, turn out on to a flat dish and stick a sprig of holly in the centre. Warm 3 tablespoons of brandy gently in a soup ladle, then set light to it with a match, and pour – flaming – over the pudding just before you set it on the table. Each of these puddings will serve 6–8 people; but two larger ones – or one giant – can be made if preferred. **AB**

## Gentleman's Pudding

A fine example of a steamed sponge pudding, made without suet or breadcrumbs. Light, delicate in flavour, and with an outstanding sauce, it is one of the best.

140g butter
70g caster sugar
140g self-raising flour
3 large eggs
3 tablespoons raspberry jam

SAUCE

2 egg yolks
1 tablespoon caster sugar
70ml dry sherry
1½ tablespoons raspberry jam

Cream butter and sugar, add sifted flour and eggs [*one at a time*] alternately. Beat well, then add jam. Turn into a buttered bowl [*holding about 1 litre*] and steam for 1½ hours. Turn out and serve with the following sauce: Whip egg yolks with sugar over hot water. Add sherry, then jam. Serve hot, either poured around the pudding, or separately, in a sauceboat. Cream may be served as well, if you wish. Serves 6. **Lady Colefax, in *Vogue***

# Marmalade Pudding

This pudding uses a mixture of equal parts suet and bread-crumbs, with no flour.

120g soft white breadcrumbs
120g shredded suet
120g caster sugar
2 heaped tablespoons marmalade, chopped
1 egg, lightly beaten

SAUCE
4 tablespoons marmalade, chopped
2 tablespoons orange juice
150ml double cream

Mix the breadcrumbs, suet and sugar in a bowl. Mix the marmalade with the beaten egg and stir into the suet mixture. Turn into a greased pudding basin holding about 825ml. Cover with greased foil, slightly domed, and tie with string around the rim of the bowl. Steam over boiling water for 2 hours, or stand in a large covered saucepan with boiling water coming halfway up the sides of the bowl. Check now and then to see that it is not boiling dry, adding more boiling water as needed. When the time is up, make the sauce. Put the marmalade and orange juice in a small pan, add 2 tablespoons of water, and heat gently. Add the cream, stirring till blended. When all is hot, pour into a sauce-boat. Unmould the pudding on to a round dish and serve with the marmalade sauce. Serves 4–5. **AB**

# Pudding Louise

I am told by a mutual friend that this was Lord Berners' favourite pudding. It is very good indeed, rather like Bakewell tart without the almonds. I have adapted it from the original, which was brief, but very precise. I tend to use Tiptree Raspberry Seedless, or Blackberry Jelly, instead of redcurrant jelly.

PASTRY
180g flour

85g unsalted butter

a little iced water

FILLING

4–5 tablespoons redcurrant (or other fruit) jelly

100g unsalted butter, at room temperature

100g caster sugar

55g flour, sifted

Make the pastry as usual. Chill for 20 minutes, then roll out to line a 23cm pie tin. Chill again, then bake blind, weighed down with foil and dried beans, for 8 minutes at 190°C/gas 5. Remove the foil and beans, and bake for a further 5 minutes at 180°C/gas 4. Remove from the oven and leave to cool.

Later, spread the jelly over the bottom of the pastry case. Cream the butter and sugar, either by hand or in a food processor. Mix in the sifted flour and spread over the jelly. Bake for 1 hour at 170°C/gas 3. Serve soon after coming out of the oven, with cream. Serves 6. This tart is utterly delicious served hot or warm, but it is not good cold, nor will it reheat well. **Adapted from** *The Alice B. Toklas Cook Book*

## Two-Tier Lemon Pudding

This is a good hot pudding, simple and quick to make, that has been all but forgotten. It separates into two parts on baking: a solid cakey top, with a lemon sauce lying underneath the surface. I like to serve it with fresh raspberries and thick cream.

15g unsalted butter

55g caster sugar

2 eggs, separated

275ml milk

juice of 1 lemon

2 heaped tablespoons flour

Cream butter and sugar. Beat yolks and add to creamed mixture. Add milk, lemon juice, and flour. Add stiffly beaten whites and put in buttered [*1.2 litre*] dish. Put dish in a bigger one [*or a roasting tin*] containing hot water and cook until nicely brown for about 45 minutes in a moderate oven [*190°C/gas 5*]. This is enough for about 3 [*or 4*] people. **Mrs Arthur James**

## Pain Perdu with Raisin Sauce

Pain perdu was originally a French pudding which became popular in England, where it was sometimes known as 'eggy bread'. This is a more elegant version, such as might have been served at a lunch party, with a hot raisin sauce.

275ml milk
2 tablespoons vanilla sugar, or caster sugar and ½ vanilla pod
6 large slices of stale white bread, crusts removed
2 eggs, beaten
55g butter

HOT RAISIN SAUCE
4 tablespoons seedless raisins
2 tablespoons sugar
15g butter
150ml water
1 tablespoon brandy
4 tablespoons double cream

Have the sauce made in advance. Put the raisins in a small pan with the sugar, butter and 150ml of water. Simmer gently for 10 minutes, until the raisins have swelled and become soft. Stand, covered, at the back of the stove while you make the pudding.

Heat the milk with the vanilla sugar. (If you don't have vanilla sugar, use ordinary caster sugar with half a vanilla pod to flavour the milk.) Bring slowly to boiling point, reduce the heat and cook gently until the sugar has melted, then leave to cool. (If using a vanilla pod, remove it once the milk has cooled completely.) Cut each slice of bread in four, and lay in a shallow dish. Pour over the milk, turning the pieces of bread over to absorb the milk without allowing them to become too soft. Beat the eggs and dip each slice in them. Heat the butter in a broad frying pan and fry the bread on both sides, until golden. Lay on a serving dish and sprinkle with caster sugar. Reheat the sauce, adding the brandy and cream, and serve in a sauceboat, with the pain perdu. Alternatively, you may omit the raisin sauce and simply serve it with a bowl of lightly whipped cream. Serves 6. **AB**

## Paradise Pudding

This is an early variant of the well-known summer pudding. It was served in its dish, with a layer of lightly whipped cream spread over the top, but I prefer to turn it out and serve the cream separately. When soft fruit is plentiful, I cook a second lot and spoon it around the pudding before serving. My favourite fruit combination is raspberries, blue-berries and redcurrants.

680g soft fruit: mixed berries and currants
2 tablespoons caster sugar
8–10 thick slices of dry white bread, crusts removed
450ml milk

GARNISH (OPTIONAL), TO BE MADE ON 2ND DAY
340g soft fruit (as above)
2 tablespoons caster sugar

Start 1 day in advance. Cook the fruit very lightly indeed: put the berries in a large bowl beside the stove. Put the sugar in a heavy pan with 4 tablespoons of water; heat slowly until the sugar has melted. Then put in the blackcurrants, if used, and cook gently for 2 minutes. Then add the redcurrants and blueberries. Cook for another 2 minutes, then pour the contents of the pan, still simmering, over the berries in their bowl. (Raspberries, blueberries and blackberries are best; strawberries are not ideal, being too watery. If used, they are best added raw, after the rest of the fruit has cooled.)

When the fruit has cooled to room temperature make a layer of it in the bottom of a bowl. Cut pieces of bread to fit the bowl, then dip each one in milk and press gently. Then lay them over the fruit. Continue to make alternate layers of fruit and bread in this way, until the dish is full. Finish with a layer of bread cut to fit exactly, so the fruit is completely covered. Cover with foil and a small plate, and lay a 680g weight on the plate. Stand overnight in the refrigerator. Next day, if adding a fruit garnish, cook the second lot of fruit exactly as you did the first lot the previous day. Leave it to cool, then shortly before serving unmould the pudding on to a shallow dish and spoon the extra fruit around it. Serve with a jug of thick cream, or a bowl of lightly whipped cream. Serves 6–8. **Adapted from** *Lady Sysonby's Cook Book*

## Toffee Pudding

This is the best of all the hot, rich English puddings, perfect for a weekend lunch party on a winter day.

120g unsalted butter
120g light brown demerara sugar
225g golden syrup
275ml milk
fingers of (white) bread, 1 day old

Put the butter, demerara sugar and syrup into a frying pan, stir until melted over slow heat, then boil more rapidly until golden brown, stirring continuously. Bring the milk up to boiling point. Arrange the fingers of bread in a large dish, pour over the milk. Lift out the fingers at once and put them into the toffee sauce to coat them well. Pile them up in a fireproof dish, and if necessary pour over a little extra toffee sauce. Serve with whipped cream. [*Serves 6.*] **The Constance Spry Cookery Book, by Constance Spry and Rosemary Hume**

# Cream of Rice (as made at the Bath Club)

A cold rice pudding, set almost solid by the addition of a small quantity of gelatine, was popular with men, who seemed to prefer it to the softer creamier version which was sometimes served.

825ml milk
120g pudding rice
2 tablespoons caster sugar
7g gelatine, or ½ a packet
1 egg yolk, beaten
3 tablespoons lightly whipped cream

Bring the milk to the boil and shake in the rice. Bring back to the boil and cook for 20 minutes, half covered. Add the sugar and cook for another 20 minutes, then turn into a basin, keeping back about 4 tablespoons of the hot milk. Pour this into a cup and dissolve the gelatine in it. Once melted, stir it into the rice, mixing well. Then stir in the beaten egg yolk and leave to cool. When it has reached room temperature, fold in the whipped cream and turn into a serving dish. Chill for a few hours, or overnight. Serve very cold, with a dish of lightly cooked fruit still slightly warm or at room temperature. Cream may be served as well, if you like. Serves 6. A useful dish in that it keeps well in the fridge, may be prepared well in advance, and is quite sustaining. **Adapted from *The Perfect Hostess*, by Rose Henniker Heaton**

# Rice Meringue

This is based on a recipe in *Minnie Lady Hindlip's Cookery Book,* but I have substituted a tart purée of apples for the layer of jam in the original.

180g pudding rice
825ml milk
1 x 5cm strip of lemon peel
55g vanilla sugar, or caster sugar

2 egg yolks, beaten
2 tablespoons double cream

APPLE PURÉE

3 Bramley cooking apples, peeled, cored and thickly sliced
3 tablespoons sugar

MERINGUE

3 egg whites
70g caster sugar

Put the rice in a pan with the milk and lemon peel. Bring to the boil and cook slowly, half covered, until the rice is tender and all the milk has been absorbed: about 25 minutes. Then remove the lemon peel and leave to cool. Then stir in the sugar, and the egg yolks beaten with the cream. Cook the sliced apples with 3 tablespoons of sugar and 6 tablespoons of water until soft, then push them through a medium food mill and leave to cool.

Spread half the rice in the bottom of a buttered fireproof dish – a soufflé dish does well – and spread the apple purée over it. Cover with the rest of the rice. Beat the egg whites until they become stiff, then add most of the sugar bit by bit. Fold in the last spoonful by hand, and pile on top of the rice. Bake for 30 minutes at 140°C/gas 1, until lightly set and golden brown. This dish is good at any temperature; hot, warm, cool, or straight from the fridge. Serves 4–6. **Adapted from *Minnie Lady Hindlip's Cookery Book***

## *Tête de Nègre*

This was a popular pudding in the 1930s, now rarely seen. The combination of the crisp chocolate shell with the creamy rice within is very good indeed.

85g long-grain rice
450ml milk
3 egg yolks
55g vanilla sugar
275ml double cream

CHOCOLATE SAUCE
85g plain chocolate
55g unsalted butter

Drop the rice into boiling water and cook for 10 minutes; drain well. Heat 275ml of milk, shake in the drained rice, cook for another 10 minutes, then drain again.

Make a custard by beating the egg yolks with the vanilla sugar. Then heat the remaining 175ml of milk until almost boiling and pour on to the egg yolks, beating well. Stand over a pan of simmering water and continue to stir for 6–8 minutes, until it has thickened slightly, just enough to coat the back of the spoon. Stir the hot custard into the cooked rice, and leave to cool. Then stir in 2 tablespoons of cream and turn into a round pudding basin rinsed out with cold water, which it fills nicely. (About 450ml.) Chill for several hours, or overnight.

Some hours later, make the sauce. Grate the chocolate into a bowl standing over a pan of simmering water. Add the butter cut in small bits, and 1 tablespoon of hot water. Once the chocolate has melted, beat well. Unmould the rice pudding on to a flat dish and pour the hot chocolate sauce over it so that it is completely covered. The sauce will set to a hard shell immediately on contact with the cold rice. Chill again before serving, or stand in a cool larder.

Just before serving, whip the remaining cream and pile on top, like a turban. Serves 4–5. **Adapted from *Personal Choice*, by Ambrose Heath**

## Lady St Just's Raspberry and Redcurrant Compote

This is an exquisite dish, both in flavour and in appearance. I cook the currant purée for a couple of minutes, just long enough to sweeten it.

450g raspberries
225g redcurrants
45–55g caster sugar

Press but do not pulp some raspberries. [*Put them under a 1.5kg weight for 1 hour.*] Put them into a glass bowl [*reserving 55g*] and cover with some of the redcurrants [*again reserving 55g*]. Continue with layers [*4 in all*] of pressed raspberries and whole redcurrants until the dish is nearly full. Sugar each layer [*with 1 tablespoon of caster sugar*]. Make a purée of the remaining raspberries and redcurrants. [*Heat 4 tablespoons of water with 4 tablespoons of sugar in a heavy pan until the sugar has melted, then add the currants and cook gently for 2 minutes. Pour them, still simmering, over the reserved raspberries in a bowl and leave to cool. Then spread over the surface of the dish.*] Put in the refrigerator for several hours [*or overnight*]. Serves 4. **English Country House Cooking, by Fortune Stanley**

## Sliced Peaches in Plum Juice

An unusual fruit dish, elegant and delicious, yet quickly made. I add eau-de-vie de framboise, when I have it, instead of kirsch, to the plum juice before serving.

140g sugar
5 tablespoons water
6 large red (ripe) plums
4 perfectly ripe peaches, white flesh for preference
1 tablespoon kirsch, or eau-de-vie de framboise

Make a syrup of the sugar and 5 tablespoons of water. When thick pour it over the plums in a saucepan, place on the fire, and cook gently until the plums burst and the syrup becomes red. Strain the juice of the plums and put part [*half*] of the plums through a sieve [*or medium food mill*] and add to the juice. Place this juice on ice to chill. [*Add spirits at this point if you prefer not to hand it round at table.*] Peel and slice the peaches, which should be very ripe, pour the plum juice over, and serve with a bottle of kirsch [*or eau-de-vie*] separately, to be added to the fruit as desired. Serves 4. [*This looks pretty served in individual glass bowls, or in one large one.*] **Vogue's Cookery Book, edited by Hilda Powell**

## Pekin Dust

This excellent dessert is an old favourite in my family, but the name of this version is new to me. The cream may be omitted if preferred, or served separately.

6 medium oranges
caster sugar (optional)
120g loaf (or granulated) sugar
150ml water
150–275ml double cream

Peel the oranges and slice them, removing all skin and pips and taking care to lose none of the juice. Mix the juice with a little caster sugar to taste [*I leave it unsweetened*], adding a little more juice if necessary, and pour over the oranges.

Put the loaf [*or granulated*] sugar in a saucepan, add the water and boil quickly till [*light golden*] brown, being careful not to let it get too dark. Pour it out on to a tin to let it get cold and set. When it is hard, crush it coarsely with a rolling-pin and shake it all over the fruit. Whip the cream and pile it on top. [*Serves 6.*] **When the Cook Is Away, by Catherine Ives**

## Compote of Oranges with Orange Jelly

An orange jelly was a favourite with children and grown-ups alike. This one is particularly good, served with a compote of sliced oranges in a light orange syrup.

JELLY
9 oranges
1 lemon
120g granulated sugar
15g gelatine (1 packet)
COMPOTE
6 oranges
30g granulated sugar

Make the jelly a day in advance. Pare the rind of 1 orange; squeeze the juice of all 9, and the lemon. Heat the sugar with 4 tablespoons of water until it boils, and the sugar has melted, then pour it over the rind and leave to cool. Dissolve the gelatine in 4 tablespoons of hot water, then add to the fruit juices, with the sugar syrup. Mix well, then pour through a strainer into a shallow bowl. Chill overnight.

Next day, squeeze the juice of 2 oranges into a bowl. Dissolve the sugar in 2 tablespoons of water, then add to the juice and leave to cool. Peel the remaining 4 oranges, removing all the white pith, and cut in fairly thick slices. Arrange them overlapping in a shallow round dish and pour the syrup over them. Chill for at least 2 hours before serving, with the jelly in a separate bowl. Serves 6. (The jelly will probably be very soft. If firm, it may be roughly chopped with the edge of a palette knife, then turned back into the clean bowl.) **Adapted from *Kitchen Essays*, by Lady Jekyll**

## Red Wine Jelly

> This was a popular dessert in England in Stuart times, but was later forgotten. It survived in the United States, however, and from there was reintroduced to England in the 1920s.

120g caster sugar
20g gelatine (1½ packets)
275ml good red wine
4 tablespoons brandy
2 tablespoons orange juice
2 tablespoons lemon juice
275ml double cream, lightly whipped

Bring 275ml of water to the boil, add the sugar and stir until it has melted. Remove from the heat, cool slightly, then shake in the gelatine. When this also has melted, add the wine, brandy and fruit juices. Mix well, then pour into a 720ml ring mould through a strainer. Cool, then chill overnight, or for several hours, in the refrigerator. Turn out on

to a flat dish to serve, filling the centre with lightly whipped cream.
Serves 4. **AB**

## Plum Croutons

> This uncomplicated dish is based on a recipe in Mrs Leyel's
> classic, *The Gentle Art of Cookery*. It must be made with
> plums ripe enough to eat.

4 slices of dry white bread, cut 1cm thick
30g unsalted butter
4 large ripe plums, or 6 medium ones
30g caster sugar

Cut the bread in neat rectangles, removing the crusts. Butter on both
sides and lay them on a baking sheet. Cut the plums in half and remove
the stones. Do this over the bread so that the juice that runs out is not
wasted. Lay 2 or 3 plum halves on each piece of bread. Sprinkle them
thickly with sugar and dot each plum half with a tiny bit of butter. Bake
for 45 minutes at 170°C/gas 3, sprinkling them once or twice with the
rest of the sugar during the baking. Take out of the oven and cool for
10–15 minutes before serving, on a flat dish, with a jug of cream. Serves
4. **Adapted from *The Gentle Art of Cookery*, by Mrs C. F. Leyel and
Miss Olga Hartley**

## Floating Island

> This is one of the few old-fashioned puddings to have
> remained popular, for it is still sometimes seen today in the
> restaurants of grand hotels like Claridge's. Nowadays, a thin
> stream of caramel is often trickled over the mound of
> meringue, which is also rather delicious.

MERINGUE
4 egg whites
6 tablespoons vanilla sugar, or caster sugar

CUSTARD SAUCE
450ml milk
½ vanilla pod
4 egg yolks
3 tablespoons vanilla sugar or caster sugar
CARAMEL (OPTIONAL)
120g granulated sugar

If using caramel, make this first. Put the granulated sugar in a heavy pan with 4 tablespoons of water and heat slowly. Boil steadily, watching constantly, until the sugar melts and starts to caramelize. When it has turned pale golden, remove from the heat and pour it into a wetted mould or fireproof dish. (This may be either a tin charlotte mould, or a fireproof glass or china bowl holding about 825ml.) Turn the mould quickly as you pour in the caramel so that the sides are evenly coated. Set aside to cool.

Beat the egg whites until stiff, then add 3 tablespoons of vanilla (or caster) sugar, little by little, as you continue to beat. Finally fold in the remaining 3 tablespoons of sugar, then turn into the caramel-lined mould and bake for 20 minutes at 170°C/gas 3.

Make the custard sauce while it bakes. Heat the milk with the vanilla pod in a small pan. Bring slowly to the boil, then remove from the heat, cover, and stand for 20–30 minutes. Then remove the pod and reheat the milk slowly. Beat the egg yolks in a bowl, adding the 3 tablespoons of vanilla (or caster) sugar. When the milk boils, pour it on to the egg yolks, continuing to beat. Then stand the bowl over a saucepan of simmering water, making sure the water does not touch the base of the bowl, and stir constantly until it has thickened very slightly, just enough to coat the back of a spoon. This may take 7 or 8 minutes. Remove from the heat and stand in a sink half full of very cold water, stirring now and then as it cools to prevent a skin forming.

When both meringue and sauce have cooled, chill them for 2–3 hours in the refrigerator. Shortly before serving, turn out the meringue by running a sharp knife round the inside edge of the mould. Pour the custard sauce around it. Serves 6. (If you prefer the old-fashioned version without the caramel, simply leave it out, and oil the mould lightly with sunflower or almond oil.) **AB**

# Prune Whip

This is like a simple soufflé, delicious served hot, with a bowl of whipped cream flavoured with brandy.

225g prunes
275ml cold (Indian) tea
55g caster sugar
3 egg whites

GARNISH
275ml double cream
1 tablespoon brandy

Stew the prunes [*which have been soaked for a few hours in cold tea*] until the stones come out easily. Crush [*by chopping, then pushing through a food mill*], add the sugar and well-beaten egg whites; [*spoon into a soufflé dish and*] place in a pan of warm water and bake in a moderate oven [*25 minutes at 180°C/gas 4*]. Serve with whipped cream flavoured with brandy. [*First whip the cream, then fold in the brandy little by little. Serves 4.*] **Caviare to Candy, by Mrs Philip Martineau**

# Bombe Favorite

This is known as cream bomb in my daughter-in-law's family, where it is made with undiluted whipped cream mixed with broken meringue. This is how it was always made before the war, but during the food restrictions an egg custard often replaced some of the cream. I prefer it made this way, for the other is very rich indeed. It was usually served with a raspberry sauce, or with stewed fruit. I like it with a garnish of very lightly cooked mixed berries.

275ml double cream, whipped
140–180g meringues, broken in large pieces

CUSTARD
2 egg yolks
1 tablespoon cornflour

1 tablespoon caster sugar

275ml milk

FRUIT GARNISH

2 tablespoons caster sugar

340g blueberries

225g raspberries

Start several hours in advance. Make the custard as usual, adding a little cornflour mixed to a paste with 3 tablespoons of water to the egg yolks, to assist the thickening. Cool quickly in a sink half full of cold water, stirring often to prevent a skin forming. When it has cooled almost to room temperature, whip the cream and fold into the custard. Fold in the pieces of meringue, trying to avoid breaking them up too much. Add as many as are needed to make a fairly stiff mixture that will hold its shape. Turn into a bowl and freeze for 2 hours.

While it is freezing, make the fruit garnish. Put the sugar in a heavy pan with 2 tablespoons of water. When the sugar has melted, add the blueberries and cook for 2 minutes, then pour them over the raspberries which are standing beside the stove in a bowl. Leave to cool.

Shortly before serving, turn out the 'bombe' on to a shallow dish and pour the fruit compote around it. Serves 5–6. Very popular with children.

Alternatively, make a fruit sauce with 450g raspberries (fresh or frozen), puréed in a food processor and rubbed through a coarse sieve or food mill to hold back the pips. Sweeten to taste, and pour around the iced pudding. **Kate Boxer**

## *Raspberry Ice*

This excellent dish is based on one prepared by Mrs Woodman, the Mildmays' cook, for a dinner party at their house in Berkeley Square. In the original version, which I have simplified, the ice was served on a base of sponge cake, with a dish of fresh raspberries handed separately, together with cream, and cigarette wafers. Raspberry makes the best of all ice creams, for the acidity of the fruit cuts through the bland mass of cream. The ice is also very good served alone.

ICE CREAM

450g raspberries

1 tablespoon caster sugar

70g granulated sugar

3 egg yolks, beaten

275ml double cream, lightly whipped

MIXED BERRY SAUCE (OPTIONAL)

225g raspberries

2 tablespoons caster sugar

1 tablespoon eau-de-vie de framboise, or kirsch

225g strawberries, cut in quarters

Purée the raspberries in a food processor, then rub through a sieve, or push through a fine food mill; add the caster sugar. Put the granulated sugar in a small pan with 120ml of water and heat slowly. When the sugar has melted, increase the heat and boil rapidly until it will form a thread between finger and thumb. Then take it off the heat and leave for a moment to cool, then pour it on to the beaten egg yolks, beating constantly with a wire whisk until the mixture is thick and foamy. Set aside to cool, then mix with the raspberry purée and fold in the lightly whipped cream. Freeze as usual. Makes just over 570ml, or 570g.

While it is freezing, make the sauce. Simply purée the raspberries in a food processor and rub through a coarse sieve, or fine food mill. Add the sugar, and a drop of eau-de-vie de framboise, or kirsch, if you have it. Then mix with the strawberries which you have cut in quarters, and turn into a shallow bowl. Serve with the ice cream, and a plate of home-made sponge fingers (see page 205). Serves 6; the ice alone serves 4. **AB**


## Caramel Ice Cream

This recipe comes from Joyce Molyneux, chef/proprietor of the Carved Angel in Dartmouth. Joyce is wholly English, despite her name, and this is just the sort of ice cream that was being made before the war, cranked by hand in wooden pails packed with ice and rock salt, in the English country houses. Joyce Molyneux is an inspired cook, and this ice cream cannot be bettered. Made with plain sugar instead of muscovado, it is simply a superlative vanilla ice cream.

1 vanilla pod
3 egg yolks
120g light brown muscovado sugar (or caster sugar)
275ml milk
150ml double cream

Slit the vanilla pod down its length. Beat the egg yolks with the sugar in a bowl until pale and fluffy. Pour the milk into a pan and add the vanilla pod. Bring slowly to the boil. Remove from the heat and pour on to the egg yolks, stirring constantly. Set the bowl over a pan of simmering water, and stir for about 5 minutes, until the custard is thick enough to coat the back of a spoon. Do not let it boil. Stand the bowl in iced water to cool quickly. Remove the vanilla pod.

When cool, add the double cream and mix well. Churn or beat by hand as it freezes. Move the ice cream from the freezer to the fridge about 15 minutes before serving. Serves 4–6. *The Carved Angel Cookery Book*, **by Joyce Molyneux**

## Brown Bread Ice Cream

To make brown bread ice cream, an old English favourite, first make toasted breadcrumbs as follows. Lay 85g of soft brown breadcrumbs on a baking sheet and bake in the oven at 150°C/gas 2 for 30–40 minutes, until light golden brown. Turn on to a plate to cool. Then make vanilla ice cream as above, using vanilla or caster sugar instead of muscovado, and fold in the breadcrumbs when it is two-thirds frozen. Continue to freeze until thick. Serves 4–6. **AB**

## Ice Cream of Roses

One of Mrs Leyel's enchanting recipes, a timely reminder that English food could be exotic as well as homely. I have substituted milk for half the cream to make it less rich, more in tune with current tastes.

275ml milk
275ml single cream
30–45g fresh rose petals, preferably old-fashioned roses
3 egg yolks
4 tablespoons caster sugar
a few drops of cochineal (optional)

Boil 570ml of cream [*or milk and cream mixed*], and put into it when it boils two handfuls of fresh rose petals, and leave them for two hours, well covered. Then pass this through a sieve [*or strain it*], and mix [*or make into a custard*] with the well-beaten yolks of eggs, and sugar to taste. Add a little cochineal [*optional*], and put it on the fire, stirring all the time, but do not let it boil on any account. [*Beat the egg yolks with the sugar, then pour on the boiling milk and cream, after straining. Stir over a pan of simmering water for 6–8 minutes, or until it has very slightly thickened, then cool quickly in a sink half full of cold water. Freeze as usual. Makes approx. 570ml.*] **The Gentle Art of Cookery, by Mrs C. F. Leyel and Miss Olga Hartley**

## Rhubarb Sorbet

This is an unusual sorbet, delicious in flavour and a lovely shade of pink. It is best made with early (forced) rhubarb which does not need peeling, as the flavour is more delicate and the skin gives it its colour. This could very well be used as a sorbet halfway through a long meal; in this case use less sugar.

680g forced rhubarb, cut in chunks
2 dessert apples, or 1 Bramley, peeled, cored and roughly chopped
180g sugar
juice of 1 orange

Put the rhubarb and apple in a pan with the sugar and add enough water to come barely level with the contents of the pan, about 275ml. Cook gently until both rhubarb and apples are soft, then drain off the juice into another pan and boil up until it is reduced by about one-third; this will take about 5 minutes. Leave to cool. Later, put the cooked fruit in a food processor with the orange juice and the cooled syrup. Process until blended, then freeze as usual. Serves 6–8. **Jane Longman, in** *Vogue*

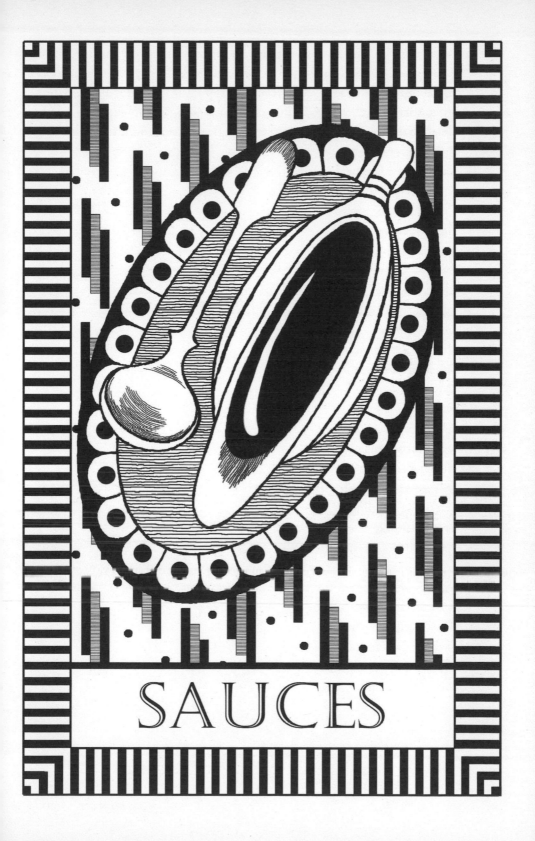

SAUCES

# SAUCES

English and French sauces differ fundamentally in that they are constructed on totally different principles. Whereas a French sauce is an intrinsic part of the dish it accompanies, often made with the juices that result from its cooking, the English sauce is a thing apart. There is no English equivalent to the sauce served with a canard pressé, for example, which is made from the blood and juices of the pressed duck. Our traditional sauce for duck is made with stewed apples. Whereas in France a sauce is used to implement and reinforce the main flavour of the main element, in England the sauce is used to give a contrast: in taste, texture and – sometimes – temperature.

Almost every main dish had its accompanying sauce, and in most households these were rarely, if ever, deviated from. To eat roast lamb without mint sauce, or at least redcurrant jelly, would have been unthinkable. Duff Cooper described such a fiasco in a letter to his wife in 1938: 'My dinner for eight was quite successful last night except when Mrs Blackman sent up roast partridge without bread sauce. I nearly had a stroke.' Roast beef was invariably accompanied by horseradish in some form; boiled mutton by caper or onion sauce. Parsley sauce was always served with boiled ham, egg sauce with boiled cod, bread sauce with roast chicken, mustard sauce with grilled herrings and cheese sauce with macaroni, cauliflower and hard-boiled eggs.

In addition to the sauces, there was also a range of traditional garnishes that were often served with the sauce, or instead of one. These included fruit jellies, either redcurrant, rowan or crab-apple, to accompany hot or cold roast mutton or lamb. Cumberland sauce is like a cross between a fruit jelly and a sauce; this was served with hot or cold ham, game pâté and terrines. Fruit garnishes were sometimes served with cold meat, especially pork, or duck. These might be composed of chopped apples, onions and celery, like an uncooked chutney. Breadcrumbs fried in butter were always served with roast pheasant and grouse, at the same time as the bread sauce. Fried parsley was the traditional garnish for fried fish, either whole, like smelts or whiting, or cut in strips, like goujons of Dover sole. It was also served with fish cakes and egg croquettes. Whole sprigs of parsley were dropped into very hot oil for a few seconds, and emerged bright emerald green, crisp and fragile as the fried seaweed (actually shredded spring greens) that we eat today in Chinese restaurants.

Typical of the 1930s were the chilled or even semi-frozen sauces that were often served with hot dishes. Since refrigerators were the newest thing in kitchen technology, iced dishes were considered very smart. Ices were made with the most surprising ingredients, ranging from Camembert cheese to horseradish, and a sorbet-like tomato mush was often served with hot fried goujons of sole. This sort of extreme contrast demanded care and precision; the plates had to be cool and the service speedy or a soupy mush was the end result.

Bottled sauces had been manufactured in Britain since the mid-nineteenth century. Firms like Lea & Perrins, Crosse & Blackwell and Burgess had been producing such things as Worcestershire Sauce, Harvey's Sauce, Anchovy Essence and Mushroom Ketchup for almost a hundred years, and they were still as popular as ever. Their appeal was for the typical Englishman who liked to combine a strong sharp taste with the basically bland flavour of English food, and who preferred to add it himself, at table. (Worcestershire Sauce and Anchovy Essence both show a similarity to the ancient Roman sauce garum, which was made with pickled anchovies and asafoetida, and used for adding to dishes.)

Some of these sauces can still be bought today – Worcestershire Sauce is still in demand for making bloody Marys – but their popularity has been usurped by the tomato- and pepper-based sauces like tomato ketchup and Tabasco. In my own kitchen, I find that soy sauce, Maggi Liquid Seasoning and Tabasco have replaced the heavier sauces mentioned above, that I remember so well from my childhood. I never ate them myself, of course, for they are anathema to children, but my father was fond of them. In the great country houses bottled sauces were never seen, for the cook preferred to make her own.

Sweet sauces for puddings were also important at this time, when hot steamed and baked puddings were popular. For these really need a complementary sauce to realize their full potential. The most usual was the excellent boiled custard, sometimes called sauce à la vanille. (Bird's Custard Powder had been around since 1846, but I found no mention of it in any of the cookery books of the inter-war period. It may be that it was only the convenience foods of recent development, like American breakfast cereals and tinned petits pois, that caught the fancy of the upper and middle classes. Certainly in working-class homes Bird's Custard was much in use, and was served with tinned fruit, or in trifle.) True custard makes the perfect accompaniment for English fruit puddings; cream was sometimes served as well, or incorporated into the custard. Hot jam sauces were popular with steamed and baked puddings. These were simply made, either with one jam or two, heated and sieved and sometimes spiked with a dash of spirits. Golden syrup was already in existence; this made an easy sauce for hot sponge puddings: just warmed through and sharpened with a squeeze of lemon juice.

A contrast in temperature was definitely the dernier cri among fashionable hostesses. In the sweet course, the contrast was reversed, with a hot sauce accompanying an ice cream. One of the most popular came from the USA: a hot butterscotch sauce which set to a hard shell when poured over a vanilla ice.

Good as they are, English sauces are rather primitive, and help to explain the term 'nursery food' used in this context. In the field of sauces our cuisine seems simplistic, especially when compared with the French. In this realm at least, we find ourselves closer to the Americans, whose cranberry sauce with roast turkey we were soon to adopt, and whose hot sauce for ice cream had already caught on.

## SAVOURY SAUCES AND GARNISHES

## *Apple Sauce with Sage*

This is an unusually good apple sauce for serving with roast pork, duck or goose.

1 medium onion, quite finely chopped
15g butter
2 teaspoons chopped sage
450g cooking apples, peeled, cored and thickly sliced
½ teaspoon sugar

Cook the chopped onion slowly in the butter until it has softened, without allowing it to brown much: about 10 minutes, covered. Then add the chopped sage and cook all together for another couple of minutes, uncovered, then set aside. Put the sliced apples in a heavy pan with just enough water to cover the bottom. Add the sugar and bring slowly to the boil. Simmer gently, uncovered, until the apples are soft, then push them through a medium food mill into a clean pan. Reheat gently, adding the sage and onion mixture. Once it is hot, remove from the heat and stand, covered, for 10–15 minutes, or until ready to serve, with roast pork, duck or goose. Serves 6. Best served warm. **Mrs Arthur James**

# Aspic Jelly

By the end of the 30s, compromises were being made in the kitchen. With fewer assistants, if any, cooks could not afford to spend hours making aspic in the traditional way, as was customary before the First World War. This was how our cook in London made her simplified version.

1 medium onion, chopped
1 medium carrot, chopped
1 tablespoon gelatine
sea salt and black pepper
570ml chicken, veal, beef or fish stock
1 egg white, lightly beaten
1 egg shell, crushed

Put in a saucepan 1 chopped onion, 1 chopped carrot, 1 tablespoon of powdered gelatine, salt and pepper. Add 570ml of stock and bring slowly to the boil, stirring all the time. Strain. When the gelatine has dissolved, drop in the white of one egg and crushed egg shell. Whisk over the flame until it boils, then put on one side and leave to settle. Strain through muslin. **Winnie, our cook**

# Celery Sauce

This is a useful sauce for serving with game birds of all sorts. Roast pheasant in particular benefits from a sauce to counteract its potential dryness.

8 stalks of celery
1 small onion, finely chopped
1 bay leaf
450ml light stock, game or chicken
30g butter
1 tablespoon flour

salt and freshly ground pepper
4 tablespoons chopped parsley

Cut the celery in small pieces and put in a saucepan with the finely chopped onion, bay leaf, and stock. Simmer over a low heat until the celery is cooked, about 20 minutes. Remove the bay leaf and put the celery and stock into a blender or food processor. Purée for about 20 seconds, then rub through a sieve. Make a roux with the butter and flour and gradually add the celery purée to make a sauce. Season well and add freshly chopped parsley. Good with all game. Serves 4–6. **Jane Longman, in** *Vogue*

## Bread Sauce

This was the traditional accompaniment to roast chicken, grouse and pheasant. It is one of those English foods which can be the best or the worst thing in the world, depending on how it is made. It is vital to flavour the milk with care, and to get the right consistency: not too smooth, or too lumpy.

340ml milk
½ medium onion
2 cloves
½ bay leaf
sea salt and black pepper
a pinch of mace or nutmeg
about 6 tablespoons soft white breadcrumbs, made from 1-day-old
    bread, crusts removed
15g butter
2 tablespoons cream (optional)

Put the milk in a small pan with the onion stuck with the cloves, bay leaf, salt, pepper, and mace, or nutmeg. Bring slowly to the boil, then turn off the heat, cover the pan, and stand for 20–30 minutes. Strain and reheat. As it approaches boiling point, shake in the crumbs gradually, stirring all the time, and stop as soon as it approaches the right consistency, remembering that it will thicken slightly on cooling. Simmer for 3 minutes, stirring often, adding more salt and pepper if required. Just before serving, stir in the butter, and a drop of cream if you have it. Serve with roast chicken, turkey, pheasant and grouse. Serves 4–5. This should be made soon before serving if possible; otherwise, keep warm over hot water. **AB**

## Cumberland Sauce

This is an old English sauce, especially useful at Christmas time, for serving with cold turkey, ham, game pâtés and terrines. It was often made with port, which I rarely buy, so I use a dash of brandy. It may be thickened – slightly – with arrowroot, if desired.

1 orange
1 lemon
340g redcurrant jelly
2 teaspoons arrowroot (optional)
2 tablespoons brandy

Pare the rind of the orange and lemon thinly, then cut in julienne strips. Blanch in boiling water for 5 minutes, then refresh under the cold tap. Squeeze the juice of the orange and lemon and add to the jelly in a small pan. Heat gently, stirring, until the jelly has melted, then push through a sieve or small food mill and return to the clean pan. Reheat slowly until it reaches boiling point. If using arrowroot, slake it in 2 tablespoons of cold water, beating to a smooth paste with the back of a spoon, then stir into the simmering sauce and remove from the heat. Stir until smooth, then add the blanched rind. Later, when it has cooled slightly, add the brandy. Pour into a jam jar; once it has cooled, seal tightly and leave for 1 week before eating. Serves 6–8. **Adapted from *A Book of Scents and Dishes*, by Dorothy Allhusen**

## Cherry Salad

Dorothy Allhusen, the author of *A Book of Scents and Dishes*, recommends serving this unusual side dish with a cold fillet of beef, but I find it is even better with the cold roast loin of pork on page 81.

225g red cherries
1 tablespoon brandy
1 tablespoon light olive oil, or sunflower oil
1 teaspoon tarragon vinegar
salt and pepper
1 teaspoon chopped parsley

A delicious salad to eat with cold fillet of beef is made as follows: Stone 225g of fresh red cherries, put them in a basin and pour over 1 tablespoonful of brandy, 1 tablespoonful of oil, 1 teaspoonful of tarragon vinegar; add salt and pepper to taste and 1 teaspoonful of chopped parsley. Serve very cold. [*Serves 3–4; easily made in double quantities. Also good with cold duck.*] *A Book of Scents and Dishes*, **by Dorothy Allhusen**

## Harvy-Scarvy

This is a good, simple relish to eat with cold meat. It comes from Norfolk, by way of American writer M. F. K. Fisher, who quotes it in one of her books. She recommends serving it with a cold, grilled pork chop; I find it excellent with the cold roast loin of pork on page 81.

4 tablespoons red or white wine vinegar
4 tablespoons olive oil
120g finely chopped celery
120g finely chopped apples, cored but not peeled
120g finely chopped onions
salt and freshly ground pepper to taste

Add vinegar and oil to celery, apples, and onion, and stir well. Chill for 1 or 2 hours, and stir again just before serving. Good with any cold meats, but preferably pork chops. [*Serves 6.*] ***With Bold Knife and Fork*, by M. F. K. Fisher**

# Devil Sauce

A popular way of using up left-over game (or chicken) was to reheat it in a devil sauce. Usually made with undiluted whipped cream, this was too rich for my taste, but this recipe, which I have adapted from three contemporary ones, uses a mixture of milk and cream.

30g butter
1½ tablespoons flour
½ teaspoon English mustard (powder)
½ teaspoon curry powder (optional)
275ml milk, heated
150ml double cream, heated
½ teaspoon sea salt
a pinch of cayenne
1½ tablespoons Worcestershire sauce
½ tablespoon mushroom ketchup
a dash of Tabasco

Melt the butter, stir in the flour, mustard and curry powder, if used, and cook for 1 minute, stirring. Then add the milk and cream which you have heated together, and stir constantly until the sauce starts to bubble. Simmer gently for about 8 minutes, until slightly reduced, adding the other flavourings as it cooks. This is a basic devil sauce, for serving with grilled or fried chicken, egg or chicken croquettes, or hard-boiled eggs. Serves 4.

To devil game (or chicken), cut the cooked bird in neat joints and spread them all over with a layer of Dijon mustard. Lay them in a shallow dish and pour over 3–4 tablespoons of game (or chicken) stock. Cover with foil or a lid, and reheat in the oven for 15 minutes at 170°C/gas 3. Then drain off the stock and turn up the oven to 200°C/gas 6. Pour the hot devil sauce over the joints and put back in the oven, uncovered, for 10 minutes, or until it has browned nicely. (Alternatively, it may be browned under the grill for 4–5 minutes.) Serve with boiled rice and a green salad, as a main course. **AB**

## Piquant Sauce

Rather like a gazpacho, this excellent cold sauce is quickly made and very adaptable. I serve it over warm hard-boiled eggs, warm asparagus, or artichoke bottoms, either as a first course, or as part of a summer buffet.

275ml fresh tomato pulp (approx. 340g tomatoes)
1 tablespoon finely chopped green pepper
1 tablespoon finely chopped peeled cucumber
1 tablespoon finely chopped celery
1 tablespoon wine vinegar
a pinch of sugar
sea salt and black pepper to taste
a pinch each of paprika, ground allspice and nutmeg

Peel ripe tomatoes and cut in pieces. Put them in a food processor and purée. Add the chopped vegetables, vinegar and seasonings, then purée again. Serve at room temperature, or chilled, over poached fish, vegetables, or hard-boiled eggs. Serves 4. **Gladys Stewart-Richardson**


## Sauce Dugléré

This is a delicious sauce, quite thin, made with fish stock, white wine and cream, with crushed tomatoes and herbs added. It is excellent served with poached fish. (See also sole Dugléré on page 30.)

1 shallot, finely chopped
30g butter
2 tomatoes, skinned, seeded and finely chopped
1 level tablespoon flour
150ml dry white wine
150ml fish stock
salt and black pepper
150ml double cream
½ tablespoon each finely chopped chervil, chives and parsley

Cook the chopped shallot in the butter for 3–4 minutes, then add the chopped tomatoes and cook for a further 2 minutes. Then add the flour, cook 1 minute, stirring, then add the white wine and fish stock which have been heated together. Bring to the boil and simmer for 4 minutes, stirring now and then, adding salt and pepper to taste. Finally, add the cream and cook for another 1–2 minutes, then remove from the heat, stir in the chopped herbs, and pour into a sauceboat. Serve with a large piece of poached white fish, preferably turbot or halibut, or the filets de sole pochés on page 29. Serves 6. **Adapted from *The Complete Hostess*, by Quaglino**

## Egg and/or Parsley Sauce

I like to combine these two traditional English sauces, both of which go so well with boiled fish, gammon, fish cakes, etc., but either can be made separately if preferred.

30g butter
1½ tablespoons flour
275ml chicken, fish or ham stock, or 450ml milk
5 tablespoons single cream (if using stock)
sea salt and black pepper
ground mace, or nutmeg
4 tablespoons chopped parsley
2 hard-boiled eggs, roughly chopped

Melt the butter, add the flour, and cook for 1 minute, stirring. Then add the hot stock, or milk, gradually, stirring till blended, and simmer gently for 3 minutes. Add the cream, salt and black pepper (unless using ham stock, in which case omit the salt), and a little mace, or nutmeg. If using milk instead of stock, omit the cream. Stir in the chopped parsley and/or hard-boiled eggs, and tip into a sauceboat to serve. This is good with boiled cod, boiled ham, gammon steaks, fish cakes and egg cutlets (in this case use parsley alone). Serves 4–5. **AB**

## Sauce Soubise

A creamy onion sauce lightly flavoured with nutmeg was often served with roast lamb, or a boiled leg of mutton. It is also delicious served over hard-boiled eggs, as a light supper dish.

3 large onions
salt
275ml milk
45g butter
2 tablespoons flour
70ml cream
nutmeg

Peel the onions and cut them into small pieces. Put them in a saucepan, cover them with hot water and a little salt, and boil them till tender [*about 15 minutes*]. Heat the milk. Melt the butter in another saucepan, stir in the flour, then stir in the hot milk gradually. Add the onions and stir till the sauce boils. Place the sieve over a basin and rub the sauce through it with the back of a wooden spoon [*or blend in a food processor*]. Put it back in a clean saucepan, add the cream and a few grains of grated nutmeg. Heat well, but do not let it boil again. [*Serves 4–5, or 2 with hard-boiled eggs.*] **When the Cook Is Away, by Catherine Ives**

## Hollandaise Sauce

This exquisite sauce was much in use, largely as a hot alternative to mayonnaise. It accompanied poached fish, especially salmon and salmon trout, also artichokes and asparagus, and was part of the popular American dish, eggs Benedict (see page 35). In pre-war days it demanded skill in the making, but today it can be made with ease in a food processor.

4 egg yolks
a pinch of sea salt
180g unsalted butter
1½ tablespoons lemon juice

First warm the container of the food processor by filling it with very hot water. Stand for 4–5 minutes, then drain and dry well. Put the egg yolks with the salt into the processor and cover with the lid, leaving the funnel open. Heat the butter in a small pan until it is almost boiling, then process the egg yolks for 30 seconds, and start adding the hot butter through the lid, while continuing to process. Once all the butter has been added, stop the machine. The sauce should have thickened slightly; if not, pour it into a small bowl sitting over a saucepan of simmering water and stir until this has happened. Add the lemon juice. Serve as soon as possible, in a warm bowl. It does not need to be hot, just warm. Serves 3–4.

Sauce Mousseline: shortly before serving, fold 4 tablespoons of lightly whipped cream into the hollandaise sauce. Serves 4. This luxurious sauce is particularly delicious with asparagus. **AB**

## Fried Parsley

> This is my favourite garnish for goujons of fried fish, egg croquettes, and other fried dishes. Alas, it now seems to have been forgotten.

Take your little sprigs of parsley, picked off the main stem, wash them, if it is really necessary, dry them well, and keep them covered with a cloth until you are ready for them; at any rate, do not let them wilt. Have ready your deep-frying oil on the fire and, when the blue smoke begins to rise, which shows that it is very hot [*about 180°C*], plunge your parsley in. It is ready almost immediately; it is a matter of seconds. I find it best to use a frying basket. It should come out crisp, bright green and neither greasy, limp, nor brown. If you fry it too long, it is apt to break to pieces. [*Use as a garnish for any crisp fried food, especially fish*.] **Come Into the Garden, Cook**, by Constance Spry

## Mayonnaise

> This was very much used between the wars, both in its own right – as an accompaniment to cold salmon, lobster,

asparagus, artichokes and hard-boiled eggs – and as an ingredient in other dishes: cold sauces, sandwiches, savoury ices, etc.

2 egg yolks
a pinch of sea salt
¼ teaspoon Dijon mustard
275ml olive oil
3 teaspoons white wine vinegar
3 teaspoons lemon juice

Have all the ingredients at the same temperature, i.e. take the eggs out of the refrigerator 1 hour in advance. The eggs should be very fresh. Drop the yolks into a large bowl standing on a damp cloth so that it cannot slip around. With an electric hand-beater, or a wire whisk, beat the egg yolks for a minute or two, adding the salt and mustard. Have the olive oil in a jug and hold it in the left hand while you beat with the right. Start adding the oil literally drop by drop, beating constantly. After a short while you can add it a little more quickly, but only a few drops at a time. When about half the oil has been added, you can start to add it in a thin trickle, then a stream, beating all the time without stopping. When all the oil is finished, beat in the vinegar and lemon juice. Taste and adjust the seasoning as you prefer. Turn into a clean bowl, cover with cling film, and store in the refrigerator until needed. Take out well in advance of serving, as it should be eaten at room temperature. Makes 275ml; serves 6 as a sauce.

Variation: A proportion of lightly whipped cream may be folded into the mayonnaise before serving: roughly half as much cream as mayonnaise. **AB**

## Mint Sauce

This was the traditional accompaniment to hot roast lamb; redcurrant jelly could be provided as well, or as an alternative. With cold lamb a mint jelly was sometimes served. The best variety of mint to use is the old-fashioned English spearmint, *Mentha spicata*.

4 tablespoons chopped mint
1 tablespoon caster sugar
4 tablespoons lemon juice

Put the chopped mint in a bowl with the sugar and lemon. Add 175ml of boiling water, stirring. Stand for 1 hour before serving, at room temperature. Serves 6. **AB**


## Sauce Tartare

This excellent sauce was often served with fried Dover sole, or with fried whitebait – indeed almost any fried fish. It also figures in the shooting sandwiches made with cold roast beef or game, on page 177.

275ml mayonnaise (see page 155)
2 tablespoons chopped parsley
2 tablespoons chopped gherkins
2 tablespoons chopped capers

Add chopped parsley, chopped gherkins and chopped capers – about 2 tablespoons of each – to 275ml of mayonnaise. [*Serves* 6.] ***Wheeler's Fish Cookery Book*, by Macdonald Hastings and Carole Walsh**


## Iced Tomato Sauce

This is an ideal sauce for light summer dishes, simple and quick to make, and very adaptable. It is best served semi-frozen, frozen thick but not yet solid. It goes well with hot fried goujons of Dover sole, or egg croquettes, or fish cakes, as well as cold dishes.

150ml mayonnaise (see page 155)
150ml double cream, lightly whipped
180g tomatoes, weighed after skinning and de-seeding, pulped
1½ teaspoons onion juice, made in a garlic press
salt and pepper

Mix together equal parts of mayonnaise, [*lightly whipped*] cream and tomato pulp. Add onion juice, salt and pepper. Freeze and serve with cold fish or with cucumber salad. [*Serves 4.*] **Come Into the Garden, Cook, by Constance Spry**

## Horseradish Sauce with Apple

> This unusual combination of grated apple with horseradish makes a most delicious sauce for serving with cold roast beef or duck. It is based on a recipe in Alice B. Toklas' last book, but it also turns up in a few English cookbooks of the period. The best horseradish to use, failing the fresh root, comes from Germany in small jars, called Kochs or Scandia.

1 Granny Smith, or other tart green apple, peeled and grated
1½ tablespoons grated horseradish, or ½ a jar
3 tablespoons sour cream
¼ tablespoon sea salt
¼ teaspoon lemon juice
a pinch of cayenne
½ teaspoon brandy

Mix grated apples with grated horseradish. Add [*sour cream*], salt, lemon juice, a pinch of cayenne, and brandy. [*Serves 4.*] **Aromas and Flavors, by Alice B. Toklas**

## Scraped Horseradish

> Rarely seen nowadays, this is the best possible way of eating horseradish, almost Japanese in its simplicity. Good for people who grow their own, since fresh horseradish is not often seen in shops.

Get a nice large single root of horseradish, peel it, and with a sharp knife scrape it so that each shaving is a long thin sliver. This is placed all down the centre of the roast beef and the carver puts a small portion on each plate with a slice of beef. It should be scraped only a few minutes before it is required, otherwise it will lose its flavour and become dry. Scraped horseradish is only eaten with roast beef, and is a most delicious adjunct. *Kitchenette Cookery*, by G. F. Scotson-Clark

## Yorkshire Pudding

> In the country houses, bastions of tradition, roast beef was always served with Yorkshire pudding, roast potatoes, gravy, horseradish sauce and a green vegetable. The pudding is best made after the beef has finished cooking, since it demands a very hot oven.

140g white bread flour
½ teaspoon salt
1 large egg, lightly beaten
250ml milk
1–2 tablespoons beef dripping, from the joint

Sift the flour into a food processor with the salt. Add the lightly beaten egg and process, then pour the milk slowly through the lid, while continuing to process. Rest for 30–60 minutes before baking, if possible.

Five minutes before the joint is ready, extract 1–2 tablespoons of dripping from the roasting tin and spread it round a shallow baking dish. Heat this in the oven for 5 minutes, then remove the beef to rest in a warm place and turn the oven up to 220°C/gas 7. Process the batter once more, then pour into the dish and bake for 35 minutes, until well risen and golden brown. Cut in sections to serve, with the beef. Serves 6. **AB**

## Bread Stuffing

> Before the war, a roast bird was almost invariably stuffed. Nowadays, with the emphasis on low-fat food, stuffings are rarely seen except at Christmas time. This is my favourite stuffing, excellent with chicken, turkey, duck or goose.

180g shallots, peeled and chopped
55g butter
180g soft white breadcrumbs
20g chopped parsley
sea salt and black pepper

Cook the chopped shallots gently in the butter until light golden, then add the crumbs and mix well. Remove from the heat, stir in the chopped parsley, and add plenty of sea salt and black pepper. Allow to cool before using. This makes enough to stuff a large chicken or capon; double the quantities for a 6kg turkey. **AB**

## Browned Breadcrumbs

This was the classic accompaniment to roast game, together with bread sauce and (home-made) game chips. The bread sauce was served in a sauceboat, and the browned bread-crumbs in another sauceboat, or bowl.

30g butter
6 tablespoons fairly coarse dry (white) breadcrumbs

In a thick frying pan, preferably non-stick, heat the butter until very hot. Just before it turns colour add the breadcrumbs and cook for about 2½ minutes, turning constantly, until they have browned evenly to a golden mid-brown. Remove from the heat, tip into a bowl or sauceboat, and keep warm until ready to serve. Serves 4. **AB**

SWEET SAUCES

## Apricot Jam Sauce

This hot jam sauce is excellent served with plain sponge puddings.

225g apricot jam
3 tablespoons kirsch
4 tablespoons water

Heat together to boiling point, in a small enamel pan, ½ cup of apricot jam, 3 tablespoons of kirsch, and ¼ cup of water. Pour into serving bowl and serve at once. [*Serves 4.*] **June Platt's Plain and Fancy Cookbook**

## Brandy Butter

This used to be called senior wrangler sauce, or hard sauce – it is still called hard sauce in the USA. It is the traditional accompaniment to Christmas pudding.

120g unsalted butter
120g caster sugar
3–4 tablespoons brandy

Cream the butter until pale and smooth. (Or blend in the food processor.) Add the sugar gradually, beating (or processing) continuously. When amalgamated, start to add the brandy very slowly, beating (or processing) all the time. Taste after adding the third tablespoon, then add the rest – if needed – very slowly indeed, for it can separate easily at this stage. Once done, pile into a small jar and store in the refrigerator until needed. It can be made several days in advance, as it keeps very well indeed. Serve very cold, with the Christmas pudding. Makes 225g. **AB**

## Creamy Custard Sauce

A jug of cream was often served at the same time as a custard sauce, with hot puddings made with fruit, bread, suet or sponge. I have chosen to combine the two in a delicious creamy custard sauce. To make a simple custard, omit the cream and increase the milk to 450ml.

½ vanilla pod
275ml milk

3 large egg yolks
2½ tablespoons vanilla sugar, or caster sugar
150ml double cream

Put the vanilla pod in a small pan with the milk. Bring slowly to the boil, then remove from the heat, cover the pan, and stand for 20 minutes. When the time is up, reheat the milk gently and remove the vanilla pod. (Rinse, dry and store in a jar of caster sugar.) Start beating the egg yolks with the sugar. When the milk is just about to boil, pour it on to the egg yolks, still beating. Then stand the bowl over a pan of simmering water and stir constantly until it has slightly thickened. This may take 7 or 8 minutes.

Once it has thickened enough to coat the back of a wooden spoon, remove the bowl from the heat and stand it in a sink half full of cold water to cool quickly. Stir now and then while it cools to prevent a skin forming. While it cools, whip the cream until just thickened, stopping before it becomes solid or it will be hard to blend with the custard. When the custard is warm, fold in the whipped cream.

If possible, serve while still warm, or at room temperature; do not chill. Excellent with hot or cold puddings of all sorts, or with compotes of fruit. Serves 4–6. **AB**

## Lemon and Vanilla Sauce

This is an unusual sauce for serving hot with steamed or baked puddings. It goes well with the seven-cup pudding on page 119. I like to serve a jug of thick cream at the same time.

55g vanilla sugar
1 tablespoon cornflour
275ml boiling water
55g unsalted butter, cut in bits
juice and grated rind of 1 lemon

Mix together sugar with cornflour. Add boiling water gradually, stirring constantly. Cook five minutes. Remove from fire. Add butter [*cut in small* bits]. Stir until melted. Add the juice and grated rind of 1 lemon. Serve hot [*with a baked or steamed pudding, or plum pudding. Makes 450ml; serves 4–6*]. **June Platt, in** *Vogue*

## Mixed Jam Sauce

Jam sauces were often served with sponge or suet puddings, with pancakes or even ice cream.

4 tablespoons raspberry jam
4 tablespoons redcurrant jelly
1 tablespoon orange juice
1 tablespoon lemon juice
½ tablespoon brandy

Warm the jam and jelly together over a low heat, until the jelly has melted. Then push through a small food mill into a clean pan. Heat again, adding fruit juices and brandy, but remove from the heat well before it reaches boiling point. Serve warm; enough for 4. **Adapted from** *More Lovely Food*, **by Ruth Lowinsky**

# PICNICS AND SHOOTING LUNCHES

# PICNICS AND SHOOTING LUNCHES

Picnics had been popular in Britain since Victorian times, and even earlier; they varied widely to suit the occasion. Perhaps the favourite sort, and one that is still much loved today, was the seaside picnic, with as wide a mixture of ages as possible. Many prosperous families sent their children to the sea for a summer holiday, even if they lived in the country all year round. Some lucky ones lived close to the sea, in which case they were inundated with summer visitors, cousins and friends, for a period of weeks throughout July and August. Other families took houses at resorts like Seaview, Cromer or Littlehampton; sometimes a family would take over a small hotel for a few weeks each summer. In some cases, like our own, the children were sent to stay in lodgings at a resort like Bognor, accompanied by nanny or governess, while their parents stayed at home, or did something more amusing.

Seaside picnics were simple affairs, not unlike those of today. The food might consist of hard-boiled eggs, bread and butter, or simple sandwiches – my favourite were jam sandwiches made with thin white bread – followed by a cake, with milk or tea to drink. At Mothecombe, the little bay where the Mildmays swam, a few miles from Flete, Helen Mildmay's grandfather had built a small stone tea-house on the edge of the beach. This had a fireplace, so that they could picnic from April onwards. (It also provided a cosy spot for the children to dress after bathing.) The Mildmay picnics sound delicious: small pasties (to rhyme with nasty), little profiteroles filled with chicken, lettuce and mayonnaise, with meringues and cake to follow, and cider or ginger beer to drink.

In Scotland, our favourite picnics were by the river, or on the moors. Our grandfather had built a small wooden fishing hut on the banks of the River Findhorn, with a fireplace, where we could shelter from bad weather. When it was fine, we would sit on the steep banks watching the river tear through narrow gorges far below, dark peaty brown and foaming like Guinness. Here my father would join us for lunch after fishing for salmon in one of the pools. We would eat little hot pies of mutton or lamb, brown bread and butter, raw tomatoes and lettuce leaves, with a piece of cheese, or cake, to follow.

Like most children's lives, ours seemed very uneventful. The highlight of the year as far as I was concerned, better by far than Christmas or birthdays, was the week we spent en famille, camping out in a small shooting lodge on the moors. This was the only time in the whole year when we were alone with our parents for any length of time, without nanny or governess, or even a cook. My mother and sisters struggled with the meals, which were erratic, despite the hampers of pre-cooked food sent up from the big house. I remember my mother trying to clean a grouse with a silver teaspoon, and my father's face of dismay on being told dinner was ready at six thirty, just as he was about to set off for a quiet evening's walk. Our bicycles were sent up on a lorry, so we could cycle to a nearby farm each morning to get milk. One of my sisters kept bees, and her beehives came up with the bicycles. The bees were left up on the moors for some weeks, so that they could make heather honey.

Our shooting lunches were much like picnics on the river: fairly simple stuff. There might be cold game, or game pie, roast beef sandwiches or cold ham in aspic, and salad. To follow, we often had jam puffs. Grand shooting lunches were a different affair altogether, especially in the great English houses. At the Duke of Westminster's shoot, a lunch was laid on for thirty guests in a small Elizabethan house in a river valley in north Wales, an hour and a quarter's drive from Eaton Hall. Here two cooks would labour in the kitchen, finishing off dishes that had been brought up from the main house at dawn. A superlative lunch would follow, served by footmen, with hot mulled claret to drink.

This degree of grandeur was unusual; each house varied in its style, but most liked to keep the food very simple, in order not to distract from the shooting. At Bolton Abbey, the Duke of Devonshire's shoot in Yorkshire, a donkey loaded with two panniers was used to carry the food up on to the moors. Mrs Shimwell, who succeeded her mother as cook to the Devonshires in the 1930s, tells me that there was always a hot soup and one other hot dish, usually a stew, packed in hayboxes. At Flete, there were always two hot courses: a stew with hot baked potatoes and another vegetable, and a hot luncheon pudding, usually steamed, or rice. Towards the end of the 30s the lunches at Flete grew simpler, and the hot pudding was replaced by a sticky ginger cake, served with a hard English cheese like Cheddar. The Mildmays drank beer or cider, with sloe gin afterwards.

Each house had its customary locale for the shooting lunch, which never varied from year to year. It might be a barn, or cottage, pavilion, folly, or small hut equipped for the purpose. They rarely returned to the big house for lunch, even when it was within reach, as it made the meal too lengthy; by the time the ladies had gone upstairs to tidy themselves, and everyone had trooped into the dining-room, half the afternoon would have been wasted.

Some houses made a habit of packing individual shooting lunches; this worked well for less grand shoots, where the lunch was more in the nature of a picnic. Ruth Lowinsky describes these in *Lovely Food*; they sound like a more elaborate version of the packed lunches we used to take out hunting, in a jointed silver case hanging from the saddle.

'Shooting lunches are best packed separately for each person, with his name written on the outside. A small aluminium box, preferably jointed at sides, back and lid, is lined with greaseproof paper. Then half a grouse is put in, some thinly cut bread and butter, a couple of savoury sandwiches, a jam puff, cheese, biscuits, and an apple, salt and pepper, each item wrapped separately in greaseproof paper.'

Elaborate shooting lunches were still going on in the 1930s, in a very few houses. At Lambton Park, in Durham, Lady Lambton was famous for the originality and perfection of her shooting lunches, which took place every weekend from the end of October to the beginning of February, and which she organized down to the smallest detail. They were held under a tarpaulin in a walled garden about a mile from the house. A rectangular table to seat eighteen was built over a charcoal brazier. The centre of the table was made of stainless steel, and was hot enough to cook on; the surround was made of earthenware tiles. Dishes were prepared in the kitchens of the big house and brought down to be finished off, or cooked from scratch, in the centre of the table. The food varied constantly; there were usually seven or eight different things, all hot.

Sardines were grilled on wire racks; kidneys, steaks, lamb cutlets and patties of corned beef hash likewise. Marrow bones were kept hot, as was saddle of lamb. Individual cauliflower cheeses were made in small bread tins; a pot of fondue bubbled away on the side. By each place was a tiny frying pan, for making blinis perhaps, should anyone produce some caviare, or just for frying eggs. Purées of root vegetables, or succotash, were served inside a giant pumpkin; roast parsnips were also popular. Tomatoes and mushrooms were filled with duxelles or herb stuffing, then cooked directly on the table. In a cool hut nearby the cold dishes were laid out: a huge ham, a tongue, Stilton, celery and puddings. Bullshots or bloody Marys were served before lunch, while the butler served mulled claret during the lunch, assisted by two footmen.

This was not all that was laid on to encourage the guns, for at some point during the morning they were joined by the ladies bringing with them hot soup in thermos flasks, and sandwiches, or hot sausages, for a mid-morning snack.

The catering arrangements at the Lambton shoots were hardly typical, being a product of Lady Lambton's fertile imagination. On a less exalted plane, the food at shooting lunches was supposed to be very simple fare, and any deviation was viewed askance. The same attitude exists today. I went to a shooting party recently where the hostess had provided a cassoulet. Perfect food, I should have thought, for a cold day, but it did not meet with approval from the other guests, being considered too exotic.

## Potage à l'Ecossaise

A sophisticated version of Scotch broth, this is recommended by Lady Jekyll for a hot picnic lunch, to take on a 'motor excursion' in a haybox. It is equally good eaten at home, in the comfort of one's own kitchen. Quite substantial, it is really more of a stew than a soup.

1.25 litres stock: beef, chicken or lamb
2 tablespoons pearl barley, washed
1 carrot, thickly sliced
1 small turnip, quartered and sliced
1 leek, thickly sliced
1 onion, quartered and thickly sliced
1 stalk of celery, thickly sliced
¼ heart of a small green cabbage, sliced, or 3 or 4 Brussels sprouts

680–900g best end of neck of lamb, divided into cutlets and trimmed, excess fat removed
2 tablespoons chopped parsley
2 tablespoons double cream
salt and black pepper
120g shelled peas, fresh or frozen, cooked
340g small new potatoes, skinned and cooked

Put into rather more than 1.2 litres of good light stock some 2 tablespoon-fuls of pearl barley [*previously washed in cold water*], a carrot, turnip, leek, onion, celery, a little cabbage or 3 or 4 Brussels sprouts, and let them cook gently together with the required number of nice cutlets from a well-selected and trimmed neck of mutton or lamb. Season [*after cooking gently, on top of the stove, for 2 hours*] with a little chopped parsley, cream, salt and pepper to taste, some green peas [*cooked separately*], and some tiny new [*cooked*] potatoes. [*Serves 4–5.*] **Kitchen Essays, by Lady Jekyll**

## Irish Stew

A simple dish of this sort was popular for shooting lunches, or for Saturday lunch in the country. This old-fashioned method of dividing the potatoes in two parts works well.

1.15kg middle end of neck of lamb
salt and black pepper
900g potatoes
450g onions

Cut and trim the meat into cutlets, put in the pot, cover with hot water, add the salt, boil up and skim. Peel the potatoes, cut about one third of them in slices, and add to the pot. Peel and slice the onions. Add these with the pepper and stir up. Then lay the rest of the [*whole*] potatoes on top and stew 2 or 3 hours, stirring occasionally. The sliced potatoes should thicken the liquid and prevent the stew being watery. [*Serves 4.*] **Irish Cookery Recipes, by Florence Irwin**

# Lancashire Hotpot

This sort of traditional dish was often served in country houses, either for a shooting lunch or for a simple family meal.

900g middle end of neck of lamb, divided into cutlets
680g potatoes, peeled and sliced
340g onions, sliced
salt and black pepper
150ml light stock
15g butter, melted
chopped parsley

Trim the meat, removing all excess fat. Butter a fireproof casserole – it does not need to have a lid – and make a layer of sliced potatoes in the bottom. Scatter some of the sliced onion over them, and sprinkle with salt and black pepper. Lay the meat on top, in one layer. Then add more salt and pepper, and the remaining onions. Pour the stock over, then cover with the remaining potatoes, the slices neatly overlapping like tiles on a roof. Brush the potatoes with melted butter, cover with the lid, or a piece of foil, and bake for 2 hours at 170°C/gas 3. Then remove the lid (or foil), and continue to cook for another 30 minutes, by which time the potatoes should be nicely browned. I like to serve this with a small bowl of chopped parsley on the table. Serves 4. **AB**

# Small Mutton (or Lamb) Pies

Small mutton pies, served hot, used to be a feature of shooting-party lunches on the moors when I lived in Scotland, as a child. They were small enough to hold in the palm of your hand, and very delicious. Nowadays they may be made with lamb, and are a useful way of using up the remains of a joint.

450g cooked mutton or lamb, chopped
180g mushrooms, chopped
45g butter

150ml meat or chicken stock
1 clove
3 black peppercorns
1 teaspoon flour

SHORT PASTRY
285g flour
140g butter
a pinch of salt
a little iced water
1 egg, beaten

Free the meat from skin and gristle and chop it fairly finely. Cut the mushrooms into small pieces and cook them with 30g butter until they are tender. Heat the stock in a saucepan, add the clove and peppercorns, and simmer gently for a quarter of an hour. Melt the remaining 15g butter, and stir in the flour. Blend well, and then strain the stock into this, stirring all the time, and cook for 5 minutes. Add the mushrooms and the meat. Mix thoroughly, and let the mixture get cold. Make the pastry. Line the patty pans with it. Fill them with the lamb mixture; give them pastry tops decorated with tiny pastry leaves. Brush them over with the beaten egg. Make a hole in the centre of each one and bake in a moderate oven until the pastry is done. [*About 25 minutes at 180°C/gas 4. Makes 12 small pies. These may also be made with uncooked lamb, minced or finely chopped, first browned briefly, with a small chopped onion, in 1 tablespoon each of butter and oil.*] **When the Cook Is Away, by Catherine Ives**

## Game Pie

Game pies were a staple winter food in the country houses, equally popular as a standby on the cold sideboard at lunchtime, or as part of a shooting lunch. They were made with a variety of game, either birds alone, or birds and animals mixed, depending on the season. They were always eaten cold.

450g stewing venison, in one piece

450g rabbit, jointed

1 pheasant, or 2 grouse, or 2 partridges (old birds may be
  used)

1 onion, halved

1carrot, halved

1 stalk of celery, halved

1 bay leaf

3 stalks of parsley

sea salt and black pepper

8 black peppercorns

8 juniper berries

15g gelatine

PASTRY

285g flour, sifted

a pinch of salt

85g butter

55g lard

1 egg + 1 yolk

4–5 tablespoons iced water

Make a day or two in advance. Put the stewing venison in a casserole with
the rabbit and the whole bird(s). Add the onion, carrot, celery, bay leaf,
parsley, sea salt and black pepper, and cover with hot water. Bring to the
boil, cover, and simmer gently for 2 hours. Discard the vegetables and
herbs and strain the stock.

   While the meats are cooking, make the pastry. Put the sifted flour and
salt in a food processor, and add the fats cut in pieces, then 1 egg. Process
until blended, then add the iced water gradually through the lid while
continuing to process, stopping when it all gathers into a ball. Turn out
and knead briefly, then wrap in cling film and place in the bottom of the
refrigerator for 2 hours. (If making by hand, sift the flour with the salt
on to a board, make a well in the centre and put in the fats in small pieces,
the egg and the water. Work together with the hands until blended, then
knead well, until smooth.)

When the meat is cooked, lift it out of the pan with a slotted spoon and strain the stock. Cut the venison into small slices about 7.5mm thick, pull the rabbit off the bone and divide into neat fillets, and cut the game off the bone, in neat pieces. Put 1 teaspoon of sea salt into a mortar with the peppercorns and juniper berries and crush them all together roughly.

When the pastry is ready, roll out two-thirds of it to line a greased cake tin with removable bottom, holding about 1.2 litres. The pastry should be about 1cm thick. Lay half the venison in the bottom, sprinkle with the crushed seasonings, then cover with half the rabbit, more seasonings, and half the game birds. Continue making alternate layers, seasoning each one, until all the meat is used up. Moisten with 4 tablespoons of the strained stock and cover with a lid of the remaining pastry. Overlap the edges by about 1cm, damp them to seal firmly, and roll to form a thick edge. Make a decorative device of some sort – rose, leaf, etc. – and stick it in the centre of the pie, then cut round it neatly and lift out. Replace, then brush all over with beaten egg yolk. Bake for 1 hour at 180°C/gas 4.

While it is baking, measure the remaining stock and add gelatine, allowing 15g to each pint. (Dissolve it in a little of the heated stock, then mix it with the rest of the cool stock.) When the pie is cooked, lift out the centrepiece and pour in the cool stock gradually, a little at a time, through a funnel. Allow time for each lot to settle and be absorbed, before adding more. When the dish is full, replace the pastry centrepiece and leave to cool. Keep for at least 24 hours before eating; it can be kept for a week in the refrigerator. This makes a pie weighing about 1.7kg, and will feed 6–8 people. Serve with pickled plums, fruit chutneys, or gherkins, and a mixed salad. **AB**

## Beef Sandwiches

This is my favourite sandwich. In the past, it would have been served at picnic lunches or shooting parties. Nowadays, it makes a perfect supper for eating while watching television.

4 thin slices of white bread, 1 day old
20g butter

2 tablespoons horseradish cream (see page 28)
85g rare roast beef, sliced
sea salt and black pepper
2 medium tomatoes, thinly sliced

Spread some thinly buttered bread with thick horseradish cream, lay a slice of beef on this [*sprinkle with sea salt*], and cover with thinly sliced and seasoned tomato and more bread and butter. [*Remove crusts. Makes 2 rounds: 4 sandwiches.*] **Lady Sysonby's Cook Book**


## Shooting Sandwiches

Another good sandwich for winter picnics or expeditions, or for a simple Sunday night supper. This is an excellent way of making a toasted sandwich that I have not come across before. I like to use a whole-grain mustard, like Grey Poupon Old-Style, which would not have been available in the 1930s.

2 slices of white bread, 1 day old, cut 1.5cm thick
15g butter
2 tablespoons sauce tartare (see page 157)
1 tablespoon whole-grain mustard
85g cold roast meat, or game, sliced

Toast neatly trimmed slices of bread on both sides [*if they are too thick for the toaster they may be done under the grill*], then split and butter half of them with plain or savoury butter, and spread the rest with a stiff tartare sauce, to which you have added some French mustard. Cover the buttered pieces with the slices of meat or game, and press the rest of the toast on this. [*Remove crusts. Makes 2 rounds: 4 sandwiches.*] **Lady Sysonby's Cook Book**


## Norwegian Sandwiches

This is a good example of the quite complex mixtures which were popular as sandwich fillings between the wars.

6 anchovies, boned and filleted
30g unsalted butter
4 medium-thin slices of white bread, 1 day old, toasted
120g thinly sliced smoked salmon
1 small egg, hard-boiled and chopped
1 tablespoon chopped parsley

Pound 6 anchovies to a smooth paste with 30g butter, and spread the pieces of toast with this. Lay thin slices of smoked salmon, sprinkled with chopped hard-boiled egg and the parsley, between them. [*This is also good made with untoasted brown bread, or rye bread. Remove crusts. Makes 2 rounds: 4 sandwiches.*] **The Gentle Art of Cookery, by Mrs C. F. Leyel and Miss Olga Hartley**

## Smoked Haddock Sandwiches

A substantial sandwich, good for a winter picnic, or a snack after the theatre.

30g unsalted butter
3 tablespoons chopped parsley
freshly ground black pepper
4 medium-thin slices of brown bread, 1 day old, or 2 slices of white
    bread, 1.5cm thick, toasted
3–4 tablespoons mayonnaise
120g cooked smoked haddock, flaked free from skin and bone
1 hard-boiled egg, coarsely chopped (optional)

Mash the butter with half the chopped parsley and some freshly ground black pepper; no salt. Spread half the bread with this. If using toast, split the slices after toasting, so that you have 4 thin slices toasted on one side only. Spread half the untoasted sides with parsley butter. Spread the rest of the bread (or toast) generously with mayonnaise and sprinkle with the remaining chopped parsley. Lay the smoked haddock on the mayonnaise, cutting the larger flakes into pieces, and scatter the chopped egg (if used) over it. Cover with the buttered bread (or toast). If making in advance, for a picnic, or late supper, choose bread rather

than toast. Remove crusts. Makes 4 rounds: 12 small sandwiches.
**Adapted from *The Gentle Art of Cookery*, by Mrs C. F. Leyel and
Miss Olga Hartley**

## Jam Puffs

At our home in Scotland, the jam puffs were somewhat
more substantial than this, being made with short pastry
and about 13cm long. They only ever appeared for shooting lunches, as a pudding. This recipe makes lighter, more
delicate puffs, just right for tea or picnic teas. If serving as
a pudding, allow two per person. To make apple turnovers,
simply use a fairly thick apple purée instead of the jam.

450g puff pastry, home-made or bought
4–6 tablespoons raspberry jam (or apple purée)
1 egg, beaten
icing sugar, sifted

Roll out the pastry to about 3mm thick. Using a small patty tin as a guide,
cut it out into circles about 7.5cm wide. Roll each one out again lightly,
just once or twice, until it is about 8.5–10cm across. Put a teaspoonful of
jam (or apple purée) on one half of each, and brush the edges with beaten
egg. Fold over and press the edges together to seal, then brush them all
over with beaten egg. Use a fork to mark the sealed edges with parallel
lines, and prick two or three times in the centre. Lay them on a greased
baking sheet and chill until ready to bake.

Bake them for 15 minutes at 200°C/gas 6, until golden brown, then
take out of the oven and sprinkle very lightly with sifted icing sugar.
Serve warm whenever possible, or at least the same day as made. If to be
eaten as a pudding, serve with cream. Makes 12; serves 6. **AB**

## Lady Moray's Fruit Cake

This was my grandmother's recipe for a spiced fruit cake,
which was served at our home in Scotland for shooting

picnics, or for tea. It may be iced for Christmas. For a richer cake, use brandy – or whisky – instead of orange juice.

180g unsalted butter
180g dark brown sugar
1½ tablespoons treacle, warmed
3 eggs
250g flour, sifted
¾ teaspoon baking powder
1 teaspoon each ground cloves, cinnamon and nutmeg
85g ground almonds
180g each currants and sultanas
4 tablespoons milk
4 tablespoons orange juice

Cream the butter with the sugar. [*Or use a food processor.*] Stir in the treacle and mix well. Break 1 egg at a time into a cup and beat with a fork, then stir into the mixture; then fold in a spoonful of flour. Repeat with the remaining eggs, adding 2 more spoonfuls of flour. Then mix the baking powder and spices into the remaining flour and fold in. [*If using a food processor, transfer to a bowl at this stage and continue mixing by hand.*] Stir in the ground almonds and dried fruit, then the milk and orange juice. Line a greased tin [*I use a loaf tin holding 1.5 litres*] with buttered greaseproof paper. Turn the mixture into the tin and bake for 2½ hours at 170°C/gas 3, loosely covered with a piece of foil. Remove the foil for the last 30–45 minutes to brown. Makes a 1.15kg cake. May be made well in advance; keeps well in an airtight tin. **Lady Moray**

## Ginger Cake

This was a very popular cake, both at the tea table and for the shooting lunch, where it was often served at the same time as an English cheese, the two being eaten together. At teatime, it was usually sliced and spread with butter. This recipe is based on one of Lady Portarlington's, who was renowned for her teas.

225g flour, sifted
½ teaspoon bicarbonate of soda
1 teaspoon ground ginger
a pinch of salt
75ml treacle
75ml golden syrup
120g unsalted butter, cut in bits
120g dark brown sugar
2 eggs, lightly beaten
2 tablespoons milk

Sift the flour into a large bowl with the bicarbonate of soda, ginger and salt. Make a well in the centre. Warm the treacle, golden syrup, butter and sugar until melted; do not let them get hot. Pour into the well and mix with a wooden spoon. Then stir in the lightly beaten eggs and the milk. Mix thoroughly, then tip into a 1.2 litre loaf tin which you have lined with buttered greaseproof paper. Smooth the surface and bake for 1 hour at 170°C/gas 3. Remove from the oven, cool for a little, then tip out of its tin, remove the paper, and leave on a rack to finish cooling. When cold, wrap in a cloth and store in an airtight tin for 1 to 2 days, if possible, before eating. Serve sliced, with unsalted butter, for tea, or a picnic. If at a picnic, add a wedge of English Cheddar for an authentic pre-war touch. **Lady Portarlington**


## Mulled Wine

Hot mulled wine was often served at shooting lunches, or other winter festivities like Guy Fawkes, or carol singing.

the peel of 1 lemon
the peel of 1 orange
6 cloves
1 stick of cinnamon
½ nutmeg
12 lumps of sugar
1½ bottles of red wine
4 tablespoons brandy (optional)

Put the lemon and orange peel, the cloves, cinnamon, nutmeg and sugar in a saucepan with 275ml of water. Bring to the boil and simmer till the sugar has melted. Add the wine and bring back to boiling point. Remove from the heat, add brandy if liked, and strain into a hot jug or bowl. Makes about 1.2 litres. **AB**

## Sloe Gin

Sloes are small bitter fruit, like tiny damsons, found growing wild in the woods in early October. Sloe gin is an excellent drink, very strong since it is made with neat gin. It is now made commercially by one or two firms, but used to be made at home. It was a winter drink, always drunk neat, usually as an aperitif, or as a quick nip to warm you up at a meet, or a point-to-point. It was also sometimes drunk after a sketchy meal, like a shooting lunch or winter picnic.

6 bottles of dry gin
3.6 litres sloes
1.15kg sugar cubes

You really need an immense earthenware crock to make this in; a bread crock does well. Don't do like a friend of mine, who made her sloe gin in a glass container which broke when she was rolling it about on the cellar floor. Prick each sloe once or twice with a darning needle stuck in a cork, or a very fine pointed skewer. Then drop them into the crock which is half full of gin. (You can make it equally well in 2 smaller containers, or in half quantities.) Finally, add the sugar and close the jar tightly. Shake the crock, or roll it over if too heavy to shake, once a week. The sloe gin will be ready in 2½–3 months, just in time for Christmas. It makes an excellent present. Makes 4.5 litres. **AB**

TEA

'The ideal tea table should include some sort of hot buttered toast or scone, one or two sorts of sandwiches, a plate of small light cakes, and our friend the luncheon cake. Add a pot of jam or honey, and a plate of brown or white bread and butter – which I implore my readers not to cut too thin – and every eye will sparkle.' In *Lady Sysonby's Cook Book*, published in 1935, the author described the essence of the English tea: a relaxed, informal meal, lacking in any form of pretension.

Tea and breakfast had much in common, in that they were both informal meals, and very English. While breakfast in the English country house was served continuously from about nine till eleven thirty, with members of the family and guests alike coming down when they chose, tea was also very relaxed, with no obligation to be punctual, or even to put in an appearance. At neither meal were the guests waited on; once the tea had been laid out, the footmen left the room, and the guests waited on each other, or helped themselves. Even when there were fifty people staying, as at Eaton Hall, the hostess was still expected to pour out the tea herself, and the guests would pass it from hand to hand until everyone had been served.

Tea was never served in the dining-room. At Flete, when Helen Mildmay and her father were alone, they had tea in the library. When there was a house party, tea was served in the drawing-room. A folding table was carried in and spread with a white cloth by the footmen, who set it up at one end of the room. Small chairs were brought in, and others already in the room were rearranged around the table. There were two teapots, with a choice of China or Indian tea, a silver kettle over a spirit-lamp, and a silver milk jug. To eat, there were usually scones with butter and Devonshire cream and home-made jam, a sticky ginger cake, an iced cake and little chocolate buns. After a day's shooting, the tea would be more substantial, with croissants baked by Mrs Woodman, who was an expert.

Various houses had their own customs, peculiar to them. In some, tea was served in the nursery, with Nanny presiding; in another, it was served in the billiard room, which was not usually frequented by ladies. Many had special dishes, like chocolate buns, orange jumbles, or ginger hats. The keynote was simplicity, and lack of ostentation, as Constance Spry explains in her classic cookbook: 'It was not considered good taste to have too many small things – one good plum cake, one light cake, perhaps of the sponge variety, or an orange cake, iced, might appear, and a hot dish of crumpets or buttered toast, anchovy toast or hot teacakes. Even on the most elegant of tea tables it was permissible to leave jam in its pot set on a plate unless you possessed a nice, plain glass jar. It was the fancy dish that was considered inelegant.'

While tea was served at five, or even five thirty, in country houses, in London it was earlier, at four thirty. This was a lighter, more elegant meal, served in the sitting-room, from a tray. A plate of cucumber sandwiches and a light sponge cake were all that most people would expect.

In some circles, bridge teas were very fashionable. The ladies would converge, all wearing hats, for an afternoon of cards and gossip combined. At some point in the proceedings the card tables were covered with white cloths, and an elaborate tea appeared. Bridge rolls were invariably served; these were usually filled with finely chopped egg and cress, the cress forming a delicate green fringe around the edges.

Lower down the social scale, tea meant high tea, which was a hybrid meal, not unlike breakfast, but with sweet things added. This was the main evening meal in working-class homes, and was served whenever the husband got home from work, some time between five and six.

The English high tea was a mixture of savoury and sweet foods, with tea to drink. The savoury element depended on the financial state of the household, and might run to sliced ham, sausages, or fish and chips when things were good. Otherwise it depended largely on bread, which could be spread with butter, margarine, jam, meat or fish paste, according to funds. This was followed by pastries, sweet biscuits or cakes. A light supper followed between nine and ten, but this was more in the nature of a snack before going to bed, and usually consisted of bread and cheese, with cocoa to drink.

It was in the country houses that tea reached its zenith. Although only a few were ever served at one time, the variety of dishes was impressive. The sandwiches alone were legion, and quite different in character from those of today. Apart from a very few, like cucumber or tomato, they were made with complex mixtures of different ingredients, all finely chopped and mixed together, similar to the sandwiches we find today in cities like Vienna and Turin. Hard-boiled eggs were never simply sliced, but chopped and mixed with mayonnaise, mango chutney, or watercress. Cream cheese was combined with chopped walnuts, dates, dried apricots or stem ginger, or with honey, or redcurrant jelly. There were many more savoury fillings than sweet, and brown or white bread was used, or a mixture of both, or soft finger rolls. For picnics or shooting lunches, substantial sandwiches were made with meat or fish: smoked salmon with anchovy butter, rare roast beef with horseradish sauce and sliced tomatoes, or cold game with sauce tartare. For the tea table, lighter versions were made on similar lines, using fillets of Dover sole, minced lobster, or potted shrimps. Vegetables were sometimes used in the form of asparagus spears, or a purée of green peas. Fruit, in the shape of sliced dessert apples, made an unusual filling, but the most exotic must be Mrs Leyel's rose petal sandwich.

In winter, a hot covered dish, in china or silver, was often to be seen on the tea table. This might hold any of the toasted breads or teacakes described by Constance Spry, or simple sandwiches of jam or marmalade that had been toasted, or even fried.

While a fairly substantial fruit cake, sometimes called a luncheon cake, was often made for picnics, those destined for the tea table were usually lighter. Plain cakes were very popular, and existed in many forms. Most were made on the pound cake principle – using equal weights of eggs, butter, sugar and flour. For a special occasion, they were flavoured with orange or lemon juice, and given a thin icing. More often, they were left very plain, like Madeira cake, seed cake, sand or rice cake. Then there were light sponge cakes, filled with butter cream, or fresh strawberries and whipped cream. For a tea party, an iced chocolate or walnut cake might put in an appearance, while a rich fruit cake was iced for Christmas. Sticky ginger cakes were always popular, often served sliced and spread with butter. All these cakes had something in common, for they shared an essentially English simplicity, unlike the rich and creamy gateaux that were eaten on the Continent.

## SAVOURY SANDWICHES

## Egg and Mango Chutney Sandwiches

A subtle mixture of flavours, far removed from the simple egg sandwiches of today.

2 large eggs, hard-boiled
2 teaspoons mango chutney
2 tablespoons chopped watercress
6 thin slices of brown bread, 1 day old
20g butter

Hard-boil the eggs; chop them finely with mango chutney and some watercress, and spread the [*buttered bread*] sandwiches with this mixture. [*Remove crusts. Makes 3 rounds, or 12 small sandwiches.*] **The Gentle Art of Cookery, by Mrs C. F. Leyel and Miss Olga Hartley**

## Egg and Prawn Sandwiches

An excellent mixture of flavours, this sandwich is equally good for the tea table, a picnic, or a television snack.

2 hard-boiled eggs, chopped
180g unshelled prawns, or 85g shelled prawns
2 tablespoons mayonnaise
sea salt and black pepper
6 thin slices of brown bread, 1 day old
85g unsalted butter
1 basket of cress

Mix the chopped eggs with the prawns cut in small chunks (3 to each prawn). Moisten with the mayonnaise and season with salt and pepper. Spread the bread thinly with butter, and lay the egg mixture on top. Scatter the cress over the top, then cover with the remaining slices of bread. Cut off the crusts before serving. Makes 3 rounds, or 12 small sandwiches. **AB**

## Lobster Sandwich

A fabulous sandwich, the best ever. Ideal for a pre-theatre snack, with a green salad and a glass of white wine, or after the theatre, with some hot consommé. Not as extravagant as it sounds: a small lobster will feed two people.

1 x 450g lobster, or 120g lobster flesh, chopped
30g finely chopped celery
2 tablespoons mayonnaise
sea salt and black pepper
4 thin slices of brown bread, 1 day old
30g unsalted butter

You should have roughly 2 tablespoons of chopped celery to 8 table-spoons of chopped lobster. Mix the two together and moisten with the mayonnaise, adding salt and pepper to taste. Spread the bread thinly with butter, and fill the sandwiches with the chopped lobster. Cut off the crusts before serving. Makes 2 rounds, or 8 small sandwiches. White crabmeat can be used instead of lobster. **Adapted from** *Vogue*

## Potted Shrimp Sandwiches

I remember eating these when I was just eighteen, at Good-wood Races. Potted shrimps are no longer so delicious as they used to be, thanks to modern technology. They are also extremely expensive, but fun on occasion. Potted shrimps can also be made at home (see opposite); when made on holiday, with freshly caught shrimps, these are a revelation.

120g potted shrimps
4 medium-thin slices of brown bread, 1 day old
30g butter
a few drops of lemon juice
freshly ground black pepper

If using bought potted shrimps, turn them out of their cartons while still very cold and discard most of the butter. (Ignore the manufacturer's instructions about warming the cartons in the oven.) Spread the bread with fresh butter, lay the little shrimps on it and sprinkle with a few drops of lemon juice. Add a little freshly ground black pepper, and make into sandwiches, removing crusts. Makes 2 rounds, or 8 small sandwiches. **AB**

## Potted Shrimps

These should really be made with clarified butter, otherwise you will get a watery deposit in the bottom of the dish. Small prawns can be used instead of shrimps; they are less fiddly to shell, although lacking in flavour.

450g unshelled shrimps, or small prawns
85g butter, preferably clarified (see below)
¼ bay leaf
freshly ground black pepper
a pinch of mace, or nutmeg

(To clarify butter: put 120g butter in a small pan and heat it slowly. When it boils, let it bubble for a few seconds, then pour it into a bowl through a small strainer lined with muslin. Leave to cool, then chill until it has set. Tip out of the bowl and scrape the sediment off the bottom.)

Shell the shrimps, put the (clarified) butter in a bowl standing over a pan of simmering water. When it has melted, add the shrimps and stir gently to mix with the flavourings. Leave over the heat for 10 minutes, stirring occasionally. Then discard the bay leaf, spoon the shrimps into a straight-sided dish (or 2 oeuf en cocotte dishes), and pour over enough of the butter to almost cover them. Leave to cool, then chill in the refrigerator. Serve in the dish, or dishes, as a first course, with warm brown toast, fresh butter and lemon wedges. Or tip out of the dishes, discard the butter, and use to make sandwiches. Serves 2 as a first course; makes 2–3 rounds of sandwiches.

Potted shrimps can be kept for 1–2 days in the fridge. If covered with a second layer of clarified butter, after the first has set, they may be kept for up to 2 weeks. **AB**

## Sole Sandwiches

This unusual sandwich is perhaps best suited to a late-night supper or TV dinner, as it is too filling for tea, and rather fragile for transporting on a picnic. I use the minimum of butter, and add a little mayonnaise.

1 Dover or lemon sole (or plaice), skinned and filleted (approx. 340g fillets)
55g butter
2 tablespoons milk
sea salt and black pepper
6 thin slices of brown bread, 1 day old
3 tablespoons mayonnaise (optional)
3 teaspoons finely chopped parsley

GARNISH

½ bunch of watercress, cut in sprigs

Fillet a sole and cook it between two plates in the oven. [*Dot with 15g of butter, add 2 tablespoons of milk, salt and pepper, and cook for 12 minutes in the oven at 180°C/gas 4, or laid over a large saucepan of boiling water.*] Let it get cold. Cut some thin slices of brown bread and butter, lay a thin fillet between [*dab with mayonnaise, if used, and salt and pepper*], sprinkle with powdered parsley, and serve the sandwiches piled up on a dish with cold watercress as a decoration. [*Remove crusts. Makes 3 rounds, or 12 small sandwiches.*] **The Gentle Art of Cookery, by Mrs C. F. Leyel and Miss Olga Hartley**


## *Watercress and Shrimp Sandwiches*

A very good combination for the tea table: sandwiches of white bread filled with fresh shrimps (or prawns), laid on a dish alternating with sandwiches of brown bread filled with watercress.

6 large slices of brown bread, crusts removed
45g butter
½ bunch of watercress
6 large slices of white bread, crusts removed
450g shrimps or prawns, in the shell
juice of ½ a lemon
freshly ground black pepper

Cut brown bread and butter it; pack sprigs of watercress closely all over half the slices; press the top slices firmly down upon the under slices. Do not trim off the characteristic little frill of green leaflets that escape beyond the brown edge of the sandwich; their stiff green border proves the freshness of the sandwich, and adds to its enjoyment. A delicious sandwich is fresh brown bread and cress alternated with white bread sandwiches of pink shrimps. [*Shell the shrimps, or prawns, and lay on slices of buttered white bread. Sprinkle with lemon juice and freshly ground black pepper, cover with more buttered bread, press down, then cut each one in half. Arrange both lots of sandwiches on a large flat plate. Makes 3 rounds, or 12 small sandwiches.*] **Food in England, by Dorothy Hartley**

## Watercress and Walnut Sandwiches

½ bunch of watercress (4 tablespoons leaves only, finely chopped)
2 tablespoons chopped walnuts
1 tablespoon mayonnaise
4 large thin slices of bread, brown or white
30g unsalted butter

Remove the watercress leaves and chop them quite finely, add the chopped walnuts, and bind with a tablespoon of mayonnaise. Butter the bread thinly, divide the watercress filling in half, and use to make sandwiches as usual. Remove the crusts and cut each round in 4. Makes 2 rounds, or 8 small sandwiches. **Adapted from June Platt, in *Vogue***

## SWEET SANDWICHES

## Apple Sandwiches

An unusual sandwich, refreshing in hot weather.

4 large thin slices of brown bread
15g unsalted butter
2–3 tablespoons mayonnaise
1 Granny Smith, cored and cut in quarters

Spread half the bread thinly with butter, the other half with mayonnaise. Slice the unpeeled apple quarters fairly thinly and lay on the buttered bread. Cover with the rest of the bread and press together lightly. Remove the crusts and cut each sandwich in quarters. Makes 2 rounds: 8 small sandwiches. **Adapted from** *Lady Sysonby's Cook Book*

## Cream Cheese and Walnut Sandwiches

This was a very popular combination, often found on the tea table. It is capable of many variations, as you can see.

*Basic Sandwich*
4 thin slices of brown bread, 1 day old
15g unsalted butter
2 tablespoons cream cheese
2 tablespoons chopped walnuts (8 halves)

Spread half the bread with butter, the other half with cream cheese. Scatter the chopped walnuts over half the slices, and make into sandwiches. Remove crusts, and cut each one into quarters. Makes 2 rounds: 8 sandwiches.

*Variation I*
Make as for Basic Sandwich, adding 2 tablespoons of chopped dates (4 dates, stoned).

*Variation II*
Make as for Basic Sandwich, spreading 1½ tablespoons of thick honey over the buttered slices of bread. Add chopped dates as well, if you like, for a very sweet sandwich.

*Variation III*
Make as for Basic Sandwich, adding 2 tablespoons of chopped stem ginger (2 pieces). **Adapted from contemporary sources**

# Honey and Oatmeal Sandwiches

A delicious and unusual combination.

2 tablespoons coarse oatmeal
4 thin slices of brown bread, 1 day old
30g unsalted butter
3 tablespoons thick honey

Bake the oatmeal in the oven until pale brown. [5–10 *minutes at 180°C/gas 4.*] Spread buttered brown bread with honey, and sprinkle the browned oatmeal over it [*after it has cooled*]. Complete the sandwich with top slice in the usual way. [*Makes 2 rounds: 8 small sandwiches.*] **Lady Sysonby's Cook Book**

# Toasted Marmalade Sandwiches

These are quite delicious: a welcome addition to any tea table. I cut them simply into 5cm squares. Untoasted marmalade sandwiches are also very good.

4 thin slices of white bread, 1 day old
30g unsalted butter
3 tablespoons orange marmalade

Make thin sandwiches well buttered and spread with orange marmalade. Remove the crusts and cut into pieces about 2.5 by 7.5cm. [*Or cut simply into quarters.*] These may be made in advance. Cover with a damp cloth till wanted. Then toast quickly on both sides [*under the grill*], and serve piping hot. **June Platt, in** *Vogue*

# Rose Petal Sandwiches

When made with the whitest of white bread and bright-pink rose petals these are incredibly pretty. Damask roses have the strongest flavour, but even this is faint, though wonderful. The texture is also interesting.

30g rose petals, preferably bright-pink Damask or old-fashioned roses
55g unsalted butter
4 large thin slices of white bread, 1 day old, crusts removed

[*Start 1 day in advance.*] Line a dish with rose petals, then place in it some butter [*loosely*] wrapped in its own paper. Cover the whole with more rose petals, pressing them closely together until the dish is full. Put it in a cool larder [*or refrigerator*] overnight. Then cut thin slices of [*white*] bread and spread them with the butter, make into sandwiches, and place [*a single layer of overlapping*] rose petals on the top of the butter so that the edges of the petals show outside the sandwich. [*Makes 2 rounds, or 8 small sandwiches.*]
**The Gentle Art of Cookery, by Mrs C. F. Leyel and Miss Olga Hartley**


## LARGE CAKES


# *Iced Lemon (or Orange) Cake*

Simple iced cakes were very popular for teatime, both with grown-ups and children. This one is typical, based on the English pound cake, or French quatre-quarts system, whereby equal weights of eggs, butter, flour and sugar are used. It is quickly made in a food processor, and is also good without the icing.

120g unsalted butter, at room temperature
120g caster sugar
2 large eggs
120g self-raising flour, sifted
1 tablespoon lemon juice
        ICING (OPTIONAL)
        180g icing sugar, sifted
        approx. 3 tablespoons lemon juice

Cut the butter in bits and put in the food processor. Add the caster sugar and cream until blended, then drop in 1 whole egg. Process again, adding 1 tablespoon of flour, then drop in the second egg and process again. Now add the lemon juice, then the rest of the sifted flour and process once more. Turn into an 825ml tin – I use a small rectangular loaf tin – buttered and lined with buttered greaseproof paper. Bake for about 35 minutes at 190°C/gas 5, until the centre is fairly firm when pierced with a fine skewer. Take out of the oven and allow to cool in the tin for 15 minutes, then turn out on to a wire rack to finish cooling.

When it has completely cooled, lay on a flat surface for icing. Heat the lemon juice, then pour it gradually on to the sifted icing sugar, adding just enough to reach the right consistency, so that it will spread easily over the cake. Beat hard until it is totally smooth. Then pour it over the cake, smoothing the sides with a palette knife. (Or just ice the top if preferred.) Leave to set before lifting on to a plate.

This makes a delicious small cake without being too rich; golden brown on the outside and creamy white within, and with a lovely texture. An orange cake may be made by substituting orange juice for lemon juice, and adding the grated rind of 1 orange to the cake mixture, to reinforce the flavour. Makes a 340g cake. **AB**

## Chocolate Sponge Cake

This is an unusually good chocolate cake: easy to make and very light, without being especially rich. One of the nicest things about it is the crust, so do not be tempted to ice it.

4 eggs, separated
180g caster sugar
120g chocolate
85g flour, sifted
½ teaspoon baking powder, sifted
FILLING
120g unsalted butter
85g icing sugar, sifted

Separate yolks from whites, add sugar to yolks with 2 tablespoons of cold water, and beat over hot water till thick and creamy. Meanwhile have the chocolate melted in 4 tablespoons of water, add it to the yolks mixture, add flour and baking powder. Now beat the whites to a stiff froth, mix whites and mixture very lightly together, pour into two well greased [*18–20cm*] sandwich tins and bake in a moderate oven [*180°C/gas 4*] for ½ hour. Cream some butter and icing sugar, put between the sponges, dust with [*sifted*] icing sugar. **Food for the Greedy**, **by Nancy Shaw**

## Sticky Ginger Cake

An excellent ginger cake, moist and rich; best made a week in advance.

340ml golden syrup
120ml black treacle
85g soft brown sugar
55g unsalted butter
1 tablespoon ground ginger
1 teaspoon mixed spice
285g flour
½ teaspoon bicarbonate of soda
150ml milk
2 eggs, beaten

Put the syrup, treacle, sugar, butter and spices in a heatproof bowl and warm through for 30 minutes at 130°C/gas ½, or until the butter and sugar have melted. Then remove from the oven and turn up the heat to 170°C/gas 3. Stir in the flour, sifted with the bicarbonate of soda, then finally the milk and beaten eggs. Turn into a 1.5 litre capacity loaf tin which you have lined with buttered greaseproof paper and bake for 1–1½ hours. Take out of the oven and leave for about 20 minutes, then turn out on to a rack to cool. Then wrap in foil and store in an airtight tin or crock for a week or so before using. Cut in thick slices to serve, spread with unsalted butter. Makes a large cake, about 1.15kg. **Mrs Arthur James**

## Madeira Cake

In the eighteenth century, a plain cake of this kind was often served in the morning, with a glass of sherry or Madeira, hence its name. By the twentieth century it was to be found on the tea table, or served with a fruit fool as a pudding. It is one of the best of all plain cakes.

180g unsalted butter
180g caster sugar
3 eggs
45g ground almonds
grated rind of ½ lemon
180g flour, sifted
1 teaspoon baking powder, sifted
1 tablespoon water

This can be made by hand, or in a food processor. (I use a food processor.) Cream the butter and sugar, then add the eggs one at a time, beating (or processing) after each one. If the mixture shows signs of separating, add a spoonful of sifted flour. When all the eggs are incorporated, add the ground almonds and lemon rind. Then add the sifted flour and baking powder, and 1 tablespoon of water. Turn into a 720–825ml loaf tin lined with buttered greaseproof paper and bake for 65 minutes at 180°C/gas 4. On taking out of the oven, cool for about 15 minutes, then remove from the tin, leaving the paper intact, and lay on a rack to finish cooling. Once it is completely cool, wrap in foil and store in an airtight tin or crock. This excellent cake keeps well for several days, and is best eaten at least 1 day after making. **AB**

## Rice Cake

Another of these plain cakes which I find irresistible. They cannot be bought and are rarely made at home. I find them an excellent staple to fall back on over a holiday: for tea, or as accompaniment to an ice, or a fruit compote, or just as a snack.

120g unsalted butter
120g caster sugar
2 eggs
120g self-raising flour
55g ground rice
grated rind of ½ lemon

Beat the butter and sugar to a cream. [*Or blend in the food processor.*] Beat in the eggs one by one [*with 1 tablespoon of flour in between each egg*]. Mix the [*remaining*] flour with the ground rice and lemon rind and stir into the creamed mixture. [*All this can be done in the food processor.*] Bake in a moderate oven. [*45 minutes at 180°C/gas 4, in a small loaf tin holding roughly 720ml, lined with buttered paper.*] **When the Cook Is Away, by Catherine Ives**

## Seed Cake

Seed cake is an English phenomenon: enormously popular with some, but anathema to others. George Lassalle, author and cook, claims that, as a boy, he 'was once frightened by a seed cake in a cricket pavilion', but I find it delicious in a somewhat austere way. It was a regular feature on English tea tables between the wars, but is rarely seen nowadays.

180g unsalted butter
120g caster sugar
2 large eggs
225g self-raising flour, sifted
½–1 tablespoon caraway seeds
grated rind of ½ large orange

Beat the butter to a cream, sieve the sugar on to it and cream both together. [*Or blend in the food processor.*] Beat in one egg, and a little of the flour, then the second egg and more flour. When all the eggs and flour are in, add the caraway seeds and orange rind. [*If making for the first time, try ½ a tablespoon of seeds, but if you are fond of seed cake use 1 tablespoon.*] Beat altogether for about 10 minutes, lifting the mixture up to make it as light as possible. [*Or continue to blend in the processor*.] Pour the mixture into the paper-lined tin [*I use a loaf tin holding 825ml*] and bake in a moderate oven. [*65 minutes at 170°C/gas 3*.] **When the Cook Is Away**, **by Catherine Ives**

## SMALL CAKES

# Brandy Snaps

Brandy snaps were a favourite feature at children's parties, often filled with whipped cream. They are not hard to make, but rolling each individual one takes a little time.

120g unsalted butter
120g caster sugar
120g golden syrup
120g flour, sifted and warmed
1½ tablespoons ground ginger
1–1½ tablespoons lemon juice

GARNISH (OPTIONAL)
275ml double cream, whipped
1 tablespoon vanilla sugar, or, for grown-ups only, 1
tablespoon caster sugar and 1 teaspoon brandy

Melt butter, sugar, and syrup, add the warmed flour, ginger, and lemon. Stir well and put out on a well-greased baking sheet in teaspoonfuls, 15 cm apart. Bake in a moderate oven until golden brown [*180°C/gas 4 for 10–12 minutes*], leave for a few moments to cool, then roll up over the thick handle of a wooden spoon and fill with whipped cream [*after they have cooled. Makes about 3 dozen. If you find the rolling too lengthy, they can be left to cool flat, on a wire rack, and served as thin ginger biscuits*]. **The Constance Spry Cookery Book**, **by Constance Spry and Rosemary Hume**

## Coconut Pyramids

Coconut was much used as a flavouring in the inter-war years, mostly in sweet dishes like cakes and puddings, but also, to a lesser extent, in savoury dishes flavoured with curry. Rice paper can still be found in old-fashioned grocers, and is very easy to use.

2 egg whites
30g potato flour
180g desiccated coconut
85g vanilla sugar, or caster sugar
¼ teaspoon vanilla essence, if using caster sugar
rice paper

Whisk the whites of egg to a very stiff froth. Sieve the flour, stir it in lightly, also the coconut, sugar, and vanilla essence [*if you have no vanilla sugar*]. Divide the mixture into small heaps, put them on the baking sheet lined with rice paper and bake in a slow oven until they are light brown. [*15–20 minutes at 150°C/gas 2. Once they have cooled, simply lift them off the baking sheet individually, breaking off the rice paper from around the edges. Makes about 12, using a heaped dessertspoon.*] **When the Cook Is Away, by Catherine Ives**

## Devonshire Splits

These small crisp scones are reminiscent of country teas in the south-west of England, where clotted cream often takes the place of butter. They are quick and easy to make, especially with a food processor.

180g self-raising flour
a pinch of salt
7g caster sugar
55g unsalted butter
75ml milk
15g butter, melted

Sift dry ingredients [*flour, salt and sugar*], rub in butter [*or blend in processor*], mix with milk to a soft dough. Knead lightly to free from cracks, and shape quickly into rounds the size of an egg. Place close together on a buttered tin [*baking sheet*], brush with melted butter, and bake in a quick oven [*25–30 minutes at 200°C/gas 6*].

When baked pull apart, and when cold split, spread with jam, and then with Devonshire cream [*or thickly whipped cream*] and put halves together. [*Makes 8–10.*] **Lady Sysonby's Cook Book**


## Melba Toast

My best friend's grandmother lived in the Ritz, in Paris. I was taken to lunch with her there, when I was sixteen, and we had Melba toast. It became for me the hallmark of a good restaurant, one that is rarely seen today. I am grateful to Prue Leith for allowing me to use her method.

Cut dry white or brown bread into very thin slices and toast them lightly on both sides. Then cut off the crusts and carefully split each slice in two, so that you have twice as many slices, even thinner than before. Lay them, toasted side down, on a baking sheet and bake for 1 hour at 130°C/gas ½. Serve after cooling, the same day as made. **Prue Leith**


## Carberry Ginger Hats

These were a country house speciality: small ginger cakes usually served at tea. They also make a delicious pudding, served warm, with the creamy custard sauce (page 161), or the lemon and vanilla sauce (page 162), or with thick cream.

85g plain flour
85g self-raising flour
120g soft brown sugar, dark or light
7g ground ginger
a pinch of mixed spice, or allspice

55g treacle
55g golden syrup
120g unsalted butter
2 medium eggs, beaten

Put flours, sugar, ginger and spices through a sieve into a basin. Melt treacle and syrup with butter in a pan. When only just warm, mix it into the dry ingredients with the well-beaten eggs. [*Turn into small greased tins.*] Bake in a moderate oven [*about 25 minutes at 180°C/gas 4. Makes about 12 small cakes, or 6–8 individual puddings, depending on the size of the tins*]. **Lady Elphinstone**

## Macaroons

Ground almonds were the flavour of the month in the 1920s and macaroons were immensely popular, both for tea and for desserts, where they were used as the basis for soufflés and mousses. Most of these dishes are too sweet for modern tastes, but the macaroons themselves are very delicious. Rice paper may be bought at good grocers; but they can always be made without if need be.

120g ground almonds
225g vanilla sugar, or caster sugar
15g rice flour, sifted
2 egg whites
rice paper
6–12 whole almonds, blanched and halved

Put the ground almonds, vanilla (or caster) sugar, rice flour and unbeaten egg whites into a food processor and blend for 2½ minutes. (If you don't have vanilla sugar, add a few drops of vanilla essence.) Have sheets of rice paper laid on baking trays, and spoon the mixture on to them in round blobs. Bake for 15–20 minutes at 190°C/gas 5. Take out of the oven and press half a blanched almond into the centre of each macaroon. Lift the sheets of rice paper on to wire racks to cool. Later, after they have cooled, lift off each macaroon, breaking the rice paper. Serve the same day, or store in an airtight tin. Makes 12–24, depending on size. **Adapted from** *Kitchen Essays*, **by Lady Jekyll**

## Orange Jumbles

These were a favourite teatime speciality in one or two country houses before the war. They are quickly made today, especially with the help of a food processor or mixer. I omit the cochineal.

85g unsalted butter
120g caster sugar
120g coarsely ground almonds
55g flour, sifted
grated rind and juice of 2 small oranges (about 5 tablespoons juice)
a soupçon of cochineal (optional)

Mix [*either by hand or in a food processor or mixer, creaming the butter and sugar together first, then adding the other ingredients*], and put on a slightly greased baking tin in quantities of about 1 teaspoon to each jumble, allowing room to spread, and bake in a moderate oven. [*10–12 minutes at 180°C/gas 4.*] They will be the size of teacup rims, and should curl their crisp edges, faintly pink as the underneath of a young mushroom. [*Makes about 25. Good served with vanilla ice cream, at lunch or dinner.*] **Kitchen Essays, by Lady Jekyll**

## Small Sponge Cakes or Fingers

These were often served at lunch or dinner, as an accompaniment to a fruit fool or ice, as well as at tea. They are quick to make and freeze well. Fat sponge fingers – as opposed to langues de chat – should be made with a piping bag, but I find this too much trouble. I use a langues de chat tin, filling it half full for thin crusty langues de chat, and filled to the brim for big sponge fingers. I have slightly adapted the following recipe in that I prefer to separate the eggs and add the egg whites at the end, but the detailed instructions for preparing the tins are particularly good.

7g clarified butter, melted (see page 191)
55g + 1 teaspoon vanilla sugar, or caster sugar
55g + 1 teaspoon flour, sifted
2 eggs, separated
½ tablespoon milk

Brush the inside of the tins carefully all over with just warm melted clarified butter. If the butter is too hot it will not coat the tins sufficiently thickly. Sift together 1 teaspoon of caster sugar and 1 teaspoon of flour; put these through a hair sieve and mix them well. Coat the whole of the inside of the tins with some of this mixture. It will adhere to the melted butter, and the whole should look evenly covered. Any flour and sugar should be shaken out of the tin. When the inside coating is set, the tins are ready for use.

Beat the egg yolks, add the sugar and beat again over hot water until thick. Then beat till cold. Fold in the slightly warmed flour [*alternately with the stiffly beaten egg whites*]. No further beating must be done. The mixture is just 'folded' together till evenly mixed. Half fill the tins with the mixture. Dust the tops with [*the remaining*] sifted sugar and flour, and bake in a moderate oven. [*180°C/gas 4. Langues de chat take 8–9 minutes, fat sponge fingers 12–14 minutes, and small sponge cakes 15–18 minutes. Makes 24 langues de chat, 12 fat sponge fingers, and 8 small cakes. Allow to cool for 3 minutes after taking out of the oven, then lift out of their tins carefully and lay on a wire rack to cool. Put in plastic bags for freezing, or in an airtight tin for 1–2 days, but best eaten the same day as made.*] **Good Cookery**, by **W. G. R. Francillon**

SAVOURIES

# SAVOURIES

Savouries were peculiar to England, having never existed in any other country. They took the form of a small, highly seasoned dish, often salty or smoky in flavour. In most cases they were made in individual servings, often laid on toast, or in a small pastry croûte. A few, like a cheese soufflé, were served in a large dish, but second helpings were not offered. They were almost always served very hot.

The Englishman has always had a preference for ending his meal on a savoury, as opposed to sweet, note. At luncheon, this was effected by the cheese, but this was never served at night, so the savoury course was devised. The explanation often given was that the men wanted something appropriate to accompany the remains of the wine, which was almost always red at this point in the meal, but this theory does not really hold water, since few savouries go well with wine, especially red. Foods like sardines, bacon, smoked haddock, and anchovies are hardly conducive to an enjoyment of wine, even white, but what they did do was to clear the palate of sweet tastes before starting on the port.

The 1920s and 30s saw the gradual decline of the savoury, as meals grew shorter and less formal. Although their place was still assured in old-fashioned houses, in more modern establishments the same dishes started to appear in another guise. As Ruth Lowinsky points out, in *Lovely Food*: 'their place is now very often taken at dinner by hors d'oeuvre served before the soup, or by a vegetable dish coming between the entrée and the sweet. It is amusing to vary this by arranging a tray with hors d'oeuvre to be served in the drawing-room with the cocktails.' Thus the old order began to crumble, as the former respect for tradition gave way to a longing for novelty.

Foreigners rarely understand the English love of savouries, although Escoffier does include a short chapter on the subject in his classic, *Ma Cuisine*. Savouries did not figure in the Italian cucina alto-borghese either, according to Lorenza de Medici in her book *The Renaissance of Italian Cooking*. In the 1920s and 30s the Italian upper classes ended their midday meal with cheese, followed by a fruit course; in the evening the cheese was replaced by a dessert, also followed by fruit.

In the days when meals consisted of four or five courses, it was considered perfectly acceptable to refuse one or two courses altogether. Thus, those without a sweet tooth might reject the pudding and merely eat the savoury, while others, usually the ladies, refused the savoury. From what I can remember – not much, since savouries were only ever served in the evening, when children were not present – savouries could be utterly delicious, or the most tedious things imaginable, depending on the skill with which they had been made, and the speed with which they were served.

The range of savoury dishes revolved around three or four themes, each with many small variations. The main ingredient was usually cheese, smoked or salted fish, bacon, or something 'devilled'. They were usually neatly contained, either in a pastry case, or on a canapé of toast, or within a wrapping of bacon. Oysters, prunes, chicken livers and grapes were all wrapped in thin rashers of streaky bacon and grilled, then served on squares of toast. Marrow bones were served wrapped in a napkin, with dry toast, and a silver scoop to extract the marrow. Toasted cheese was always popular, usually in the form of Welsh rarebit. Herring roes were served on toast, as were flaked smoked haddock and devilled kidneys. Eggs were sometimes used, since they would not have featured in the first course, as they often did at lunchtime. Scotch woodcock was made with scrambled eggs topped with anchovy fillets and capers. Cheese pastry cut into straws or small biscuits made a simple savoury, as did thin strips of streaky bacon, coated with grated Parmesan and grilled.

There were a few cold dishes, like a cheese or horseradish mousse. Savoury ices were not unknown, and recipes for a Camembert ice turn up in various books of the period, although I have never managed to make them work. Far more delicious, to my mind, is Nancy Shaw's glace pomme d'amour, a tomato cream ice made with a mixture of mayonnaise and cream. Other very simple savouries were made with pastes of pounded game, anchovies, smoked cod's roe or potted cheese, spread on little rounds of toast. These provided useful ways of using up the remains of other dishes. Unsweetened ice cream wafers could then be bought, and were used for making light savouries, spread with grated cheese and mustard and cayenne, then baked briefly in the oven.

Savouries at the end of a meal are just not practical today, since they demand help in the kitchen. The dishes themselves are still useful, however, served at another time. Almost without exception, they make good hot canapés or snacks to serve with drinks, before a meal. In this context, they are very similar to the small appetizer which many restaurants produce today, while you are studying the menu and choosing the wine. (But savouries were never served two or three at a time, as these little appetizers often are.) Made on a larger scale, many make good first courses. The French always serve croque monsieur as a first course, and this is merely a fried cheese and ham sandwich, very similar to many of our own hot savouries. Some of the simplest and best savouries, like cheese straws or bacon crisps, are very good indeed served with a hot consommé, as part of the first course. A few, like the cheese soufflé, or the tomato ice, could be served instead of a pudding.

I have been surprised to find some luxury foods like foie gras, black truffles, and smoked salmon quoted in this context, served as savouries at the end of a meal. And, in Siegfried Sassoon's diaries, while staying in Nuremberg in 1922, he recorded: 'We dined at the Bamberger Hof, which at first seemed disappointing. But the wine was excellent, and we concluded our meal with caviare.'

## Potted Cheese

Useful either as a savoury or as a snack, this is a good way of using up the remains of large cheeses. It can be made in any amount by simply doubling up the ingredients in the same proportions.

180g Cheshire or Cheddar cheese
30g butter
2 tablespoons single cream, or rich milk, or an extra 30g butter
2–3 tablespoons beer, sherry, red or white wine
2 tablespoons finely chopped chives

A good soft cheese can be made from ordinary Cheshire or Cheddar. Pound up in a mortar or put it through a sieve and add about one-sixth of its quantity in butter. A little cream or rich milk may also be used. When all is soft, add 2 or 3 tablespoonfuls of beer or wine and any chopped herbs you like. Chives are good and so is pennyroyal. Press into pots and keep in a cool place. [*Serve with hot toast, French bread, or water biscuits. Serves 4.*] **Come Into the Garden, Cook, by Constance Spry**

## Water Biscuits

Home-made water biscuits are unusual, and good for serving with cheese, or with a clear soup.

30g butter
120g flour, sifted

½ teaspoon baking powder, sifted with the flour
a pinch of salt

Rub the butter well into the [*sifted*] flour with a pinch of salt and mix with a little [*4–5 tablespoons*] cold water; roll them very thin [*cut in rounds*], prick, and bake in a good oven. [*20–25 minutes on a greased baking sheet, at 170°C/gas 3, until lightly coloured. Serve warm, soon after baking. Makes about 10 of 6cm diameter.*] **A Medley of Recipes, by Dorothy Allhusen**

## Bacon Crisps

These tasty little snacks are excellent for serving with drinks, or as part of an hors d'oeuvre, with the corn meal soufflé on page 56, for instance.

8 very thin rashers of green streaky bacon
7g butter or lard

Remove the rind and any small bones, and cut into very thin narrow strips [*about 10cm x 5mm*]. Put 1 teaspoonful of either butter or lard [*in a frying pan*] and when very hot, put in the bacon. Fry on a quick fire till the bacon begins to curl, and is very brown and crisp, but not burnt. Drain on greaseproof paper [*or soft kitchen paper*]. When free of all grease, and quite dry, place in a glass dish and serve instead of salted almonds. A very attractive novelty at a cocktail party. [*Serves 4 as part of an hors d'oeuvre, or 8 with drinks.*] **Lightning Cookery, by Countess Morphy**

## Parmesan Bacon

This is an unusually simple hors d'oeuvre, and can be easily made without help in the kitchen. The crisp bacon strips are also very good served with the corn meal soufflé (see page 56), or with a soup, or with drinks before dinner. They are easily eaten in the fingers.

12 very thin rashers of unsmoked streaky bacon
55g freshly grated Parmesan
55g fine, dry, white breadcrumbs

Cut the rind off the bacon. Mix the grated cheese and breadcrumbs. Heat the grill, laying the bacon rashers under it for a moment, just until the fat starts to melt. Then dip them in the mixed cheese and breadcrumbs, patting it on well. Set aside until ready to serve. Then put back under the grill and cook slowly, until crisp and golden, turning once. Drain briefly on soft paper, then lay on a flat dish to serve. Serves 4 as a savoury or light snack. **AB**

## Toasted Cheese Sandwiches

These make a delicious mid-morning snack, or late supper, or TV snack. Their only disadvantage as a savoury is that they have to be made at the very last minute.

quite thickly sliced white bread, 1 day old
butter
strong cheese, i.e. Cheddar
cayenne pepper

For each sandwich make two pieces of toast and butter them while still hot so that the butter sinks into them. Over one of them spread a good layer of strong cheese with a dash of cayenne. Place it under the broiler [*grill*] for a few moments and then put the other buttered slice on top of this and pop the sandwich under the broiler for two or three minutes, just long enough to warm the whole through. **Kitchenette Cookery, by G. F. Scotson-Clark**

## Cheese Biscuits

These small cheese biscuits can be served equally well as a canapé, with drinks, with a clear soup, or at the end of the meal, with the last of the red wine, after, or instead of, a pudding. When made in the shape of small sticks, 5cm x 5mm x 5mm], these become cheese straws, for serving in the same way.

30g butter
30g flour
30g freshly grated Parmesan
15g grated Cheddar
1 small egg yolk
salt and cayenne

Rub the fat in the flour, add the rest of the ingredients, mix thoroughly, and bind with the egg. [*Roll out about 5mm thick.*] Stamp the paste into small rounds [*about 5cm wide*], prick these, and bake in a cool oven till golden brown. [*8–10 minutes at 170°C/gas 3. Makes about 8 biscuits; can easily be made in double or treble quantities. The mixing is speedily done in a food processor.*] **Good Cookery**, by **W. G. R. Francillon**

## Parmesan Fingers

This was originally served as a savoury, but I find it useful to serve with drinks, or to accompany a hot consommé, like the one on page 19. It is best made with stale, rather than merely dry bread, and only prepared shortly before baking. Made in this way, the fingers stay crisp and delicious; otherwise they may be slightly limp.

3 large slices of stale white bread, approx. 1cm thick, crusts removed
150ml double cream
55g freshly grated Parmesan
freshly ground black pepper
7g butter

Cut stale white bread into fingers [*about 8.5 x 1cm square*]. Soak [*or better still, dip briefly*] in cream then roll in grated Parmesan and pepper and pat with knife so that cheese sticks well. Butter baking sheet and bake in a hot oven. Serve very hot. [*Bake for 6 minutes at 200°C/gas 6, turning them* over halfway through. Makes about 15; serves 4–6.] *A Medley of Recipes*, by **Dorothy Allhusen**

## Fried Cheese Sandwiches

These are very good and quite unusual, like a savoury version of pain perdu. Like many old-fashioned savouries, they are not very practical today, since they must be eaten the moment they are made, which demands some help in the kitchen. They are more useful served as a first course, or a hot snack with drinks.

12 large thin slices of dry white bread
150ml milk
1 egg, beaten
salt and cayenne
a pinch of dry mustard
70g butter

CHEESE FILLING
55g grated sharp cheese, i.e. Cheddar and Parmesan mixed
75ml milk
30g butter
sea salt and black pepper
a pinch of cayenne
1 egg, beaten

Put the grated cheese, milk, butter, salt and pepper and cayenne in a double boiler and heat slowly until all has melted, stirring all the time. Then raise the heat slightly and stir hard, over boiling water, until it is smooth. Remove from the heat and stir in the beaten egg bit by bit, stirring constantly. Put back over a low heat and stir until it has thickened slightly, like mustard, and is perfectly smooth. Tip into a bowl and leave to cool.

Later, use it to make sandwiches with thin slices of unbuttered white bread. Remove the crusts, and cut each round into two, or four, small sandwiches. Dip each one briefly in milk, then in egg beaten with a pinch each of sea salt, cayenne and mustard powder. Heat the butter in a broad frying pan and fry the sandwiches quickly on each side, until pale golden brown. Drain on soft paper and serve at once. Makes 6 rounds, or 12 sandwiches, or 24 small ones. **Adapted from contemporary sources**

## Mushrooms on Toast

An elaborate version of this homely dish was considered suitable for a dinner party. Made on a larger scale, it can serve as a first course. This method for making croûtes comes from *English Country House Cooking*, by Fortune Stanley.

4 small slices of dry white bread, 7.5mm thick
70g butter
340g mushrooms
1½ tablespoons flour
150ml milk, heated
sea salt and black pepper

Cut the bread in circles, or squares, removing crusts, and spread both sides very thinly with butter. Lay on the oven rack and bake for 10–15 minutes at 200°C/gas 6, until golden and crisp. Remove and keep warm.

Reserve 4 small mushrooms and chop the rest roughly. Cook them in 30g butter for about 8 minutes, until soft. Make a thick white sauce with 30g butter, flour, hot milk, sea salt and black pepper; mix with the chopped mushrooms. Dot the 4 whole mushrooms with tiny bits of butter and grill. To serve, divide the purée between the croûtes, piling it in mounds, then lay a grilled mushroom on top. Serves 4, or 2 as a first course. **AB**

## Canapés Fumés

This popular savoury also makes a good snack, or light main dish, made in double quantities. It can be prepared a little in advance, then reheated at the last moment, while making the toast.

340g smoked haddock
275ml milk
15g unsalted butter
½ tablespoon flour
black pepper
1 egg, beaten
2 thick slices of bread, brown or white
½ tablespoon finely chopped parsley, or paprika

Put the haddock in a pan, add the milk and bring slowly to the boil. Cover the pan and remove from the heat; stand for 10 minutes, then drain off the milk through a strainer, reserving it. Flake the fish, discarding skin and bone, then chop the flakes roughly by hand. Melt half the butter and add the flour, stirring. Cook for 1 minute, then measure 120ml of the milk the fish was cooked in and add to the pan. Stir till blended, adding some black pepper, and simmer gently for 3–4 minutes. Then remove from the fire and stir in the beaten egg, then the flaked fish. Put back over a low flame and cook gently, stirring, until the egg has cooked and thickened slightly. Remove from the fire. Make the toast, using white or brown bread as preferred. Spread the toast lightly with the remaining butter, cut each slice in half, removing crusts if serving as a savoury, and lay on hot plates. Pile the smoked haddock on top of the toast and sprinkle with very finely chopped parsley, or paprika. Serves 4 as a savoury, or 2 as a light main dish. **Adapted from *A Year's Dinners*, by May Little**

## Smoked Cod's Roe Paste

This is the English version of taramasalata, now forgotten in favour of the Greek one. I like both, and make this often in the old way, using a pestle and mortar. (A food processor can well be used instead.) In pre-war days, this would have been served as a savoury, but it is more useful today as a first course, or snack, with spirits or beer – it does not go well with wine.

225g smoked cod's roe, weighed after skinning
120g unsalted butter, at room temperature
1 tablespoon lemon juice
freshly ground black pepper

Put the skinned roe in a mortar and add the butter cut in bits. Pound until amalgamated, adding lemon juice and black pepper. (This can be done in a food processor.) Pile into a small dish, filling it to the brim. Chill for 2–3 hours before serving. Serves 4–6 as a savoury, piled on small squares of toast, or 2–3 as a first course, in its dish, with hot toast. **AB**

## Scotch Woodcock I

8 anchovy fillets
4 tablespoons milk
16 capers
4 thick slices of dry white bread, crusts removed
30g butter
6 eggs
sea salt and black pepper

Soak the anchovy fillets in the milk for 10 minutes, then rinse under the cold tap and pat dry. Rinse the capers in a small strainer, and pat dry. Toast the bread and cut into neat squares about 5cm wide. Spread them with half the butter and keep warm. Beat the eggs, adding sea salt and black pepper, then scramble as usual in the remaining butter. Pile on to the squares of toast and lay the anchovy fillets crosswise over the top, laying a caper between each angle. Serve immediately. Serves 4 as a savoury, or 2 as a first course, on larger pieces of toast. **AB**

## Scotch Woodcock II

This is a simplified version of the above. Instead of the anchovy fillets and capers, spread the buttered toast with Gentleman's Relish (Patum Peperium), or anchovy paste, then pile the scrambled eggs on top.

# Herring Roes on Toast

This was one of the best savouries. Made on a larger scale, it makes a very good first course, or even a light main dish.

4 large soft herring roes, or 8 medium ones
30–55g flour
30g butter
1 tablespoon sunflower oil
2 thin rashers of unsmoked streaky bacon
2 large slices of fairly thick brown or white bread, toasted
1 teaspoon anchovy paste, or Gentleman's Relish (Patum Peperium)
salt and cayenne pepper
2 teaspoons chopped parsley
lemon wedges

Get fine, fresh, plump roes, about four per person. Wash under running hot water; this will remove the slime and stiffen them. Drain on paper kitchen towels. Put enough flour in a plastic bag, then gently shake the roes in it to coat all over. Remove from the bag, shake off surplus flour and lay on some greaseproof paper. Melt the butter with a slurp of oil in a good heavy frying pan; when it is just sizzling put in the roes and cook gently until golden brown on both sides. If you are dealing with more than one panful, keep the cooked roes warm in the oven having removed them from the pan and drained them on some kitchen towel. Grill the bacon until brittle. Have ready some hot toast spread with anchovy paste or Gentleman's Relish. Pile the roes on to the toasts, sprinkle with cayenne pepper and a pinch of salt, crumble the bacon over the top and strew with chopped parsley. Serve with wedges of lemon. [*Serves 4 as a savoury, or 2 as a first course.*] **Feast Days**, by **Jennifer Paterson**

# Glace Pomme d'Amour

Since savoury ices are almost unknown today, except in the form of sorbets between courses, this exquisite pale-pink ice cream is probably better suited for use as a first course.

When made with fresh tomato juice and home-made mayonnaise it is truly delicious. The original version was filled with mayonnaise, surrounded by lettuce leaves and cheese made into balls. I prefer to add a cleaner, fresher taste: see below.

275ml freshly made tomato juice
150ml mayonnaise (home-made) (see page 155)
150ml double cream
sea salt and white pepper
a dash of Tabasco, or 2 teaspoons lemon juice

Fold the three main ingredients together, adding sea salt and white pepper, and Tabasco or lemon juice to taste. Pour into an ice cream machine (or freeze in icetrays) and run until it is about two-thirds frozen. Then spoon into a 570ml ring mould and complete the freezing process.

This is easily turned out by dipping into warm water for about 30 seconds. Fill with one of the following: a) halved and seeded white grapes; b) the avocado filling on page 43; c) large prawns, cut in chunks, dressed with olive oil and lemon juice; d) a ceviche of sliced, raw scallops; e) chunks of lobster or white crabmeat, with oil and lemon. Serves 4.
**Adapted from *Food for the Greedy*, by Nancy Shaw**


## Salted Almonds

These were laid on the table in small dishes for people to nibble between courses in the evening. The service was often slow, since it was frequently some considerable distance from kitchen to dining-room. They are also very good served with drinks.

whole almonds
butter
sea salt

It is best to buy the almonds unskinned and blanch them yourself, if you have the time. Put them in a small bowl and pour some boiling water over them. Leave for a couple of minutes, then take out 3 or 4 and rub the skins off between your fingers. If it is hard to do, put them back in the hot water for a moment or two longer. They will get progressively harder as the water cools, so drain them once or twice and refill with more boiling water.

When all are blanched, dry them thoroughly by patting in a cloth. Heat some good butter in a frying pan and, when it is very hot, put in the almonds and fry them quickly, turning frequently, until they are a pale straw colour on both sides. Lift them out and drain on soft paper, then lay them on a plate and scatter some Maldon sea salt over them. (Some people add cayenne, but I prefer them simply salted.) Best eaten the same day as made, but they can be kept for a few days wrapped in foil and stored in a tin. **AB**

# DRINKS

# DRINKS

The variety of alcoholic drinks, and the manner of their serving, has not changed greatly since the 1920s. While the English still figured highly among the world's top buyers of French wines, their annual consumption was only one-sixth what it had been in 1900. This was largely due to heavy taxes levied on imported wines after the close of the First World War, making French wines very expensive. This did not deter the upper classes, however, for they had become dependent on claret and hock, champagne and brandy. Arnold Bennett, complaining of feeling unwell in 1922, blamed the 'four Cs – Cocktails, Caviare, Champagne and Cognac'. For over 250 years the English had been addicted to such luxuries. In 1688 they imported 20,000 barrels of French wine, and it was only when Queen Anne levied a tax of £55 per barrel (to favour the import of port from Portugal) that the figure dropped sharply, and levelled out at an average of 2,000 barrels a year for most of the eighteenth century.

In the large country houses between the wars, wine was drunk at dinner, at least when there were guests, but not at lunch. Then cider or beer was usual, with ginger beer as a Sunday treat for the children. (No one seemed aware that ginger beer has much the same alcoholic content as light ale; no wonder we all enjoyed it so much.) The wines were chosen with great care by the master of the household and laid down in the cellar for future use. The wine was left in total control of the butler; often his employer might have preferred to keep charge of the cellar key himself, for many butlers were secret drinkers.

The choice of what to drink with what was much the same as it is today, with a few exceptions. (The custom of drinking Sauternes with foie gras, at the beginning of a meal, only recently became fashionable.) In his book *What Shall We Have To Drink?*, published in 1933, Marcel Boulestin gives suggestions for fine wines to serve at a formal dinner. These could be followed today with advantage, could we afford it. It is interesting to note that, of the twenty-three wines mentioned, only two are unfamiliar today.

At the start of the meal, he suggests sherry with hors d'oeuvre or soup, or, with oysters, Chablis or champagne. With the fish, he offers a choice of white Burgundies – Pouilly, Montrachet or Meursault – or a dry Loire wine like Muscadet; a Chablis, Moselle, or white Côtes-du-Rhône; or a dry white Bordeaux like Ch. Filhot, a white Haut-Brion, or the white Margaux called Pavillon-Blanc.

With the entrée, usually a meat dish served in a sauce, M. Boulestin suggests a second growth, or light claret, thus keeping back the best wine for the second meat course. This was traditionally a roast bird, either game or poultry depending on the season, which showed off the great wines to their best advantage. He recommends a fine Burgundy – Chambertin, Corton or Romanée; one of the great Médocs – Latour, Lafite or Margaux; or a Saint-Emilion like Ausone or Cheval-Blanc.

With the pudding comes a sweet dessert wine. This would probably be a Sauternes – Yquem, Guiraud or Rieussec; or a wine from Saumur or Anjou, of which Boulestin was very fond, or of course champagne. To conclude, with the coffee, a glass of old brandy.

This account demonstrates how much better the formal dinner of the 1930s, with its two meat courses, suited the serving of fine wines. For in this case the second red wine, always the best, accompanied the simple roast bird. Whereas today, even in Bordeaux, the second red wine invariably accompanies the cheese, which makes for a less happy combination.

In the 1920s, drink began to prove a vast divide – larger by far than food – between the different socio-economic groups. Whereas the well-off upper-middle classes and the aristocracy liked to keep their cellars well stocked, the impoverished and the lower classes never kept alcoholic drinks in the house. For one thing, it was expensive, and what housewife would pay for beer when food was her main priority? And social drinking in the home no longer figured below a certain level, where the man of the household preferred to go out and meet his friends in the pub. (The same is true today, but was not always so; before the First World War families often sent out to the pub for a jug of ale with their Sunday dinner.) Gradually drinking had become a separate activity, no longer connected with eating, but with smoking, playing darts and chatting.

At a higher social level, cocktails provided another chasm between the generations. While old-fashioned families like the Mildmays never drank before a meal, not even a glass of sherry, the young fashionable folk in London became addicted to cocktails almost overnight. Loelia Westminster felt obliged to offer her weekend guests cocktails, despite the fact that her husband abhorred them, and that the butler had never mastered the art of making them, so that a tray of lukewarm concoctions already poured into glasses was the best she could do.

This was one field where the Americans excelled, and none more so than Mrs Simpson, who introduced the Prince of Wales to old-fashioneds during a cruise on Lord Moyne's yacht, in 1934, and found him an enthusiastic convert. The number of different cocktails was legion; some had silly names, like Rosebud, Mimosa, the Doctor and Between the Sheets. The barmen in London clubs and bars vied with each other in inventing new combinations, and cocktail parties became the rage.

Wine cups were also very popular for parties; these were based on white wine, vin rosé and champagne, as well as non-alcoholic mixtures of fruit juices. Over and above its use in cocktails and cups, champagne continued to be hugely popular, just as it always had been, ever since its invention in the late seventeenth century. All through the eighteenth and nineteenth centuries it was drunk by the English in great quantities; in 1887 imports reached a peak when 9½ million bottles were drunk in the UK. In the 1860s, the English developed a taste for dry champagne. The French did not become converted till the First World War; until that time they made it expressly for the English, who were their biggest buyers. Until the 1930s, the French continued to export more champagne than they drank themselves.

Immediately after the end of the First World War, champagne sales in England rocketed, but soon fell again by half, thanks to a heavy duty imposed by none other than the then Chancellor of the Exchequer, Winston Churchill. By 1926, however, the tax had been lifted, and sales rose again. Champagne fitted perfectly with the mood of the late 20s: effervescent, irresponsible and hedonistic. It was drunk as an aperitif, throughout a meal, or just with the first course or pudding, or after dinner. The most popular after-dinner drinks for men were port or brandy, while the ladies might be offered a sweet liqueur like crème de menthe. At about ten thirty, in country houses, the butler would carry the 'grog tray' into the drawing-room. This held whisky and soda syphons for the men, and the inevitable barley water – or still lemonade – for the ladies.

Certain drinks were considered appropriate for outdoor activities, like sloe gin, cherry brandy and mulled wine. Sloe gin was made from wild sloes in early October and kept for two months before using. Thus it was ready in time for Christmas, but some would have been kept from the year before for drinking in November and early December. This was drunk before lunch, as an aperitif, and after shooting lunches, at meets or point-to-points. Cherry brandy was served on similar occasions, when a quick nip of something strong and warming was required: after a shooting lunch, or at a race meeting. Mulled red wine, drunk hot, was also popular at shooting lunches, or at any outdoor evening activity in wintertime, like firework parties, or carol singing.

Perhaps the greatest difference between the inter-war years and now lies in their fondness for mixtures of drinks, in the form of cocktails and cups. A few of these are popular today, like bloody Marys, kirs and Buck's fizz, but on the whole we prefer to drink our wines and spirits on their own, or in fairly austere combinations with tonic or mineral water.

## Barley Water

This was often made, not just for invalids, but to serve after dinner parties for the ladies, who rarely drank spirits. When made for the sickroom, the lemon juice was usually omitted.

3 tablespoons pearl barley
juice of 2 lemons
sugar to taste (about 2–3 tablespoons)

Wash three tablespoonfuls of pearl barley in 1.2 litres of water two or three times changed and thrown away. Put a fresh 1.2 litres of water with the barley, bring to the boil, simmer slowly for 10 minutes. Strain into a jug, add juice of 2 lemons, sugar to taste, and set on ice till wanted. Enough for three or four. *Kitchen Essays*, **by Lady Jekyll**

## Lemonade

Lemonade or barley water were usually on offer in the country houses, as many women preferred soft drinks. This is how it was made, and still is, at Sledmere, home of the Sykes family, in Yorkshire.

6 lemons
140g sugar
825ml water

(Do put the lemons in a warm place before you squeeze them; this way you get the maximum juice from them.) Wash the lemons and dry. Grate the rind and put it in a pan with the sugar and water. Stir till the sugar has dissolved. Turn off the heat and let it stand till you squeeze the lemons. Strain the juice and when the syrup is cold, strain this also. Combine the juice and syrup and stir well. Serve in a glass jug with thinly sliced lemon, and ice in hot weather. The sugar can be adjusted to taste. For a less strong lemonade use 1.2 litres of water. **Sir Tatton Sykes**

## Orangeade

Fresh orangeade was traditionally served at parties where young people were present; the grown-ups preferred lemonade, or the ubiquitous barley water. Orangeade is especially pretty when made with a proportion of blood oranges, perhaps half as many as the others, when they are in season.

85g granulated sugar
pared rind of 2 oranges
pared rind of 1 lemon
juice of 6 oranges

juice of 1 lemon

GARNISH

3–4 thin slices of orange, unpeeled

3–4 thin slices of lemon, unpeeled

Put the sugar in a heatproof jug with the rinds. Pour on 275ml of boiling water and stir until the sugar has dissolved. Then leave to cool almost to room temperature. Strain out the rinds, add the juice of the oranges and lemon, and a further 825ml of water. Pour into a glass jug and chill until ready to serve. Add the garnish shortly before serving. Makes about 1.2 litres. **AB**


## Mrs Gibson's Iced Tea

As American dishes started to infiltrate the social scene, iced tea began to supplant lemon barley water at tennis teas and garden parties. This is a particularly good recipe; I have reduced the sugar since our tastes have changed in this way, and I like to add some ginger ale at the last moment.

8 tablespoons (45g) Indian tea leaves

4 tablespoons sugar

juice of 1 lemon

juice of 3 oranges

approx. 825ml ginger ale (optional)

GARNISH

lemon slices

sprigs of mint

Put 8 tablespoons of Lipton's tea [*leaves*] in a large pan. Pour over 1.2 litres of boiling water. Add sugar, stir well. Squeeze juice of 1 lemon and 3 oranges. Pour juices over a tray of ice [*or through a strainer filled with ice cubes*]. Strain tea [*also through ice*], and add to juices. Add 570ml of iced water and chill. [*Makes 2 litres. I pour it over ice cubes in tall glasses, adding half as much ginger ale just before serving, and garnish with lemon slices and sprigs of mint.*]**Mrs Nancy Lancaster**

# Raspberry Vinegar

Flavoured vinegars are not a modern invention, as might be supposed, but have been around for many years. In France, as many as sixty-five different flavoured vinegars were being manufactured by the great mustard firm of Maille, in Dijon, in 1800. In England, a sweet fruit vinegar was often used as a cordial, for diluting in water or soda water. This makes an excellent and inexpensive drink in hot weather.

450g raspberries
570ml red or white wine vinegar
340g sugar

Take 450g raspberries to every 570ml best wine vinegar. Let it stand for a fortnight in a covered jar in a cool larder. Then strain without pressure, and to every 450ml put 340g white sugar. Boil 10 minutes, let cool, and bottle in nice-shaped medium-sized bottles. A teaspoonful stirred into a tumbler of water with a lump of ice, or introduced to a very cold syphon [*or sparkling mineral water*], will taste like the elixir of life on a hot day, and is as pretty as it is pleasant. [*Makes approximately 450ml.*] **Kitchen Essays, by Lady Jekyll**

# Pussy Foot Cup

This is pale green in colour, an utterly delicious non-alcoholic mixture to serve on a summer's day. Especially pretty served in a clear glass jug, with a mixture of pale and dark green fruit, with a few strawberries.

1 litre fizzy lemonade
450ml dry ginger ale
450ml tonic water
450ml soda water or sparkling mineral water
175ml orange juice
175ml lemon juice
1 green apple, unpeeled, quartered, cored and sliced

peel of ¼ cucumber
3 large sprigs of mint
a few strawberries

Serve in a large jug with ice. [*Makes about 2.75 litres.*] **The Complete Hostess, by Quaglino**

## The Doctor

This is the classic rum punch formula, which someone must have brought back from the West Indies: one of sour, two of sweet, three of strong, four of weak. It makes a delicious long (alcoholic) drink for a hot summer day, with lots of ice. For a shorter, stronger version, reduce the 'weak' content, i.e. the water, by as much as half. I use white Bacardi rum.

1 part fresh lime juice
2 parts sugar syrup (see page 235)
3 parts rum
4 parts water

Shake up with frappé [*crushed*] ice. **The Perfect Hostess, by Rose Henniker Heaton**

## Champagne Cocktail

Nothing conjures up the spirit of the 1920s better than a champagne cocktail, redolent of Noël Coward's lyrics, and the Café de Paris.

*In each champagne glass put:*
1 small lump of sugar
2 or 3 drops of Angostura bitters (on the sugar)
1 teaspoon brandy

Fill the glass with champagne. Place a slice of lemon or orange on top. **Mrs Nancy Lancaster**

## Cup Quaglino

This is a good cup for serving at parties, like a cross between a champagne cocktail and a Buck's fizz, only less alcoholic.

1 bottle of non-vintage champagne, chilled
275ml fresh orange juice
75ml brandy
75ml orange curaçao
250ml soda water, or sparkling mineral water
sliced fruit in season: oranges, apples, peaches, lemons, etc.

Put a large piece of ice in a big jug and add the liquid ingredients. Decorate with different kinds of fruit in season. *The Complete Hostess*, by **Quaglino**

## White Wine Cup

An unusually delicious cup, easily made by anyone who makes their own elderflower syrup. Otherwise, use Belvoir Elderflower Cordial.

2 bottles of dry white wine (Alsace wine is good for this)
450ml soda water
1 wine-glassful of brandy
1 wine-glassful of elderflower syrup or cordial
sliced lemon
strawberries
cucumber rind
borage
ice

Mix all together one to two hours before serving. *Party Food and Drink*, **by Rosemary Hume**

# Wine Cup

This recipe came from Justerini & Brooks, one of the leading wine merchants in the inter-war years, by appointment to King George VI. Justerini & Brooks were established in the 1750s, and are still going strong. This is a most delicious cup, pale pink in colour. It is slightly too sweet for drinking at a meal, but perfect for a pre-lunch drink, or at a party, on a summer day. The original recipe called for maraschino as well as brandy, but this is very hard to find nowadays, so I leave it out.

1 bottle of good vin rosé
75ml brandy
450ml fizzy lemonade
450ml soda water or sparkling mineral water
a few slices (unpeeled) of green apple, oranges and lemons
a few strips of cucumber peel

Serve very cold. **The late Edward Tatham, former Managing Director of Justerini & Brooks**

# Sugar Syrup

Sugar syrup is a necessary adjunct for making cocktails, since sugar alone does not dissolve properly. The exception is the champagne cocktail, where a lump of sugar is the traditional sweetener. It can be prepared in larger amounts, as needed, and stored in the refrigerator in a covered jar.

120g granulated sugar
150ml water

Put sugar and water into a small pan and bring slowly to the boil. Simmer for about 3 minutes, until the sugar has completely melted, then pour into a small jug and leave to cool. Once it has cooled, store in the refrigerator and use as needed. It can be kept for a week under refrigeration. If making in larger quantities, and keeping for longer, it is best kept in an airtight container. Makes 150ml. **AB**

# BIBLIOGRAPHY

## Cookery Books

Acton, Eliza, *Modern Cookery*, London, 1845.

Allhusen, Dorothy, *A Book of Scents and Dishes*, London, 1926.

Allhusen, Dorothy, *A Medley of Recipes*, London, 1936.

Beeton, Mrs, *Mrs Beeton's All About Cookery*, London, 1961.

Boulestin, X. Marcel, *Simple French Cooking for English Homes*, London, 1923.

Boulestin, X. Marcel, *The Conduct of the Kitchen*, London, 1925.

Boulestin, X. Marcel, *What Shall We Have Today?*, London, 1931.

Boulestin, X. Marcel, *What Shall We Have To Drink?*, London, 1933.

David, Elizabeth, *Spices, Salt and Aromatics in the English Kitchen*, London, 1970.

David, Elizabeth, *English Bread and Yeast Cookery*, London, 1977.

Escoffier, *Ma Cuisine*, Paris, 1934.

Fisher, M. F. K., *With Bold Knife and Fork*, New York, 1968.

Floyd, Keith, *Floyd on Britain and Ireland*, London, 1988.

Francillon, W. G. R., *Good Cookery*, London, 1920.

Grigson, Jane, *The Observer Guide to British Cookery*, London, 1984.

Harben, Philip, *Philip Harben's Cookery Encyclopedia*, London, 1955.

Hartley, Dorothy, *Food in England*, London, 1954.

Hastings, Macdonald, and Walsh, Carole, *Wheeler's Fish Cookery Book*, London, 1974.

Heath, Ambrose, *The Queen Cookery Book*, London, 1960.

Heath, Ambrose, *Personal Choice*, London, 1970.

Heaton, Rose Henniker, *The Perfect Hostess*, London, 1931.

Heptinstall, William, *Hors d'Oeuvre and Cold Table*, London, 1959.

Hindlip, Minnie, *Minnie Lady Hindlip's Cookery Book*, London, 1925.

Hume, Rosemary, *Party Food and Drink*, London, 1950.

Irwin, Florence, *Irish Cookery Recipes*, Belfast, 1937.

Ives, Catherine, *When the Cook Is Away*, London, 1928.

Jekyll, Lady, *Kitchen Essays*, London, 1922.

Leyel, Mrs C. F., and Hartley, Miss Olga, *The Gentle Art of Cookery*, London, 1925.

Little, May, *A Year's Dinners*, London, 1930 (approx.).

Lowinsky, Ruth, *Lovely Food*, London, 1931.

Lowinsky, Ruth, *More Lovely Food*, London, 1935.

Lowinsky, Ruth, *Food for Pleasure*, London, 1951.

Lucas, Elizabeth, *Vegetable Cookery*, London, 1931.

Luke, Sir Harry, *The Tenth Muse*, London, 1954.

McDouall, Robin, *Robin McDouall's Cookery Book for the Greedy*, London, 1963.

McDouall, Robin, *Clubland Cooking*, London, 1974.

McNeill, F. Marian, *The Scots Kitchen, Its Lore and Recipes*, Glasgow, 1929.

Marion, Lucie, *Be Your Own Chef*, London, 1948.

Martineau, Mrs Philip, *Caviare to Candy*, London, 1927.

Martineau, Mrs Philip, *Cantaloup to Cabbage*, London, 1929.

Martineau, Alice (Mrs Philip), *More Caviare and More Candy*, London, 1938.

de Medici, Lorenza, *The Renaissance of Italian Cooking*, London, 1990.

Molyneux, Joyce, *The Carved Angel Cookery Book*, London, 1990.

Morphy, Countess, *Lightning Cookery*, London, 1931.

Paterson, Jennifer, *Feast Days*, London, 1990.

Platt, June, *June Platt's Party Cook Book*, Boston, 1936.

Platt, June, *June Platt's Plain and Fancy Cookbook*, Boston, 1941.

Powell, Hilda (ed.), *Vogue's Cookery Book*, London, 1939.

Quaglino, *The Complete Hostess*, edited by Charles Graves, London, 1935.

Rohde, Eleanour Sinclair, *A Garden of Herbs*, London, 1936.

Rohde, Eleanour Sinclair, *Vegetable Cultivation and Cookery*, London, 1938.

de Salis, Mrs, *Tempting Dishes for Small Incomes*, London, 1892.

Scotson-Clark, G. F., *Kitchenette Cookery*, London, 1925.

Shaw, Nancy, *Food for the Greedy*, London, 1936.

Spry, Constance, *Come Into the Garden, Cook*, London, 1942.

Spry, Constance, and Hume, Rosemary, *The Constance Spry Cookery Book*, London, 1956.

Stanley, Fortune, *English Country House Cooking*, London, 1972.

Sysonby, Lady, *Lady Sysonby's Cook Book*, London, 1935.

Toklas, Alice B., *The Alice B. Toklas Cook Book*, London, 1954.

Toklas, Alice B., and Cannon, Poppy, *Aromas and Flavors*, New York, 1958.

White, Florence, *Good Things in England*, London, 1932.

Wijk, Olof, *Eat at Pleasure: Drink by Measure*, London, 1970.

de Wolfe, Elsie, *Elsie de Wolfe's Recipes for Successful Dining*, New York, 1934.

## General Books

Asquith, Lady Cynthia, *Haply I May Remember*, London, 1950.

Beaton, Cecil, *Self Portrait with Friends, Selected Diaries of Cecil Beaton*, edited by Richard Buckle, London, 1979.

Beauman, Nicola, *Cynthia Asquith*, London, 1987.

Campbell, Susan, *Cottesbrooke, An English Kitchen Garden*, London, 1989.

*Carrington, Letters and Extracts from Her Diary*, chosen by David Garnett, London, 1970.

Cecil, Hugh and Mirabel, *Clever Hearts, Desmond and Molly MacCarthy – A Biography*, London, 1990.

Channon, Sir Henry, *Chips, The Diaries of Sir Henry Channon*, edited by Richard Buckle, London, 1967.

Cooper, Artemis (ed.), *A Durable Fire, The Letters of Duff and Diana Cooper 1913–1950*, London, 1983.

Coward, Noël, *The Noël Coward Diaries*, edited by Graham Payn and Sheridan Morley, London, 1982.

Crawford, Sir William, and Broadley, H., *The People's Food*, London, 1938.

Davidson, Caroline, *A Woman's Work Is Never Done*, London, 1982.

Devonshire, The Duchess of, *The House, A Portrait of Chatsworth*, London, 1982.

Donaldson, Frances, *Edward VIII*, London, 1974.

Driver, Christopher, *The British at Table, 1940–1980*, London, 1983.

Drummond, J. C., and Wilbraham, Anne, *The Englishman's Food*, London, 1958.

Field, Rachael, *Irons in the Fire, A History of Cooking Equipment*, London, 1984.

Fitzgibbon, Theodora, *The Food of the Western World*, London, 1976.

Fleming, Anne, *The Letters of Anne Fleming*, edited by Mark Amory, London, 1985.

Forbes, Patrick, *Champagne, the wine, the land and the people*, London, 1977.

Jones, Chester, *Colefax & Fowler, The Best in British Interior Decoration*, London, 1989.

Lindsay, Loelia, *Grace and Favour*, London, 1961.

Lutyens, Mary, *Edwin Lutyens by his daughter Mary Lutyens*, London, 1980.

McKendry, Maxine, *Seven Centuries of English Cooking*, London, 1973.

Meynell, Francis, and Mendel, Vera (ed.), *The Week-End Book, a new edition*, London, 1928.

Mitford, Jessica, *Hons and Rebels*, London, 1977.

Murphy, Sophia, *The Duchess of Devonshire's Ball*, London, 1984.

Nicolson, Harold, *Harold Nicolson Diaries and Letters*, vol. 1, edited by Nigel Nicolson, London, 1966.

Olivier, Edith, *Edith Olivier's Journals*, edited by Penelope Middleboe, London, 1989.

Orwell, George, *The Road to Wigan Pier*, London, 1937.

Palmer, Arnold, *Moveable Feasts*, Oxford, 1952.

Partridge, Frances, *A Pacifist's War*, London, 1978.

Partridge, Frances, *Memories*, London, 1982.

Ritchie, Charles, *The Siren Years, Undiplomatic Diaries 1937–45*, London, 1974.

Saintsbury, George, *A Scrap Book*, London, 1922.

Saintsbury, George, *A Last Scrap Book*, London, 1924.

Sassoon, Siegfried, *Siegfried Sassoon Diaries 1920–1922*, edited by Rupert Hart-Davis, London, 1981.

Sebba, Anne, *Enid Bagnold*, London, 1986.

Shand, P. Morton, *A Book of Food*, London, 1927.

Soyer, Alexis, *The Modern Housewife*, London, 1872.

Stobart, Tom, *The Cook's Encyclopedia*, London, 1980.

Sykes, Christopher Simon, *Country House Camera*, London, 1980.

Sykes, Christopher Simon, *Private Palaces*, London, 1985.

Tannahill, Reay, *Food in History*, London, 1973.

Tims, Barbara (ed.), *Food in Vogue*, London, 1976.

Tims, Barbara (ed.), *Food in Vogue*, London, 1988.

Toynbee, Philip, *Friends Apart, A Memoir of Esmond Romilly and Jasper Ridley in the Thirties*, London, 1954.

Visser, Margaret, *Much Depends on Dinner*, London, 1989.

Warren, Geoffrey, *The Foods We Eat*, London, 1958.

Waterson, Merlin (ed.), *The Country House Remembered*, London, 1985.

Wilson, C. Anne, *Food and Drink in Britain*, London, 1973.

Wilson, C. Anne, *The Book of Marmalade: Its Antecedents*, London, 1985.

Woolf, Virginia, *The Letters of Virginia Woolf*, vols. 3–6, edited by Nigel Nicolson, London, 1977–80.

Wyndham, Ursula, *Astride the Wall*, London, 1988.

# MAIN INDEX

Page numbers in **bold** refer to recipes.

Cakes – *cont.*
    chocolate sponge 197–8
    fruit cake, Lady Moray's
      179–80
    ginger cake, Lady
      Portarlington's 180–81
    ginger cake, sticky 169, 198
    lemon cake, iced 196–7
    luncheon cake 185, 188
    Madeira 199
    pound 196
    rice 199–200
    sand 188
    seed 200–201
    small sponge cakes, or fingers
      205–6
Canapés fumés 217–18
Canary pudding 118
Caper sauce 81
Caramel ice cream 137–8
Carberry ginger hats 203–4
Carrots, new, with curry 91–2
Castle puddings 117–18
Cauliflower gratin 45–6
Caviare xliv, xlviii, 212
Celery sauce 147–8
    soup 23–4
Champagne 226–8
    cocktail 233
    cup 234
Charlotte, apple 112–13
Chasse 13
Chatsworth House xx, xxii–xxiii,
    xxvii, xl, l
Cheese
    biscuits 214–15
    fried sandwiches 216–17
    macaroni 44
    potted 212
    toasted sandwiches 214
Cherry brandy 229
Cherry salad 149–50
Chicken
    baked, with noodles 56–8
    devilled 151
    pulled and grilled 58–9
    roast, in cream 59–60
    Roman pie 60–61
Chicory, *see* Endives au jus
Chips, game 63, 97–8
Chocolate sauce 128–9
Chocolate sponge cake 197–8

Christmas pudding 120–21
Clarified butter 191, 206
Cocktails 227–8
    champagne 233
    doctor, the 233
    old-fashioned 227
Coconut pyramids 202
Cod, curried 53
Cod's roe paste, smoked 218–19
Colbert, sole 53–4
Colefax, Sibyl (Lady) xxxi–xxxii,
    xxxiv–xxxv, 121
Compôte of oranges, with jelly
    131–2
    of raspberries and redcurrants
      129–30
Concombres, escalopes de veux
    aux 82–3
Consommé 17, 19–20
    à l'estragon 21
    à l'Indienne 22
    garden nectar 22–3
Corn meal soufflé 56
Côtelettes soubises 79–80
Cottage pie 68–9
Crab, dressed 18
Cream, horseradish 28
Cream cheese and smoked salmon 32
    and walnut sandwiches 194
Cream of rice 127
Creamy custard sauce 161–2
Croquettes, egg 36–7
Croutons, plum 133
Cucumber, *see* Escalopes de veau
    aux concombres
Cumberland sauce 149
Cunard, Emerald (Lady) xxxi–
    xxxiv, xlv, 111
Cups 228
    pussy foot 232–3
    Quaglino 234
    white wine 234
    wine (rosé) 235
Curried cod 53
Curry, new carrots with 91–2
Custard, Bird's 111, 145
Custard sauce 161–2
Cutlets, *see* Egg croquettes
Cutlets, lamb
    grilled rack of lamb 77–8
    pâte Don Pedro 78–9
    soubises 79–80

**D**

Date and cream cheese sandwiches
194
David, Elizabeth 35
Délices de sole Murat 28
Devil sauce 151
Devilled chicken, or game 151
Devonshire splits 202–3
Doctor, the 233
Dover sole 19, 51
Drinks 225–9
Duck, roast 60
Duglèré, sauce 152–3
sole 30–31

**E**

Egg sandwiches 188
and mango chutney 188–9
and prawn 189
Eggs 17–18
baked with shrimps, cold 34
Benedict 35–6
Breakfast dish, a 12–13
Cendrillon 37–8
croquettes 36–7
cutlets 36–7
mimosa 39–40
mollets à l'Indienne 38–9
mousse 39–40
oeufs à la gelée xlvii, 40
poached, with smoked haddock
7–8
pochés, surprises 40–41
summer first course dish, a 41–2
Eggy bread 124
Eiffel Tower 1
Elderflower cordial, or syrup 234
Endives au jus 90–91
Escalopes de veau aux concombres
82–3
Estragon, consommé à l' 21

**F**

Fingers, sponge 205–6
Fish cakes, Mrs Anderson's 8–9
another fish cake 9–10
Fish mayonnaise 31–2
Fish sandwiches 187
lobster 189–90
Norwegian 177–8
potted shrimp 190
prawn, egg and 189

shrimp, watercress and 192–3
smoked haddock 178–9
sole 191–2
Fish soups
bouillon de poisson 24–5
souchet of slips 26–7
Floating island 111, 133–4
Food rationing xxv
Fried cheese sandwiches 214
Fried parsley 155
Fried tomatoes in cream 102
Fruit xli, 111–12
Fruit cake, Lady Moray's 179–80
Fruit fools xiv, 206

**G**

Game 49, 50
devilled 151
pie 174–6
roast 62–3
shooting sandwiches 177
venison, roast 65–6
Game chips 63, 97–8
Garden nectar 22–3
Garnishes 49–50
Gentleman's pudding 121
Gibson, Mrs, iced tea 231
Gin, sloe 169, 182, 229
Ginger
cake, Lady Portarlington's 180–81
cake, sticky 198
and cream cheese, sandwiches
194
hats, Carberry 203–4
Glace pomme d'amour 220–21
Glazed onions 93
Golden syrup 118, 145
Goujons of sole 25–6
Grape salad, with cold quail 63
Grapes, muscat 112
Gratin, cauliflower 45–6
onions, au 93–4
Green peas, see Peas
Grouse salad 63

**H**

Haddock, smoked 3, 209
canapés fumés 217–18
Monte Carlo 54–5
with poached eggs 7–8
sandwiches 178–9
Hard sauce 161

Sponge cakes, small **205–6**
Sprats 19
Spring vegetable pie, steamed
    **98–100**
Squab, roast **62**
Steamed spring vegetable pie
    **98–100**
Stew, beef **72–3**
    Irish **172**
Sticky ginger cake 169, **198**
Sugar syrup **235–6**
    vanilla 124
Summer first-course dish, a **41–2**
Symons, A. J. A. xx

**T**

Tart, Bakewell 110, **116–17**
    Lady Portarlington's apple
    **114–15**
Tartare sauce **157**
Tea 185–8
    bridge 186
    iced **231**
Tête de nègre 111, **128–9**
Toast, cabbage **20–21**
    herring roes on **220**
    Melba **203**
    for savouries **217**
Toasted cheese sandwiches **214**
    marmalade sandwiches **195**
Toffee pudding **126**
Tomato(es), and rice pie **101**
    fried in cream **102**
    glace pomme d'amour **220–21**
    iced, and horseradish sauce **102–3**
    iced sauce **157–8**
    jelly ring **42–3**
Truffes, salade aux **103–4**
Two-tier lemon pudding **123–4**

**V**

Vanilla, and lemon sauce **162–3**
    ice cream **138**
    sugar 124
Veal, escalopes de veau aux
    concombres **82–3**
Vegetables 87–9
    pie, steamed, spring **98–100**
    soufflé 18, 87, **100–101**
Vermicelli soufflé **46**
Vinegar, raspberry **232**

**W**

Walnut and cream cheese
    sandwiches **194**
    and watercress sandwiches
    **193**
Watercress and shrimp sandwiches
    **192–3**
    salad **104–5**
    and walnut sandwiches **193**
Westminster, Duke and Duchess
    xxix–xxxx
Wheeler's 53
Whitebait 19
Whiting 19
Wine xx, 225–7
    mulled 171, **181–2**
    red wine jelly **132–3**
    white wine cup **235**
    wine (rosé) cup **235**
Wine and Food Society xx
Wood pigeon 62
Woodcock, roast **63**
    Scotch **219**

**Y**

Yorkshire pudding **159**

# INDEX OF SOURCES

## S

Salis, Mrs de 13
Scotson-Clark, G. F. 158–9, 214
Shaw, Nancy 41–2, 102–3, 197–8, 211, 220–21
Spry, Constance xiv–xv, xxxviii–xxxix, 38–9, 110, 112–13, 126, 155, 157–8, 186–7, 201, 212
Stanley, Fortune 58–9, 129–30, 217
Stuart, Sarah 14
Stewart-Richardson, Gladys 152
Sykes, Sir Tatton 203
Sysonby, Lady xxxvii–xxxviii, 40–41, 78–80, 88, 125–6, 177, 193–4, 202–3

## T

Tatham, Edward 235
Toklas, Alice B. 59–60, 98–100, 122–3, 158

## V

*Vogue* (magazine) xx, xxi, xlvi, 19–21, 66–7, 81–2, 114–15, 121, 147–8, 162–3, 189–90, 193, 195
*Vogue's Cookery Book* 22–3, 28, 42–3, 102, 103–4

## W

Walsh, Carole 54–5, 157
Wijk, Olof 32
Winnie 147
de Wolfe, Elsie (Lady Mendl) xxxv–xxxvi, xlvi, xlviii, 56–8, 104, 110, 115–16